Living Your Dream

Opening a Financially Successful Fitness Business

Thomas Plummer

HEALTHY LEARNING™

A previous version of this book was published as *Open a Fitness Business and Make Money Doing It.*

ISBN: 978-1-60679-169-1
Library of Congress Control Number: 2011923852
Cover design: Studio J Art & Design
Book layout: Studio J Art & Design
Front cover photo: Hemera/Thinkstock

Healthy Learning
P.O. Box 1828
Monterey, CA 93942
www.healthylearning.com

Dedication

This book is dedicated to every brave individual who ever dreamed about opening a fitness business and then took the risk to make it happen. In the fitness industry, we are in the business of changing lives, and living your dream by opening your own business makes the world a better place for a lot of people who might never have found fitness without you.

This book is also dedicated to the entrepreneurial spirit that has fueled the incredible growth and success of the health and fitness industry worldwide. In many ways, we are just getting started in this industry, and the best days of the fitness business are yet to come.

Acknowledgments

I can honestly say without a doubt that I have been in front of more fitness business owners and operators of every type than anyone else in the history of this industry and I think I have learned something from each and every one. Thank you to all who have passed through my seminars for the questions and experience you have brought with you.

I am also profoundly grateful that I have been able to live my life pretty much on my own terms through my involvement with the fitness industry and through the owners and vendors who have supported my efforts all these years. There are far too many to list, but to all those who have helped me along the way, I would like to say thank you once again.

As I have said in my other books, no one really goes it alone. Everyone who has achieved any type of success has had the helping hand of someone else—and I am no exception. My thanks to all who have made my business and my life a wonderful journey.

I couldn't end this note without a special thought for Susan, who makes the journey worthwhile, and for Jillian, Madison, and CJ, special people who give me new reasons to enjoy my life beyond work and fitness.

Noted author Stephen Covey once wrote about the four levels of competence. Level one is unconscious incompetence. You don't even know that you don't know what you're doing. That's where most people in the fitness business are: blissfully ignorant.

Level two is conscious incompetence. This is the level when you are cruelly made aware that you don't know what you're doing. This is where Thom first takes you. And this is where you hate him. It's the worst feeling in the world—but you are getting closer.

The next level is conscious competence. It takes a while, but Thom will get you there. You'll now be making smarter decisions and running your business based on tracking and numbers. You start to make a little money.

This is when you start to love Thom!

The final level is unconscious competence. You're now a business owner, who thinks, acts, and operates like a business owner (instead of playing one). If you let Thom be your guide, this is the mastery level.

Everyone needs a coach. Everyone.

Whether it's a team sport such as football or basketball, or individual sports such as boxing or tennis, behind every great performer there is a great coach, advising, pushing, and directing.

In the fitness business, the number one guy is Thomas Plummer. He's been my personal coach for years and my life and business are dramatically different thanks to his knowledge and input.

This book embodies everything you need to know about opening your own fitness business, and it should be mandatory reading for anyone involved in fitness—whether you are opening a studio or a bigger gym, or even if you are just a trainer looking to get to the next level.

Alwyn Cosgrove
Author and Lecturer
Owner of Results Fitness

Foreword

contents

NOTE TO THE READER

Use this material at your own risk. Much of what is written here is based upon my own opinion, derived from my own research and experience in this industry. All the material included in this book is offered as a simple starting point for an owner or manager to use as you build your first business or simply improve the one you already own.

In all cases, and especially in legal issues concerning your business, such as leasing, you are advised to seek the advice of qualified professionals that support your business locally, including accountants, attorneys, and other business professionals who may know your business and your situation on a more intimate level.

Neither the author, nor publisher, nor any party related to the information and development of this book assumes any responsibility or liability for the consequences, whether good or bad, of your application of this material.

Also please note that some examples or bits of information are repeated in several different chapters in this book. Many of the readers of the earlier books have reported that they read this material by choosing specific chapters that are relevant to their interest or business problem at hand and don't always read the book straight through in order. If you are opening a new business, and it is your first, it is recommended that you read the book straight through, highlight what you need, and then start conversations with your team of professionals. Experienced owners should concentrate on the issues they encountered during their first venture that they wish they might have had some guidance on at the time.

SO YOU WANT TO OPEN A FITNESS CENTER?

Hemera/Thinkstock

Chapter One

Whatever possessed you to want to get into the fitness business? You can be sure that you will be asked this question often as you ponder opening a fitness facility for the first time. Your potential investors, your banker, your significant other, your family, and your friends will all want to know why you're getting into a business that is perceived by those on the outside as so easy, yet is known by those who own and operate fitness businesses as one of the most challenging and intensive small businesses you could own.

Opening a small business is a very serious matter involving a high degree of risk that is compounded by the high level of stress stemming from the constant application of member service. Risk generates from the fact that you will invest your money, along with other people's cash in most cases, in a project that has a possibility of failure, as do all small business ventures.

Failure, while not life-threatening, always feels like it at the time when you have to turn that key in the door for the last time and walk away from your dream. Clubs do fail, although in smaller numbers than in the past because today's owners are better prepared to run their fitness dream as a business compared to many of the owners in past years.

This new generation of fitness businesses demands a significantly higher investment than clubs of just 10 years ago, and this increase has brought in a new breed of owner that is not only faithful to the tenets of fitness, but also understands business at a higher level due to the increased cost of getting started. The increased cost of opening a traditional fitness business, along with the revival of functional training and sports performance, has also spawned a surge in the development of new generation training centers that in many cases generate the kind of revenue that was unknown even by the large chain clubs just a few years ago.

Any small business can fail and often it is the unexpected, unknown, or emotional mistake that takes it down. The unexpected might be delays by your builder that eat up your reserve capital. The unknown might come in the form of another competitor opening in the same market that you didn't know about (because you failed to do your homework) and who is chasing the same target market.

Emotional mistakes are perhaps the most frequent among young owners who become impatient and try to force the business even if it is obvious that he needs to back away. Taking a location, no matter what you are told by your support team, that is too expensive or in the wrong part of town is a sign that you're emotional. Signing a lease and making other obligations when you're short of money for the overall project means that you're too emotional. Believing that it doesn't matter that 12 clubs are already in the market going after the same target members and defending that decision because you are going to build a club like no one has ever seen—and besides, you're the best trainer in town anyway—is a sign that you're making bad, emotional decisions.

The stress factor kicks in when the enormity of creating a new business where one had not existed before overwhelms you in the middle of the night. You will be stressed, your family will be stressed, and people you don't even know will hate you because it will become hard to talk about anything else but your new business and how it is coming along.

Many new owners often become as obnoxious as first-time parents who can't talk about anything but their new baby and will irritate you with the need to give you every detail of the birth, the first dirty diaper, the first steps, and basically the whole first year. The only difference between this over-the-top parent and a new club owner are the pictures. The club guy probably has more pictures of his new club on his phone than the 30 kid pictures the parent carries around.

"Why?" is also the most important question you should be asking yourself as you investigate getting into a new fitness business. Why do I want to get into this? What is the expected outcome from my decision to open a fitness facility? Am I opening this club for the right reasons, and do I understand that this is a business and not just a hobby for a crazed fitness person?

The expected outcome is the end result of opening your new business, usually projected five years down the road. Again, more questions will help you determine the expected outcome of your new venture. Are you opening this first unit to start a small chain and become regional? Do you plan to build up this business and then sell it at some point in the future and go on to something else? Can you build from the ground up, sell the business in the future, and hold the real estate? Is this first club all you want, as long as it can provide a good living for you and your family?

All of these questions are important and worth considering during this first phase, where you just sit back and let your imagination run wild. At this point, no limit exists to what you should be considering and all possibilities should be thought through and discussed.

One of the most important questions to consider during this "What if I opened a fitness center?" stage is that of lifestyle versus risk. Someone pursuing lifestyle, for example, is not always someone who makes a successful business owner.

Lifestyle people are those who love working out everyday or might be personal success stories when it comes to fitness. These folks are the ones who have lost the extreme weight, battled through an unhealthy situation in their life, or have had fitness somehow be a life-changing experience. These people are passionate and want to share with the world what fitness has done for them and they see opening a fitness center as the best avenue to reach that goal.

This group of fitness purists often have the hardest time in the fitness business as owners and operators because they enter a very demanding field least prepared for the business aspects. The fitness business is truly rewarding in that you have the chance to change lives every day, but the business skills such as raising capital, managing a staff, mastering marketing and sales, and developing programming all have to be in place for that new business to survive and prosper in a competitive market. Passion alone doesn't guarantee success, but a passion for changing lives, accompanied by a desire to create a sustainable business, is the proper approach.

Risk is the other side of the lifestyle coin. As mentioned earlier, opening any new business is always accompanied by the prospect that the business might fail. Your job, as you consider getting into the fitness industry as an owner, is to minimize this risk by learning as much as you can about how the business works, acquire the skills you need as a businessperson to succeed, and go into your new company with your eyes open to the risk involved in betting your money, and usually someone else's money as well.

Look at other fitness businesses carefully and learn to see beyond the pretty equipment and classes. What basic business principles enable one club to succeed where others merely survive? What "best practices" separate financially successful club owners from those that flail away at the business, never really making any money?

Lifestyle is the benefit of being in this industry, but the only way you will succeed financially over time is to understand that it is a business and that you are willing to run it as such every single day you own it. People call them gyms, clubs, and training centers, but the real term you need to understand is that they are all fitness businesses, with the operative word being "business."

If lifestyle is your ultimate choice, meaning that you want to get into the fitness business because you love to work out or you want to share your personal fitness success with others, then you might be better off working in a club as a trainer or some type of other fitness professional. But if you're like Braham Akradi, founder of Life Time Fitness (NYSE: LTM), the last fitness group to go public; Joe Cirulli, owner of several financially successful fitness centers in Florida; or Joe Millet, managing partner of the Big Sky chain in Connecticut, you can figure out how to be both financially successful and enjoy the fitness lifestyle. All three of these outstanding business professionals started small and grew into major players, either nationwide or in their respective areas, and all started with a love for fitness that they maintained long after their success was secured.

There is also an entire generation of new training businesses that are shaking up the industry and forcing us to rethink what it means to open a fitness business. Owners such as Alwyn and Rachel Cosgrove, Todd Durkin, and Rick Mayo have created training businesses that often generate more money per month than a traditional, mainstream fitness business did in the 1990s. These professionals represent the best of what the new generation of trainer can accomplish in today's competitive fitness market.

What sets these business owners apart, and many other men and women like them, is that they had a love for the fitness business but also took the time to develop themselves as businesspeople along the way. In the end, to be successful in this business, you have to have both a passion for helping people and changing lives and the drive to master all aspects of the business itself.

Common Mistakes You Should Recognize

As you take your first step into the world of owning a fitness business, be aware of the common mistakes you can make at this stage that will negatively affect the outcome of your business later. These mistakes are not the only ways that you can end up in trouble, but they are definitely shared by the largest percentage of new fitness owners.

Sticking with the wrong concept. Many people latch on to a concept and then won't let it go, even if it doesn't really fit them or their market. For example, you might have dreamed of opening your own training center specializing in upscale adults, but if your marketplace already has three or four of those, you must decide if the area can support another one. Forcing a concept will almost always end in financial failure. Can you take your concept to another market that is underserved, or can you change your plan and perhaps open a women's-only gym or a sports performance center for children, demographics that may be underserved in your town?

Overpaying for someone else's dream or mistake. It is amazing how many people get into the fitness business after being drawn in by someone else's passion. This happens often, for example, when a passionate trainer hooks up with a client (the money person) to open a new center. The trainer hasn't taken the time to learn how a business works as a business, and the money person trusts his trainer to know the business because the trainer has done so much to help the client. In this scenario, the investor will often end up with the business because the trainer, who was never prepared to run the business, can't make money and walks away, leaving the person who signed for the money and the lease behind in the fitness business. Are you opening this facility because it is a good business plan or because you're caught up in someone else's dream?

Doing it for the wrong reason. As mentioned previously, if you're opening this new business because you just want a place to work out that's better than the other places in your town, or because you love the dream of changing hundreds of lives the way yours changed when you first discovered the wonders of working out, then you're doing it for the wrong reasons. Can you take this passion and make money with it? That question is the most important one to ask yourself at this stage of preparation.

Being too emotional. It is not unusual for a person to rush into business too quickly when first thinking about opening a fitness facility. A common mistake, for example, is to put together a little money and look for your first location. The first location isn't exactly right and might be lacking the right amount of parking or the rent is too high, but your passion gives you a sense of urgency and you force your new business into something that will increase your chances of failure later. It is hard to do, but set your emotionalism aside and remember that it's a business you're opening, and that you need to be able to walk away from any deal that doesn't make sense in your business plan or that has to be forced to make happen. It might take months to open your first place, but it might also be several years from the time you commit mentally to opening a business and you work out your first client.

So, why do you want to get into the fitness business? If you're creating a practical business plan and are willing to learn all the aspects needed to be financially successful over time, then you will make it. If, on the other hand, you're opening this business because your dream is working out every day in your own place, standing at the counter greeting your members as if you're the mayor of Fitnessville, and thinking you will hire the experts you need to actually run the place while you work out a handful of fitness fanatics who refuse to train with anyone but you, then getting a job in someone else's fitness business might be a much more practical idea than actually owning one yourself.

Focusing Your Project

At some point, you have to turn your dream into the first few steps of reality. The expected outcome is to take that vague idea of owning a fitness business and start to give it a shape, a rough cost, and a target market for your new business and to find out if owning a small business is the avenue you want to pursue to realize your dream of working in the fitness industry for a living.

Giving your dream a shape and a focus early also allows you to have those initial talks with bankers or investors and lets you start to develop an initial cost factor. You may be dreaming, for example, of opening a large multipurpose club, but after spending time developing your initial focus, you might find that your personal interests and skills, or your capital limitations, push you in another direction such as opening a 6,000-square-foot training facility centered on sports performance.

Going in with a focus up front also can save literally hundreds of thousands of dollars later in the project by eliminating costly wrong turns such as investing too much money too soon and then finding out you don't have the funding or support you need to finish the project. Even the money you will spend on a business plan, a vital tool to raise money and to develop a working concept, can be wasted if you don't have an idea going in about what you want and can afford.

Think these points through thoroughly and start to build your project notebook based upon your thoughts and research. Most of the ideas defined in this chapter will also be covered in depth in other chapters. Again, all you're trying to do at this point is start developing a firmer concept of your new business. Ask yourself the following questions:

- Can my community support another fitness facility similar to the one I want?
- What is my target market for this club? Can I define this group by age, affluence, and location?
- Can I find a home for my business by becoming a specialist and taking a smaller or different space?

- Should I attempt to make this a real estate project or is renting my best option? Would my potential investors be better served by committing to real estate?
- Success in other businesses doesn't always guarantee success in this one. What do I need to learn in this business to be successful? How is this business different than what I have done in the past? What are the key skills that I need to learn to survive during the first year?
- Do I really know what I am getting into with this business? Do I understand that this is a seven-day-a-week business that is capital-intensive and will have all the staff and member problems associated with opening any type of service business? Am I willing to work the 60 or more hours a week it takes to be good in this business during my first year? Do I really understand that I will have to be in this business most evenings until 8 p.m. or later during my first year?
- Am I aware of how long it takes to actually open a new business? Have I thought about how long it takes to raise capital, get permits, use an architect, and build my new business? Do I have the personal reserve capital to support myself during the first six months I am open so I can give my business a chance to get healthy?

Can your community support another fitness facility similar to the one you want?

An interesting thing about fitness centers is the true market area they command. Most new owners go into their projects looking at their marketplace as being much bigger than it really is, when in reality your market is always smaller than you think. Consider the following: 85 to 90 percent of your membership will most likely come from within a 12-minute drive time of your club if it is a mainstream fitness business and about a 20-minute drive time if you have a specialty business such as a training center or sports performance business.

This translates to most clubs having at best a three- to five-mile radius around their business that comprises their market. You can figure this out without being too scientific. Find the area of town you are thinking about, pick a street corner, and then, at about 6:00 p.m., which should be rush hour for most markets, drive 12 minutes in one direction and mark that spot on a map. Then go back to your corner and head out in another direction for 12 minutes. Eventually, you will build a rough circle around that site that highlights your potential market.

This low-tech method will determine how hard it would be for your potential members to get to your club during what are normally the busiest hours for most fitness businesses. Once you establish a ring, you can mark off competitors that would be in your competition area and get an idea about how many different clubs are in your ring. Also, try to establish the target market for each one of these competitors.

For example, you might have a Y that caters to families, a few mainstream fitness businesses, a circuit club, a specialty high-intensity workout business, and maybe a few training clubs. The question to ask is whether you are trying to service a segment of the population that is being neglected or are you trying to directly compete with someone already existing in business?

What is your target market for this club? Can you define this group by age, affluence, and location?

When you think about your target market, you're trying to determine who will use your club. When asked whom their club is designed for, many rookie owners respond with somewhat vague answers. "Well, it's for people with money," or "I'm going to specialize in older people," or "I'll have something for everyone."

Target market is defined as the core 80 percent of your membership. In other words, about 80 percent of your membership may come from one specific target market. This market usually encompasses about two generations, although you obviously will have a large number of members over or under your target age.

For example, you might be an upscale adult club that has a target market of 30 to 50 year olds with average household incomes of over $60,000. In this example, about 80 percent of your members would be in this age category.

An important thing to remember is that likes attract likes. In other words, people like to socialize and hang out with people like themselves. Therefore, knowing your target population is important because every decision you will make, from the color of the paint to the programming choices in your business, should be based upon acquiring members in your target group. Another way to look at this is how can you market a business if you don't know whom you are trying to reach? Knowing your target market is the first step toward building a workable business plan.

Can you find a home for your business by becoming a specialist and taking a smaller or different space?

If three good pizza places were on three corners of a busy intersection, would you open another pizza place on the fourth corner or would you consider opening a burger place or a Chinese restaurant? Specializing, or finding a niche, is nothing more than trying to determine which segments of your market are being served by existing clubs, and which areas or target populations are underserved. For example, if your area has four or five clubs all vying for the same 18-to-34-year-old market, would it make sense to open another club that goes after those same demographics or would you be better off to open an upscale adult club, women's-only facility, or perhaps a lifestyle enhancement center (personal training center)?

Specializing is also usually cheaper than trying to open a big box-style club. Many markets don't have the square footage available to develop a large facility, yet many of these same markets could benefit from smaller facilities that are going after more narrowly defined target markets.

As a side note, the economics of the last few years will change the fitness market for years to come. The large box club, meaning 35,000 square feet and larger, will become a rarer phenomenon as a start-up business or as a normal expansion for most chains because the cost of building these kinds of businesses has risen dramatically. Additional factors include increased risk, greater competition for this segment of the market (18- to 32-year-old members), lack of borrowing power, and the cost of rebuilding and maintaining clubs already owned and operated by most of the chains.

The majority of growth in the coming years in the business will be in clubs that are less than 20,000 square feet, with probably the largest increase coming from the training clubs in the 3,000 to 12,000 square foot sector. Why would you build a new, franchised gym, replicating a big box 1995 club business model, for a high-risk $4,000,000 or more (usually in rental space), when you can open a 6,000 square foot club that will gross $100,000 or more a month with a net pre-tax return of 20 percent or higher?

The economy, and other factors such as maturing markets with more competition that force the need for retention, will force change upon the market and the coming years will see far more training facilities being built rather than traditional box clubs replicating the business model of the 1990s.

The question to ask yourself is: Are more narrowly defined markets (such as sports performance for children, training clubs, or women's-only clubs) available that would make more sense in my market, rather than opening a typical box club that needs more capital and has already been done too many times in my desired area? Another way to ask this question is: Can I specialize in a specific niche and still make money and still live my dream?

Should you attempt to make this a real estate project or is renting your best option? Would your potential investors be better served by committing to real estate?

Building from the ground up is often a possibility that is not considered by a new fitness business owner, but you should take a look at this option, especially if you have investors and the right market. Most people that are thinking about getting into the fitness business start with rental space, assuming that it will be cheaper and easier to get into initially. Rental space, however, can often be harder to get into because of the collateral needed to get the project funded through traditional sources and because of the difficulty of attracting investors.

For example, an upscale club of 10,000 square feet could cost as much as $1.3 million, and often much more, to build based upon the following numbers, which are averages for this type of club. In some markets you might be able to build for less or have a lower rent factor, which would affect the operating cost per month as well the reserve.

- Build-out for the interior at $50 (not common anymore) to $60 to $90 per square foot (becoming the new standard) = $600,000 to $900,000

- Equipment = $300,000 (heavy on cardio and functional and based upon open space for training lanes, possibly turf, and a lot of functional necessities such as kettlebells, ropes, sleds, core balls, medicine balls, suspension training with racks, etc.)
- Reserve capital = $225,000 (three months reserve at $75,000 per month operating expense)
- Miscellaneous = $75,000 (computers, software, stock and inventory, licenses and certifications, etc.)
- Architectural fees = $80,000
- The total money needed for this project would be $1,280,000 to $1,310,000, and you would need at least $250,000 to $400,000 in cash (depending on the bank) to make it happen.

This size club might represent a newer version of a mainstream fitness center using a strong emphasis on building a large training income. This model could easily be reduced to about 6,000 square feet, which would lead to across-the-board reductions such as a much lower internal build-out, less fixed equipment, smaller architectural fees, and less reserve capital.

The business goal for this model would be to create two income streams within the business: one based upon the traditional membership model and the other based upon a layered training model where you replace sessions and packages, the outdated standard of trainers everywhere, with long-term commitments for training done in groups lead by a trainer or using a limited version of one on one.

This dual income approach is one of the reasons there has been a breakout in the training club category where owners using this model are generating $60,000 and more per month in small training clubs, something unheard of just a few years ago. This same training model, which will be mentioned later in this book, is also something a mainstream fitness owner can adapt to any fitness business.

In this example, you have two problems to consider when you are trying to do this project in rental space. First of all, a banker may want you to have at least 20 percent down for this project for traditional financing and you would have to collateralize the balance at 80 to 100 percent. In other words, the bank might give you the money, but you have to put up real property or other collateral such as stocks or CDs, which have to cover at least 80 percent of the money you borrow.

The reason the banker has this requirement is that if you fail, the bank has nothing to go after to recoup its losses because everything you spend the loan money on such as build-out and equipment, really doesn't have any value to the bank. The build-out stays with the building in most leases and becomes the property of the owner of that building, and the equipment is hard to sell for any real money. In other words, you have nothing the bank can seize to liquidate to get their money back when you open in rental space.

The second issue is that this scenario is difficult to use to attract investors. You're in essence asking your money people to get into the fitness business with you, which is something most don't want to do. Few money people want to invest in things they don't know anything about or can't ultimately control if the business doesn't perform. This type of business might provide a great living for you, but paying back investor money with a decent interest rate puts extra strain on the business. Investors are usually looking for a way to make a good return on their money and want the principal back in a decent amount of time rather than acting like a bank that might be willing to structure the debt over a longer time and at a lower interest.

The investor is also faced with the same issue that the bank is: What happens to his money if you fail? Again, no worthwhile assets would be available to go after that are worth selling off to pay back the debt. If you fail, everyone loses, which is why putting this much money into rental space is so hard for many potential owners.

IT Stock

On the other hand, it is a lot easier to attract people who want to be in real estate. Even the banks like real estate projects more than they like rental space in many towns, because if you fail, something concrete exists that can be sold to pay back the money that was borrowed.

Investors especially like to be in the real estate investment business. If the plan looks good, an investor can put some cash in and then the investment becomes passive, meaning that he can go after other projects instead of being tied up with this one. He also gains equity over time, appreciation in the real estate, and is probably also getting a return on his investment as well.

The problem is that many potential owners never consider real estate because the number is too big and it scares them. For example, that same 10,000-square-foot club might cost $2.7 to $3 million to build from the ground up based on these general figures:

- Land = $800,000 (an acre-and-a-half minimum in most areas)
- Site preparation = $100,000 (prepare the site, retention ponds, utilities)
- Shell of the building = $700,000 (based on $70 per square foot)
- Build-out = $600,000 (based on $60 per square foot)
- Equipment = $300,000 (heavy on cardio and functional and based upon open space for training lanes, possibly turf, and a lot of functional necessities such as kettlebells, ropes, sleds, core balls, medicine balls, suspension training with racks, etc.)
- Architect = $150,000
- Reserve = $225,000 (three months based on $75,000 monthly operating expense)
- Miscellaneous = $75,000
- The total for this project would be approximately $2,950,000.

Sticker shock is high when you ask a potential owner to consider this number, but again, this project might be easier to complete in many markets. First of all, the Small Business Administration (SBA) has certain programs, such as the 504, that make getting into this type of project much easier. These programs are handled through banks that specialize in working with the SBA and usually only require 10 to 15 percent down. Bankers that understand SBA loans often like them because the government actually guarantees a substantial percentage of the total loan package if you fail, eliminating their exposure. Raising $270,000 to $400,000 might be easier to raise for a building project than coming up with the same amount of money and then still having to come up with the collateral to cover the rest of your loan using the rental space example.

This project could also be tweaked in a number of ways to increase investor potential, such as by adding 10,000 square feet of rental space on the first floor and putting the fitness facility on the top floor. If the rental spaces were done well, and in the right location, the rents for the first floor would offset a great deal of the monthly debt for the entire project.

In the real estate example, if the project turned out to cost $3 million, and the owner raised $500,000 through investors looking for a real estate project, the monthly payment would only be about $18,000 for everything (using a payback of approximately $6,000 per million over 25 years), which would be largely offset by having 10,000 square feet of rental space available.

The final point in this debate is that the owner in the rental space might be paying $10,000 to $14,000 for rent alone in his space, not counting debt service to the bank, while the owner in the second example might be paying just $18,000 per month for the entire project, not counting offsets for the retail space that could be rented.

As you focus your project, consider building or buying an existing building if it fits your market. You might find it easier to get a bank to work with you or to find needed investors who would rather own real estate rather than a fitness center.

Success in other businesses doesn't always guarantee success in this one. What do you need to learn in this business to be successful? How is this business different than what I have done in the past? What are the key skills that I need to learn to survive during the first year?

Every business has its own nuances, needed skill sets, and learning curve. Being a competent businessperson in another area obviously does give you an edge when getting started, but the rules in the fitness business are different—as they are in all other small businesses—and many experienced businesspeople are surprised, and often angry, when they find that the fitness business looks so easy on the outside but is so difficult once you own your own facility.

When you consider opening a fitness business, you don't need all the answers, but you do need to understand the questions, and these questions come from understanding all the moving parts of a typical fitness business. These areas of needed expertise are as follows:

- *Management and numbers*: How does a club make money? How do you collect money from your members? What is a good payroll percentage? How do you market to attract enough leads to drive your business? Why do clubs fail and how can you avoid these mistakes? All of these questions, especially those that pertain to the financial foundation of the business, have to be answered before you build your first business plan.

  You must also consider the question: Who is going to run the back shop part of your new business on a daily basis? The back shop person is the one who normally controls the money for the new company as well as other vital functions such as payroll, marketing, banking, accounting, and staffing. Most new fitness owners are so wired about the front side, where the training and fun stuff takes place, that they allocate little thought to who will actually run the business portion on a day-to-day basis.

- *Working people out*: Fitness is your base product. Who can certify your trainers? How do you find and hire trainers? What is current in the training field? What is the culture you need to establish that will help the largest percentage of your members get results and achieve success? Building a successful fitness program is not a random act, and it takes thought to match your club's offerings and programming with your target market and to find your niche in often crowded, competitive markets.

- *Weight management*: More than 60 percent of the American population is overweight. The fitness business has to provide leadership in this area in the future to further expand its penetration to reach new folks who don't yet use a fitness facility.

- *Customer service and staffing*: Member retention and staffing will be the two biggest issues in the fitness business during the next 10 years. How do you keep the members you get? How do you find and develop a staff that can drive revenue in your business? How do you pay employees and keep them motivated over time? What are real retention numbers and how do you achieve them?

- *Sales*: Selling memberships and services are always going to be part of owning a fitness facility. In fact, sales can be defined as follows: 95 percent of what you do every day is sell somebody something. The other 5 percent involves management of the business. A fitness business is a production-based business that depends on daily cash flow, which only comes from selling new memberships and services in the business each day you are open.

As a potential owner of a fitness business, you need to have a grasp of all of these skills, especially when it comes to sales. You can hire expertise to cover your weak areas, but you have to have a working idea yourself if you want to be successful. In sales, for example, you would find it hard to hire and manage a sales team if you have never sold memberships yourself in a fitness business—and the same is true for the other skills. You don't have to be an expert, but you do have to have a working concept concerning all the main parts of a typical fitness business.

Do you really know what you are getting into with this business? Do you understand that this is a seven-day-a-week business that is capital-intensive and will have all the staff and member problems associated with opening any type of service business? Am I willing to work the 60 or more hours a week it takes to be good in this business during my first year? Do I really understand that I will have to be in this business most evenings until 8 p.m. or later during my first year?

How hard could it really be to own a fitness business? You get to work out anytime you want. You get to hang out with a lot of semi-naked people who are just there for fun and fitness. And everyone wants to work in a fitness business so finding staff shouldn't be an issue, should it?

Opening a fitness business is like opening any other customer-service intensive business. You will have to put in a lot of hours and hard work (think work weeks of 60 hours and more during your first year and longer), especially during the initial growth period of the business, to make it work.

The fitness business is also capital-intensive, meaning that it costs a lot more to open than many other small businesses you might consider. Reinvestment is also a considerable cost over time often consuming about 7 to 9 percent of your gross income per year to just stay competitive.

Opening a small business is often a surprise for many people. You must enter your new business with the understanding that owning a fitness business has a unique set of challenges and that you've just bought yourself the right to put a lot of hard work into your dream.

Are you aware of how long it takes to actually open a new business? Have you thought about how long it takes to raise capital, get permits, use an architect, and build your new business? Do I have the personal reserve capital to support myself during the first six months I am open so I can give my business a chance to get healthy?

The lengthy timeline is often the biggest surprise of all for potential owners, especially those that think opening a new business will take only a few months. Look at this typical timeline for opening in a rental space. It represents an average project, which may vary depending on the project, but this list does cover all the stages you'll most likely go through on your journey:

- Getting a focus and conceptualizing your business: 1 to 2 months
- Writing a business plan: 2 months
- Working with banks and investors to raise capital: 3 months
- Negotiating rental space: 1 to 2 months
- Using an architect and acquiring permits: 2 to 3 months
- Build-out: 4 to 6 months

From the moment of, "Hey, I want to get into the fitness business," to the moment of, "Welcome to my new place," may take anywhere from a year to 18 months in a rental-space facility for a mainstream fitness facility and 3 to 12 months for a training facility. If you want to build, it will take at least a year and maybe as long as two if you encounter any code issues in your area or need to attract more than one investor into your new real estate project.

If you have capital already in place and an inventory of rental space in your area to choose from, then you might get it done in as little as nine months, but that is quicker than normal for most projects. The key is to not be surprised about the length of time it may take, and don't force the project because of the emotional need to get it done in a hurry and to get in and get working. All projects have a natural flow, and the most common mistake is to go too quickly and make bad decisions that cost you time and that hurt your business once you're open.

Build It to Sell It

Every decision you make as you build your new business should enhance the ultimate value of your business, because at some point you are going to want to get out. It might seem a little backward, but many owners are more successful because they get in with a plan to get out, and that plan is based upon getting the maximum dollars for their business at some point in the future when they are ready to leave the game.

For example, if you build in rental space, as mentioned previously, you will have to sign a lease with a landlord for your new business. The length of the lease, the option periods, the value of the lease compared to market value, and any build-out you might negotiate all can affect the value of the business when you sell in the future, because having the right to perpetuate the business into the future at a below-market rate is much more valuable then buying a standard lease with limited options.

The Key Concept in This Chapter

At some point, you have to take the steps necessary to turn your dream of being in the fitness business into reality. The first step is to start taking all of those random ideas and focus them into one set concept that fits you and your market. Be open to new ideas and don't force a concept by being too emotional. Opening a small business is a big step in most people's lives and you want to give yourself every chance to be successful, both financially and in your dream to help people change their lives for the better through fitness.

Additional Resources

McCarthy, J. (2004). *IHRSA's Guide to the Health Club Industry for Lenders and Investors* (2nd ed.). Boston, MA: IHRSA.

CONCEPTUALIZING YOUR NEW BUSINESS

Chris Clinton

chapter Two

The first step in conceptualizing your new business is asking yourself, "Who is going to be the client of this new business?" In other words, who is this business designed for in your mind? You can't build a generic business and expect to become financially successful. If you want to make money over time, you have to build a business that has a specific target market in mind before you commit and start the building process.

The modern fitness business has been around since approximately 1945 in its present form, which can be defined as fitness clubs and businesses for the general public that are based upon membership sales. Clubs existed in this country prior to 1945, but the fitness business really began to take off in the late 1940s and early 1950s.

Perhaps the most surprising fact about our business is that the industry has only managed to capture 16 percent of our entire country's population according to IHRSA research. In other words, after more than 60 years of commercial fitness, only 16 percent of the people in America belong to fitness centers.

The fitness industry has done a decent job of attracting people who are already interested in fitness, but it hasn't yet done the work necessary to attract the other 84 percent who don't belong to any type of fitness facility.

There are a number of reasons for this failure to penetrate the market that need to be explored at this stage, prior to you building your first club or perhaps opening a second unit in a new market.

First of all, has the fitness industry developed a model that will attract the other 84 percent of the population who have yet to discover commercial fitness? Secondly, does the consumer have the "need" to join a club and make visiting a commercial fitness center a part of his daily life?

The answer to this first question is that the industry is evolving faster now during the last several years than it has during the last 60. This evolution is based upon the simple fact that the mind-set of the consumer is forcing the clubs to change. In the past, mainstream fitness centers were not much more than membership mills that could attract a large number of new clients, burn them up through poor service and questionable results due to poor training, and then replace the lost members with fresh blood the next month.

Changes in the market are forcing the commercial operators to change their approach or die. Many markets are saturated with large numbers of clubs, which hurts an owner's ability to easily replace lost members due to such heavy competition—no matter what price point they use to attract members.

The business models that most of the chains still use, and far too many of the independents, are still based upon the factor that an unlimited number of new members exist somewhere out there in the market to replace the ones they lose every month due to their inability, or lack of desire, to properly take care of their members. This model worked in the 1980s and 1990s when there wasn't much competition, but it is a failing model when you have too many clubs chasing too few members.

The consumer is also more educated about fitness and less tolerant of paying for a membership that doesn't result in a change in his appearance or health. Most of this new breed of member wants more from a facility than just renting a treadmill, but they do not want to pay thousands of dollars a month for help that should be offered more affordably and to a wider range of members at a lower cost.

Most importantly, the smaller training clubs, once the poor hideout for the single trainer on his own, are now emerging as serious players in the game, introducing training that gets serious results for clients, and the trainers are doing this in larger and more serious physical plants. These clubs attract a significant percentage of the better-educated and more affluent clientele that might have been members of the mainstream club in the past but no longer support those clubs because of a lack of options, serious equipment, and support.

One of the keys that will need to be considered as you build your new facility is the consumer himself and how his life is changing. We all know, and can literally see, that our culture is leading toward having a higher percentage of our population that is fat, obese, and just plain out of shape. The year 2009 was the first year in America that the obese segment (32 percent) passed the overweight segment (31 percent).

Many experts in our field dispute the actual numbers because any serious kettlebell guy that is in shape is probably also obese according to Body Mass Index charts. This fact is undoubtedly true, but it does not negate the overall trend. Even if you plan to do sports performance, this trend will affect your business since you will still need to draw from this population of future fitness people who have not yet discovered a life of fitness and health.

Industry pundits call these groups the "Get Its," representing the 16 percent, and the "Don't Get Its," representing the other 84 percent who have not yet found us. Those who understand fitness and the importance it can play in their lives—those who get it—already work out and belong to fitness clubs. The rest don't yet make the connection—for the obvious reason that these clubs have failed the consumer in the past—that if you want to get into shape, you start with a fitness club.

The mistake club owners make, and the opportunity of the future, is that almost everything they do in their clubs regarding the attraction of new members is targeted at people who get fitness and understand it (the 16 percent), and almost nothing in their marketing approach, club design, sales policies, or training philosophy is really aimed at those who are not yet involved in commercial fitness, which, at 84 percent, is obviously the biggest untapped market.

Who are the "don't get it" people and what do they want from you?

Start with the premise that about 300 million people live in this country. Out of this number, roughly 45 million belong to fitness facilities of some type. IHRSA research shows that approximately 30 million more may have belonged to a fitness center at some point in their lives, but currently do not.

Using these numbers, approximately 225 million potential members are out there who have most likely never stepped foot into a fitness facility. If the industry can change its image and the product we offer to attract a wider range of clientele, then if we only converted 5 percent more, or 11.25 million, we could change the very nature of what we do in this industry. Divide that number by the roughly 30,000 mainstream fitness centers in America and every gym currently in business would get 383 new members, which is a significant number for most clubs. If our goal as an industry is to change lives and the culture of sedentary living and obesity in this country, then we really haven't even begun as an industry since we have touched so few people after more than 60 years.

Keep in mind that we are only referring to mainstream fitness facilities. There are a significant number of small training facilities that are very successful in changing a lot of lives that only need about 15 to 20 new members a month to become very financially successful. In many ways, these training clubs that are being built in the 3,000- to 12,000-square-foot range represent the club of the future. These facilities are cheaper to build, generate a solid return on investment, fit into more affluent markets due to their lesser space requirement, and are actually based upon the premise that they exist to get clients into real shape, something mainstream clubs often can't claim since they are built to simply generate memberships on a monthly basis.

Where the club industry goes wrong is that we try to change the world by going too big too soon. Not everyone is a fitness candidate and not everyone will join a gym. You need to think about the fitness business as more of a continuum, with those who will never, ever join fitness centers on the extreme left and the hard-core workout fanatics on the extreme right. Figure 2-1 depicts this continuum, including the 16 percent that represents all current

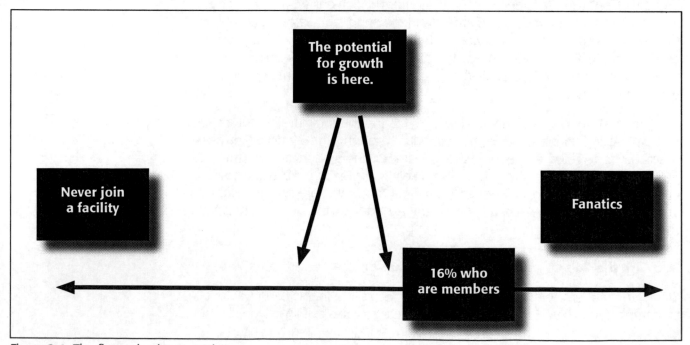

Figure 2-1. The fitness business continuum

club members. Fitness professionals live and work on the right side of the continuum, and the potential market for your business is the people closest to that side. In other words, we already have the 16 percent as part of the current club market and we only need to move toward the left a few points to make big changes.

According to IHRSA, the number of people joining gyms has slowly been rising at a rate at about 5 percent per year. That slow-but-steady growth, representing the future of the industry, will continue to come from those folks closest on the continuum to the 16 percent number. These are the folks who fit the rest of your demographics and who sort of understand what you do, but for whom fitness hasn't yet become important in their lives.

An example might be a former housewife who has raised her kids, returned to the workforce at age 40, and now wants to spend some time working on herself. She might have never belonged to a gym, but she is a strong candidate because she has everything you need: awareness, income, education, and opportunity.

The challenge is to take advantage of this opportunity in your market by building facilities and creating a business plan that goes after this group of aware-but-as-of-yet-uninvolved potential members. The fitness people already in the market (16 percent) will find you on their own since fitness is a part of their lifestyle, but future success in this industry lies in developing new markets that are being underserved.

How big is your potential market?

Capture rate is the term that defines how much of your market you should be able to acquire as members in your club. The problem with any type of capture-rate formula is that it is hard to develop just one formula that covers every type and size of facility and price structure. For example, a 10,000-square-foot club and a 40,000-square-foot club in a market of 50,000 people, using a set capture rate of 4 percent, would both come up with answers that would be unrealistic for their business plans.

Remember from Chapter 1 that your market is within an approximate 12-minute drive time from the club during rush hour. The 4 percent number in this example would mean that each club in this market would capture 2,000 members, which is unrealistically too high for the smaller club in most markets, yet too low for the larger club to survive.

Again, price structure, profit centers, and other competition are all factors that would affect the actual numbers that each club would get and need to survive over time. For example, the smaller club might have an extremely low price, which would lead to larger sales numbers and memberships, but would at some point mean that it might become unable to sustain those numbers due to market saturation and loss rates.

Other factors such as the kinds of programs offered, the focus on training in the club, the club's marketing niche, and the affluence of the marketplace also affect how many members a club can attract. No two clubs or club markets are alike, and too many new owners build their business plans on unrealistic numbers that they plan to attract as new members.

Determining Market Potential

Two methods can be used to help you get an idea of your market potential. The first is a sliding scale model, and the second method is based upon actual expenses in the club. Both methods represent the **minimum** numbers you need to make the business work.

An important side note is to always build your business plan on the minimum numbers you need to stay in business, not on the unrealistic numbers that every potential owner dreams about but seldom realizes in his business. The old rule used to be that you should create three business plans for any new business. The first one is the best-case scenario, which you create and then throw away. The second plan is the middle-case version, which you create and give to your bankers and investors. The third plan is always the worst-case version, and that is the one you use to actually run your club on a day-to-day basis.

It is important to know as a new business owner when you have to hit the following numbers. The most important month in your new business is the 25th month, which is when your business plan should mature and when you should reach the target number of new members that your club needs to be financially successful. It will not take this long, however, to start generating revenue in your business, but this is the point where the club matures and where it should be a fully functioning, stable business.

Most clubs can cover their base operating expenses (meaning you are now breaking even and the monthly cash flow covers all operating expenses) somewhere during the seven- to nine-month mark of operation, assuming that the club opened somewhere between August 15 and February 15 and has at least two months of operating capital in reserve.

You will have higher expenses than revenues during that growth period, and the reserve capital ensures that you have enough money to pay your bills without having the need to panic, which leads to poor decisions. Stated again, you will lose money for the first few months you are in business. Operating loss is a normal part of being in business during the first year and you should expect it to happen. If your business turns profitable earlier, "Congratulations, you have beaten the odds," but that doesn't happen too often for a new fitness business, so assume the loss is going to come and prepare for it with reserve capital.

If you open your club in May or June, which is the hardest time period to open a new facility in most markets, your new business won't come together until about the tenth month you are open, and you will need a full three months of operating reserve rather than just the needed two months if you open the club during one of the more optimum times of the year.

Method 1: Percentage of population

This method is based upon square footage and the percentage of the population in your 12-minute drive time that you can capture. It is a sliding scale and represents the minimum number of paying members you need to have in your system during the 25th month of operation.

Again, the 25th month is important because it reflects the full maturation point for a typical club. You've had two full years of business and are now entering your third year. By this point, your club has passed through two full member-retention cycles and your net receivable check (accumulation of all monthly member payments) should be at its highest point. At this point in time, this check should be covering at least 70 percent of your base operating cost each month, with an ultimate target of 100 percent coverage.

It is important to note that most of the successful personal training centers have moved away from selling packages and sessions and have adopted long-term agreements for their clients. For example, someone who wants personal training might pay $300 a month for 12 months for four sessions a month or as much as $2,500 a month for unlimited training including assessments, supplements, and other support items. This topic is discussed in greater detail in later chapters.

Many mainstream clubs are learning from the success the smaller training clubs have had with this method and have begun to build this system into their training departments, replacing the more ineffective and dated system of limited one-on-one training sold to a very small percentage of the members in the club.

These clubs have also adopted the semi-private and group personal training models as well that reflect the move toward offering a layered pricing structure that allows a larger number of clients in the facility to share the cost of the trainer rather than being completely eliminated due to the cost of the one-on-one sessions.

Your total membership at this maturation point is also important for the new business owner. Loss rates (members that move away from the club or don't pay) and retention rates (members who finish an initial term of membership and then continue into future years) are known, and often your membership at this point reflects the highest point possible in your club. It is possible to increase membership beyond this point, but the combination of losses and retention issues often flatten the membership growth potential at this point.

The example presented in Figure 2-2 is based upon a market of 50,000 people in a five-mile ring of the club, or about 12 minutes of driving time, and the target number represents memberships and not the total number of actual members.

Keep in mind that memberships represent a single financial instrument to be collected by the club, but this membership might have more than one person included. For example, you might generate a single membership for

Club's Total Square Footage	Total Population	x	Multiplier (Based on Total Square Footage)	=	Target Members
5,000	50,000	x	.015	=	**750**
10,000	50,000	x	.025	=	**1250**
15,000	50,000	x	.03	=	**1500**
20,000	50,000	x	.035	=	**1750**
25,000	50,000	x	.04	=	**2000**
40,000	50,000	x	.05	=	**2500**
50,000	50,000	x	.06	=	**3000**
60,000	50,000	x	.07	=	**3500**
75,000	50,000	x	.08	=	**4000**

Figure 2-2. Percentage of population

a husband and wife, which represents one membership but two members. The calculation is based on using the multiplier as a derivative of the total population.

In this case, the multiplier is a percentage of the population you can hope to attain as members in your new club. Also, remember that this number is nothing more than an estimate based upon a typical mainstream facility. For example, if the 10,000-square-foot facility was a sports performance center with adult personal training, it might have fewer than 800 members and still be very successful financially.

Method 2: Sales needed compared to operating expenses

This method, based on what is called the one per thousand rule, calculates your total needed memberships as a factor of your monthly operating expenses and membership price for a single member to join the club. This rule may be the single most important concept for you to understand in your new fitness business because if you break this rule, you will have a hard time surviving and the business could fail from a lack of enough memberships to feed your business.

The Rule

You need one new member per month, per thousand dollars of operating expenses, based upon a monthly rate for one member of $39.

This rule stems from one of the most frequently asked questions by a potential owner developing a business plan: How many new members do I have to get each month to make it? Looking at needed monthly sales allows you to get a feel for if your business plan sounds logical for your market. For example, if you live in a town of 20,000 people, but your expenses are $80,000, you might need more members per month than your market can handle. In this example, if your price was $39 per month per member, you would need 80 new members a month to support the club over time—something not sustainable in a market of only 20,000.

Keep in mind that expenses are situational. The rent factor, or mortgage number, may be substantially lower in some markets, thereby lowering your overall operating expenses. For example, you might spend $6 per square foot in a southern market as compared to $48 per square foot or higher in a major metro market such as San Francisco.

Your expenses may also vary due to the type of club you choose. For example, the interior finish and operating expenses for a 25,000-square-foot, women's-only club in Boston may be twice as much as that of a smaller club in a more rural market in the same state. Lower-end clubs, basing their business plan on volume such as those in the $19 per member per month category, often will have less monthly expense than a full-service club with a full array of group classes and a full staff of trainers.

This rule is based upon the new, annual memberships—either contractual or paid-in-full—you generate each month. This rule does not include renewal members or account for short-term memberships. Your goal as an owner is to average the needed number over the last three-month period in your business, because in the fitness business you might get 150 new members in March, but only 30 in July, so you must keep your average above the needed number over time.

To calculate this number, divide your cost of operation by the number closest to your monthly price, as depicted in Figure 2-3. For example, if your expenses are $70,000, and your anticipated price is $39 per month for an individual membership, then divide $70,000 by 1000. In this example, you will need 70 new members on average per month to become financially successful.

This rule does not account for the club's other profit centers such as personal training or weight loss programs, which generate money on top of these sales numbers. It also does not take into account retention numbers. This rule simply gives you the minimum number you need to average each month in new, annual memberships to stay in business. If you hit these numbers, you have a good chance of surviving and even being financially successful. If you consistently fall short, your chance of failure is higher.

Remember, in the fitness business, hardly anyone fails during their first year or so. The analogy is that you don't die in this business from a brick to the head and go quickly. In this business, death comes slowly and it is like lying naked in a field and having 100 chickens slowly peck you to death. This slow death comes from never hitting your minimum sales numbers (the one per thousand rule); although, if you are somewhat close each month, you can hang on for several years before you are finally forced to close due to a slow starvation of new business.

Monthly Membership Price	Cost of Operation (Total Monthly Expenses)	÷	Factor (Based on Monthly Membership Price)	=	Minimum Number of Monthly Members
$19	$70,000	÷	600	=	116
$29	$70,000	÷	800	=	87
$39	$70,000	÷	1000	=	70
$49	$70,000	÷	1200	=	58
$59	$70,000	÷	1400	=	50
$69	$70,000	÷	1600	=	43
$79	$70,000	÷	1800	=	38
$89	$70,000	÷	2000	=	35

Figure 2-3. The one per thousand rule

Sales are your lifeblood in the business, and when you conceptualize your business plan, you need to start with getting an understanding of how many sales, and how many new memberships, your business will need. Then, you must determine if those sales are reasonable for the type of club you are considering opening in your market.

There is also a minimum number you need to hit if you are a smaller club. No matter how small your business is—meaning you "trainer types" in those 3,000-square-foot clubs (the recommended smallest club you should ever open)—you still have to add a minimum number of new members each month to replace lost clients and to add new blood into your business. This minimum number is 15 to 20, depending on the concept and the market. If you can't add this number each month or you don't think this rule applies to your business, you should reconsider opening because failure is very painful.

Training clubs that can't sustain at least a 15-new-clients-per-month minimum end up buying themselves jobs that are paid for each month by having just enough members. These owners get their 50 to 60 clients in the stable and then only add a few new clients per month that barely replace their lost clients. Over time, you find yourself working hard, all by yourself, and become trapped in the business. Growth is just as important in the training business as it is in mainstream clubs, although the numbers are different and you can live with 15 to 20 new members a month in most training clubs.

Where Is the Growth Going to Be in the Future?

When you start to conceptualize your new club, you have to consider your market and what it would take to compete. Markets can be divided into four distinct subgroups. Each group, or level, includes certain types of clubs that would work in that level but might not work in others.

Level 1 markets

Level 1 markets are the major metro markets that have 250,000 residents or more. During the past years, the large chains have been aggressive in these types of cities, often opening on the same street in the same part of town.

Rent factors are usually high, which limits your space and the type of club you might want to open. If you want to get into this type of market, such as Denver proper or Chicago, you may want to find a niche and think nontraditionally. It is hard to get significant space in these markets for a mainstream facility at a rent that makes sense, so independent owners often open target-specific clubs, such as hybrid training centers or upscale women's clubs. These owners also put clubs on upper floors in buildings where the rent might be lower the higher you go, or they look for basement space, which is also often cheaper.

Hybrid training centers are defined as small clubs, usually in the 1,500- to 5,000-square-foot range, that specialize in training but also offer memberships on a limited basis. These clubs are a more advanced version of the old personal training studios that were too dependent on too few people to survive.

These major metro markets can be very productive if you can get opened in one. Clubs in downtown Chicago, for example, can do quite well due to the neighborhood effect. Your club wouldn't have a lot of parking, but you might draw from your immediate eight-block surrounding area or neighborhood.

Availability is usually the limiter in these markets. There is simply seldom enough space to open a traditional club in the 10,000-square-foot or larger category, and if there is enough space, it is then often priced out of the range of the typical first-time club owner.

As discussed later and often in this book, the rent factor can take a new club down if the business concept doesn't match. Many new owners will sign a lease with a rent factor that is too high with little chance of ever getting enough members to feed the business plan.

Level 2 markets

Level 2 markets are the suburban markets or smaller population cities with populations in the 100,000 to 250,000 range. The big chains are beginning to expand into these areas as the Level 1 markets become saturated, but a lot of growth potential is still available if you are patient enough to research and find the right area.

These markets can support the larger clubs, such as the 40,000-square-foot boxes, but smaller clubs that go after narrower niches, such as 12,000-square-foot, women's-only facilities, can also do well. The franchise clubs, such as AnyTime Fitness® or Gold's Gym®, also do well in these markets because they can vary their size to suit space concerns. Some of the newer franchises, such as Planet Fitness®, also do well in certain segments of these markets that have strong turnover and density.

The newer model training clubs thrive in these markets. This kind of model that is usually between 3,000 to 12,000 square feet and built as a fully functional club with turf, training space, endless functional tools, decent locker rooms, and good cardio is appealing to the more sophisticated training client who is bored with the dated one-on-one circuit concept.

These clubs can have up to 1,500 members with an emphasis on training, but there is a still core membership base that enjoys access to this type of training and this type of equipment. In many markets, this type of facility is becoming the new generation upscale adult club.

It is interesting to note that at the end of 2010, the typical 1995 big box, 35,000-square-foot club, characterized by the Gold's Gyms of that era, were becoming much more difficult to build and support. The economy, issues with banks and financing, the emergence of the smaller, more efficient training clubs, and the intense competition at the national chain level all led to fewer of these boxes being built.

Level 3 markets

Level 3 markets have 50,000 to 100,000 residents and may represent some of the last great club markets left. Operators already exist in these markets, but many of the existing clubs at this level are old and out-of-date, and a newer operator with a more modern concept can often do well. This level is often the forgotten market in the sense that club owners established themselves in the 1980s and 1990s and very little competition followed. For example, there were a large number of big racquet facilities built in the 1980s that still serve as the primary fitness sources in many towns represented in this level that are ugly, dated, and ripe for competition.

Depending on the actual size of the market, the smaller, full-service, mainstream clubs in the 5,000- to 15,000-square-foot range do well, and space is usually available at a reasonable cost; although in a large segment of Level 3 markets, a 25,000-square-foot club would also work. You can also buy a building or a building lot in these markets and build your own fitness center/

retail space using the concept discussed in Chapter 1, where it describes a combination of retail space on the ground floor with a fitness facility upstairs.

The chains aren't likely to hit these areas too hard because they often don't fit their model or going-public plans. This opens the market to an aggressive local owner who wants to open a small, regional chain or to open with vertical segments in mind, which means that you open a variety of clubs with different names that target different groups. Vertical expansion ties up the market to new competition by filling all the possible categories the consumer would seek.

You might, for example, open a mainstream fitness facility under one name, a women's-only club three miles away under a different name, and perhaps even a sports performance center for kids somewhere in the middle, giving the illusion to outsiders that the market is full.

Level 4 markets

These markets have fewer than 50,000 people—small-town America at its best. These markets represent great opportunity for an owner who loves small-town living or perhaps has other commitments in the area and wants to open his first club with little risk. It is also the case that these clubs are successful because they are often the only game in town. These clubs are usually lifestyle facilities, meaning you pick this town because you grew up there or because you really want to live there.

Clubs in these markets often attract a bigger market share because they fulfill a more social role in the community and become the place to hang out and see people. This market is also underserved—with many small towns only having an old, storefront type of club built on 1990s circuit training concepts and dated group exercise programs.

Newer clubs, with group fitness, a pool, and multipurpose rooms that can be rented out to the public, would do well in these communities. Small training-specific clubs are difficult in these markets since you would not normally have enough clients to financially sustain this business model.

Clubs in towns this size that have a large number of tourists also do well if they focus on their two separate markets: the locals who support the club year-round and the tourists who hit it hard during limited seasons.

Building a Gym for a Specific Target Market

You can't be everything to everyone in the fitness business anymore. Multipurpose facilities that cater to the vast masses are getting scarce and harder to build due to the expense, and those that are being built are usually beyond the financial means of most people trying to get into the fitness business as individuals.

Before you open, you have to have a specific target market in mind. Start your thinking with the question: Who is this club designed for and who is my target member? This target market is based upon age and affluence.

Remember that likes attract likes, and successful clubs in the future will be built upon more narrowly defined populations that share common interests and desires. For example, the programming in a club for those who are 24 to 40 years old would be much different from the needed programming in a club that specializes in members who are 35 to 55 years of age.

The common response to this viewpoint is that you can offer programming for everyone in the same facility by just changing classes or by just adding rooms that offer fitness opportunities for all the different users of the facility. The remaining proponents of the "one size fits all" model often cite the non-profit fitness businesses such as the Ys as a business idea that supports the entire population of the community. The answer to this statement is, "Would this type of club, and its business model, survive if it wasn't being propped up with community money that covers all the losses and shortfalls?"

The emergence of the smaller 5,000-square-foot model, the functional training-specific club, the circuit clubs, and other smaller business entities that drain away members from the big boxes also make this "club for all the people" a tough idea to support over time.

There is another question that also needs to be asked: Do all of these different groups of people that make up the typical three-mile market for most clubs really want to belong to the same club? Do old people want to get run

Hemera/Thinkstock

over by the kids that are there for sports performance classes? Do the 20-something people want a club filled with deconditioned people who, in their eyes, are clueless about fitness? And can you really expect an upper scale adult population to enjoy working out with members who are there just because the club might have a cheap membership? Likes attract likes and the different layers of affluence seldom mix well in a club.

This type of club also opens a wide range of management issues for the owner. How would you dress your staff if you are trying to attract the 20-something crowd and older clients in the same business? What kind of music do you play that makes everyone in one club happy at the same time if the ages range from 18 to 80? What colors and degree of interior finish do you go with in your design? What's cool for the 24 to 40 crowd won't work for the older, more upscale group, and the programming that gets a 40-year-old, deconditioned housewife excited might bore a 30-year-old young business professional to death.

Remember, your target market is defined as the members that comprise 80 percent of your total membership. This grouping also usually represents a narrow two-generational grouping. For example, your target market might be 24 to 40, which means your club will specialize in this age group and you will have a base membership of about 80 percent of your members in this age range, and every decision you make as an owner will be with the end goal of attracting more of these people and making the ones you have happy. You will have younger and older members, but your club is designed for that one target market. Consider the following suggested markets and the strengths and weaknesses of each.

Ages 18 to 34. This market is tough to compete in because most of the major chains go after this group on a national scale. Clubs built for this market generally go after high volumes and require a lot of sales to keep them going due to the turnover associated with the members in this age range. Training clubs actually do well in a certain segment of this population. Many of the more athletic people in this grouping are drawn to group personal training and are still actively involved in many sports. This segment within a segment will gravitate away from a mainstream fitness facility toward one that is more challenging and has the tools and information they need to stay active in their lives.

Ages 24 to 40. This age range probably doesn't seem much different from the one discussed in the previous category, but in reality it represents a whole different business plan and a much more sophisticated client. Most of the folks in this group are in their second job or beyond, are more stable in the community, and are looking for a high-energy place to work out that might be of a little higher quality compared to the mass produced box club and that has the equipment and training options available that they read about in the popular fitness magazines. This type of club is like a nightclub without the alcohol and it would be okay to have a DJ and free drinks a few times each month if that fits your personality. Clubs targeting this market fit best in the 12,000- to 25,000-square-foot range, although smaller clubs in the 6,000-square-foot category could do very well if the focus is functional training.

Ages 25 to 45. This group supports the more rural markets or the family clubs. In small towns, you often have to cater to a wider range of members, but your general target market in these types of locations is going to be a slightly younger overall group due to the presence of so many families. Rent factors often dictate the size of club for these markets, but in most cases lower rents in the rural areas will lead to a larger size club. Clubs as small as 7,500 square feet work and can handle the load in the smallest markets, while the family clubs, such as those in the southern states, will often be in the 60,000 to 150,000 square-foot category.

Ages 30 to 50/35 to 55. This emerging group will become even stronger in the coming years. The predicted boomer influx will happen; it's just going to be later than most people think. Boomers that were born prior to about 1950 were not really affected by the fitness boom influences—such as Jim Fixx and the running craze or the advent of Nautilus® equipment—that impacted their younger brethren, and not enough of this group will ever join clubs to make a dent. Fitness simply wasn't part of their early life and won't be part of their later life in big enough numbers to drive a business plan.

Those born after 1950, however, are coming to the gym and will do so in bigger numbers in the next decade. At this point, your target market for this type of total-support, upscale facility will be those in the 30 to 50 range, but that will change slowly toward the 35 to 55 age group. These clubs can range in size from 5,000 square feet on the low end to 25,000 square feet. The key is to build a slightly smaller club but to go after the upscale market in your area with higher prices and a higher degree of finish. In this category, perhaps think of a specialty club such as a training club for those seeking fitness after 50.

If you're looking for a narrower niche to fit your particular market or personal interest, consider the following subcategories. Keep in mind that it is easier to compete in a crowded market if you have a unique marketing position. If one of the following types of clubs is lacking in your area, and you have a personal interest in either category, then consider becoming a specialist in one of these growth areas.

Over-50 clubs. Owners who specialize in the fitness-after-50 group can do well in specific markets where the density is high for this age classification. This smaller club would be based upon functional training and lifestyle enhancement.

Sports-performance centers. Few owners have been successful trying to get children to engage into adult fitness. Children don't want to work out on shrunken adult equipment or go through group classes that are nothing more than watered down adult classes done to different music. A booming market, however, is developing in sports performance that fits almost any child. These clubs, developed by pioneers in this area such as Bill Parisi, work to develop the speed, agility, and quickness needed by any child who wants to be more successful in any given sport. Kids of all shapes and sizes do well in this model, and units can be built as small as 3,000 square feet up to freestanding models that have adult components in the 15,000-square-foot range.

Kettlebell/functional training clubs. These clubs are becoming a hot topic in the field and many new owners are gravitating toward this model due to the low start-up cost, ability to generate substantial revenue over time in group training, and the fact that functional training is becoming something the general public recognizes from the magazines and current television shows such as *The Biggest Loser*.

Women's-only businesses. This model still works in many areas, especially in the clubs that have moved away from the old circuit concept toward getting women more involved in fitness as real athletes. The industry has made a huge mistake over the years when it came to training females, sending women to the corners of the club to hide in group exercise rooms or to do high repetition training with pink dumbbells. Women, and in most cases men over 50, were always second-class citizens in the fitness community and suffered because of this thought process.

Perhaps one of the biggest contributions we have seen from the training boom in the early 2000s was the idea that all clients are trained as athletes in much the same way you would train anyone seeking the best results in the shortest period of time. Training gurus driving this concept were people such as Alwyn and Rachel Cosgrove, Mike Boyle, Todd Durkin, and Pavel Tsatsouline, who all train their female clients as they would any other athlete in the group. This breakout in thought has led to women's-only clubs that are generations ahead of the old circuit clubs of the 1990s.

Mastering One of the Big Three Concepts

The fitness business has slowly been moving toward more specialization and niching over the years. Competition and the cost of building larger units have forced many new owners to go after narrower niches in their marketplaces.

When you start to piece together that ideal club in your head, keep in mind that many of the old-school clubs offered almost everything but really did few things well. These clubs might have had group classes, but they were offered in one, plain room. They might have also had training, but rented out to outside trainers instead of building an internal program. These clubs felt compelled to offer almost anything someone might ask for in a membership, but because the club owner didn't really specialize in anything, most of the offerings were weak or incomplete. They had everything in the club but nothing was done well enough to give the club a competitive edge in the market.

Increased competition, the rise of the more sophisticated consumer, and the increased cost of running a fitness facility have all combined to force the next generation of owners to do fewer things, but to master those that they do decide to offer. The words to remember are "kill the category." Word of mouth comes from offering the ultimate experience for the consumer, and as an owner you simply can't offer this business-changing experience in multiple categories every day in your business.

In other words, what do you want to be known for in your market? If you're going to do something, absolutely kill that category and the business will follow. Master one of the following categories and be competent in the others:

- Group exercise
- Weight management
- Lifestyle enhancement-functional training/children's performance training

Think of these categories as the major definers of your business. The one you pick needs to match your market, who you are as a fitness person, what you believe in as a fitness philosophy, and the type of facility you can afford to open at this stage of your life. For example, a club owner in the Atlanta area is so into group exercise that he built a new 20,000-square-foot club with half the space dedicated to five group exercise rooms. He likes group exercise and made it the center focus of his business plan.

Another owner from Texas, on the other hand, built a 27,000-square-foot upscale club but dropped his group program after only six months. His heart was in functional training and he ultimately used the entire facility to meet his needs. The club generated an average of $83,000 a month in training revenue with 3,500 members, but he couldn't make group exercise work at all because his personal interest centered only on training.

Both of these owners are successful in their markets and both built their businesses around their personal strengths. Whatever you do, do it better and with more depth than anyone else in your market and you will have a higher chance of success.

Become the Third Stop in Their Daily Lives

Work and then go home. Work and then go home. Work and then go home. At some point, a person wants to get away from bosses, spouses, kids, phones, and the stress of their everyday routine. The clubs of the future should strive to become that spot in the person's life, but owners first have to change how they think about their clubs and, especially, their thoughts about what kind of business they are really in.

What's really neglected in most clubs is the social aspect. The majority of new clubs have everything a person needs to get in shape, but they lack the social heart that makes that club a necessary part of the consumer's life over time.

The important thing to remember is that the consumer's expectations are changing. According to *The Experience Economy: Work is Theater and Every Business a Stage* by Pine and Gilmore, consumers are raising their expectations regarding what they expect to get for their money. They have moved beyond service as a differentiator and the newer, better educated, and more sophisticated consumer will spend more for a great experience.

Most fitness businesses can adequately service the consumer and meet his fitness needs, but few can entertain and delight. Sports bars, stretching areas that serve as socialization zones, cardio theaters, and plush locker rooms are all things that will set you apart in the future from clubs that merely offer fitness.

Even the training club owner should build his new club with the idea that he wants to be more than just a place to work out. Small sports bars, decent locker rooms, and strong social events such as team race participation or club-offered bike rides all add to the member's belief that the club is a part of his life beyond just a place to get his workout in and go home.

Fitness, even at its best, isn't always fun, but no reason exists why your club can't be something that delights the person during every visit and becomes the best part of his day. New owners should remember that the industry is moving beyond fitness and that we are actually in the entertainment business, where every visit becomes an energizing experience that leaves the member wanting more tomorrow. Fitness is the key, but it's how the fitness is delivered that will make your club stand out and be more financially successful.

The Key Concept in This Chapter

Be patient, do your research, look at other clubs and your competitors, and then spend time trying to develop an idea that will help you differentiate your business. Your plan has to match you and your personal interests as well as your market. And remember, master the central focus in your business and *kill that category* in your marketplace.

FINDING A HOME FOR YOUR NEW BUSINESS

Jupiterimages

chapter Three

Once you've conceptualized your new business, you have to find it a home. One of the most frequently asked questions by potential owners considering their first fitness facility is whether to rent, build, or buy a used club. The answer to this question has to match you and your business plan, and it will ultimately be determined by how much capital you can raise for your project. Understanding your options with each of these possibilities will help you make a more informed decision and guide you to the choice that will give you the greatest chance of succeeding financially.

Let's review some of the possible business concepts you might be thinking about at this time. The following options are just a few of the ones you have to work with, although many owners end up combining concepts to meet their personal goals, to match the market, or to take advantage of unusual space or opportunity in their areas.

The simple training studio

- This size is about 1,500 square feet or smaller.
- This model is usually a storefront.
- It is typically stuffed with too much fixed equipment.
- There are no locker rooms, but changing areas are provided.
- The prime product is one-on-one training.

This type of fitness business was the standard model for years in the training world, but it is not recommended now due to changes in how we go about training the clients. First of all, the space is too small for anything but one-on-one, which is the least productive business tool you can use as a trainer.

Successful training businesses in this decade have moved toward the group training experience with an emphasis on groups of 10 to 12 people doing fixed workouts or semi-private training with groups of about two to six people doing more personalized workouts with more coaching.

The size of these facilities is their biggest limiter. Most of the early models were nothing more than shrunken mainstream fitness centers with cardio and fixed equipment crammed into a small space. This size limits the number of people you can train, as well as the number of trainers that can use the space at the same time.

Many trainers embraced the model because of the illusion that it was safe and a lower risk to get started. Why pay $3,000 for a larger space when you can get into one of these for $1,000 a month? The issue is that the larger space would give the trainer more credibility, more of a chance to expand his tools and concepts, and a much higher chance of making more money over time since he would most likely be able to service a much larger number of clients, and a much wider range of clients, by being able to move beyond just one-on-one sessions into sports performance, group experiences, and special workshops.

The exception to the rule is the kettlebell clubs that have sprung up in recent years. These clubs do fill a need, can be started for as little as $5,000 to $25,000 in most markets, depending on flooring needs and build-out requirements, and can throw out a decent net profit over time. The revenue potential varies as much as do the trainers who start these facilities. Some can do as little as $8,000 a month and provide a decent profitability for the owner, and others—in bigger markets and with a more business-savvy owner—can generate $40,000 and more per month.

The hybrid membership base training facility

- This size is about 3,000 to 7,500 square feet.
- This model has limited cardio (6 to 12 pieces), a lot of functional equipment, turf areas, training lanes, suspension training and other tools that allow for group training, sports performance, children's groups, as well as more advanced one-on-one training.
- This type of model allows the clients to use the facility without being with a trainer by either using open space or the cardio area or by the client having access to unlimited group workouts each week as part of their overall membership package. Keep in mind that you never want to create a situation that forces a client to have to buy a membership somewhere else. For example, most old-style training clubs only allow the clients to work out with a trainer while in the club. If that client just wants to come to the club and do something on his own, he is denied and he is forced to get a membership at another club, which is something you don't want to have happen as an owner of the training studio.
- Once this business model gets to 4,000 square feet or bigger, changing areas are replaced by small, but full-service, locker rooms.
- This model is becoming popular in the industry, as the cost of opening mainstream is getting prohibitive. In many cases, these are the people who would have opened a more traditional fitness business but now opt to build one of these models. These facilities are cheaper to open compared to mainstream fitness businesses—often in the $150,000 to $400,000 range—they have strong profitability and are easier to place in a crowded market due to the smaller footprint.

This is the model that has probably changed the fitness industry more in this century than any other business type, even surpassing the impact the circuit clubs had on introducing the deconditioned person to fitness during the 1990s.

These clubs service a much larger client base than typical old-style training facilities and can often have memberships as large as 1,200 to 1,500 members but can be extremely profitable with as few as 150 members. This business model is also changing how we think about how money is made in the industry. These clubs can easily generate $60,000 to $100,000 plus per month, numbers that the smaller box clubs of just a few years ago counted as good for annual revenue.

The small fitness facility

- These are full-service fitness clubs with cardio, strength, free weights, and perhaps a limited group presence.
- The clubs in this business model are usually between 4,000 to 8,000 square feet depending upon the market.
- These are membership-driven clubs that offer a base membership to join and then offer training or other services to its members, emulating the larger, mainstream fitness facilities. Memberships might begin at $39 per month per member. These clubs do not work well based upon the $19 pricing model.
- The businesses in this category are often franchises based upon circuits or some other franchise differentiator, such as being open 24 hours through computer access. There are a lot of different players in this class representing a number of different business plans. Independents do well in this class too, depending upon the market.
- These differ from the training facilities in concept, equipment, revenue sources, and often locations. These are smaller versions of a traditional fitness club as opposed to a training club that derives its income from layered pricing where everyone is involved somehow in coaching of some type. Training income does, however, need to be a large factor to make these sustainable over time since the space is the limiter for the number of members the club can hold, which also limits the total membership revenue available.
- These clubs work well in smaller markets or in areas that the larger box clubs won't pursue. The newer generation owner of these facilities often incorporates training into the model, giving it an additional edge as a membership club but also lessening the dependency on new sales by generating a higher return per member through the increased training.
- This club model will be very important in the future. Small, intimate neighborhood clubs can be opened almost anywhere and are less risky due to the smaller start-up cost and lower membership numbers needed to support them. Add training revenue that obtains a deeper penetration into the membership, targeting at least 33 percent as opposed to about 3 to 6 percent for a typical mainstream fitness club, and these can be great business models.
- Depending on the market, this club may or may not have group exercise. If you want to have a full group program, and yet still be able to open one of these more compact models, you should have at least 7,500 square feet. If you want to keep the concept smaller, then consider just cycle classes, which can be done with as little as 10 bikes. What you don't want to become is nothing more than a shrunken mainstream center that is too crowded and has just a little bit of everything but not really enough of the right things, where none of the programming or services are done well because the place is simply too small to do anything right.

There have been a lot of these clubs built since about the year 2000. This format allows someone to get into a club cheaply, service a small town or suburb, and make a decent living. The weakness, however, is that you are still competing heads up against larger, more fully equipped clubs in most markets. The key to opening a smaller, pocket fitness center is to find ways to differentiate yourself from the boxes that surround you.

These clubs also have to be adapted to the local market and culture. Some of these clubs that open in markets with little competition can do well as the only local fitness option. When there is heavy competition, however, this model gets tougher to run without adding something such as a layered training model. Circuit clubs are dying and should be avoided, but there is still life in 24-hour models in some markets, especially if that concept is part of a broader-based business plan that includes training.

There has also been a trend in recent years to open this concept in more square footage. Some of the newer generation of these clubs are getting as big as 12,000 square feet but are filled with more of the equipment you would see in a more sophisticated training facility. This new model has been especially popular in the Midwest and is often an ideal model for a more isolated or rural market.

The low price/full-service model

- This club would be in the 12,000- to 25,000-square-foot range.
- This would be a full-service model with full group, locker rooms, training and other amenities such as a sports bar/juice bar.
- Membership prices for this model would begin at about $19 per month per member. The club attempts to make it on membership sales volume hoping the club can attract more members with the lower price but still be able to offer a range of programming.
- This type of business model would be heavy on cardio equipment, meaning the 25,000-square-foot model might have 100 pieces or more. This club also would have a lot of traditional strength equipment with a large number of fixed plane equipment (traditional selectorized circuit equipment) and free weights, and the newer models would have more functional equipment and less of the traditional bodybuilder-type stuff.

This club model started to appear in larger numbers for two reasons. First of all, the low end/value players that introduced the $10 club drew a lot of attention during the first years they were opened, but many owners don't like a business concept based upon the continuous replacement of members you have lost month after month. Owners in markets affected by the low price players countered with a $19 entry-level price, but still offered a full-service club as compared to the $10 clubs that in reality do nothing more than rent circuit equipment and cardio.

The second reason these clubs have appeared is due to the economy from 2008 and forward. Many club owners that had enjoyed success at a membership rate of $39 or higher felt forced to lower the price to compensate for the financial decline in their marketplaces. This strategy worked to a certain degree, but the ones who originally opened at that price seemed to do better in the long run than those who merely dropped their price as a reaction to the market.

There have been a number of chains that have attempted to open using this business model with mixed success. This model still needs a lot of volume to work and is nothing more than a newer version of what the industry has been opening for the last 30 years. The surprising thing to learn when you open this model is that your price might be lower, but your expenses really aren't that much lower. In other words, you have dropped the price to attract more members, but your cost of operation really hasn't gone down that much.

Despite the limitations, this model would work in markets where the demographics are flatter. The term flatter, in this case, means that there is a wider range of people in the middle to lower income categories, typical of many towns in the more rural parts of a state. Areas with heavy competition make this a tough business plan since a certain segment of the market will seek out a club with nicer amenities and fewer people for a slightly higher price if given a choice.

Again, if you can develop a dual income stream derived from layered training that goes beyond the $19 attraction price, these clubs can and will work for years. Without the training, however, this will be a much harder model to run since there will be a lot of clubs in this category fighting for a limited market share.

The mainstream box club

- This club would be 25,000 square feet or bigger, and some clubs in this model are over 100,000 square feet. You will not see clubs in this category opening at the rate they were being opened prior to the economic problems we encountered during the later part of the first decade of this century. Opening a club that is 40,000 square feet or bigger is simply becoming a matter of risk versus return. Opening a 30,000 square foot club in rental space in today's market might cost as little as $2,000,000 and could be substantially higher. Building one of these from the ground up could easily cost $6,000,000 or more.

- This model is the full-service approach that was so favored by the chains during the last 20 years, and what is in these clubs hasn't really changed that much since 1990. This club would have large locker rooms, several group rooms, a restricted personal training area, acres of fixed plane equipment and plate loaded lines, and large cardio and free weight areas.

- Pricing for this model might be as low as $19 per month for a single member but might be substantially higher in some markets such as the Northeast, where the prices might begin at $59 per month or higher. Most of these clubs are still nothing more than membership mills whose prime function is to attract endless streams of new members. Extreme competition in this category from all the big chains, more sophisticated potential members who now favor results over do-it-yourself fitness, and the cost of opening one of these makes this a tough model to get into these days, especially if you're trying to open one in a major market that is populated by the chain players.

This club used to be everyone's dream in the fitness business, but there will be fewer and fewer of these built in the coming decades. They are simply too expensive to build and operate in competitive markets for most players.

These clubs do have a place, however, and that is when they are focused more on being family clubs in markets outside of the major metro areas or in secondary markets such as major towns in the South or Midwest. In these markets, this type of club fulfills the role of the social center in the town. Towns that have limited outside activities or extreme winters are ideal markets to build a family-focused fitness center of this size. In these markets, the club becomes the place to meet and greet folks in the community, and everyone feels a certain status by being a member.

The real play with opening one of these clubs is owning and developing the real estate. If you can turn this project into a real estate play, then it becomes a much better concept to explore. It is also easier to attract investors and banks if there is real estate involved in the project. In the 1980s, many of the large racquetball facilities were built with the idea that the fitness would pay for the building over 20 years and then you would tear it down and have prime dirt paid for in a good location.

This tactic worked if the owner picked the right location for the project and the dirt was still valuable 20 years later. Pick right and you were successful, but often the city moved away from these dinosaurs, leaving run-down buildings in areas of the town where no one wanted to build. If you are considering one of these as a real estate investment, do the homework and meet with city planners to figure out what you might own 20 years into the future.

Again, there will be fewer of these models in the future. Would you want to build a single large unit for $2,000,000 to $4,000,000, or would you prefer to build four hybrid-training facilities for a total of $1,000,000 for all four? It is worth noting that the newer generation owner who is getting into the industry has a different mind-set than the guys who developed all these early chains and who, therefore, pioneered the box club concept.

The new owners actually understand that there is no business today without understanding retention. This means that whatever you open has to be designed to retain as many members as you can over time, as opposed to the old-style box that was really built just to drive memberships and then replace people once they failed in fitness and left the club. The larger the box, the more difficult it is to deliver intimate customer service, which is the heart of retention. In other words, it is very difficult to deliver service in a 100,000-square-foot facility with thousands of members.

A final note about this business model is that a few of the chains are beginning to dramatically change what is in the box. Equipment that used to be for the exclusive use of the trainers and their limited clientele is now being made available as standard equipment on the floor. This model is being rebuilt and might be viable again in the future, but the market and competition has changed so quickly that unless the concept is reinvented, you will see fewer of these in the coming years.

Franchise clubs

Franchise clubs have not been mentioned specifically because they most likely fall into one of the categories mentioned previously. Buying a franchise means you are buying a proven business model that can be duplicated over and over again—something very few of the franchises that have appeared in the fitness industry over the last few decades can validate or actually deliver.

If you are looking for a franchise club and feel safer using someone else's business ideas, make sure you understand their business concept and what it takes to start and run one. Most new franchise owners need a lot of help and are grossly unprepared to be in the business. Hiring and supervising a trainer, for example, is a lot more difficult than hiring someone at minimum wage to make sub sandwiches.

If you anticipate needing a great deal of help mastering your new business, verify what is available, not just through the franchise itself but also through a lot of calls to a lot of their franchisees. Also, spend time with a number of their franchisees and go beyond just the few they normally use as references. This project is a big investment and you need to understand what it takes to be successful with their business model.

Is Rental Space Right for Your New Business?

When working with rental space, someone else owns the building and you rent that space from the owner for whatever price the market will bear. Your space might be in a strip mall, an office park, or it could be a freestanding building with your own parking.

When you rent space, you bring your equipment, finish the interior (called leasehold improvements), and open for business by paying the landlord rent for your portion of his building. Each month you pay your rent as well as your share of the property taxes, common area maintenance, and insurance for the property, depending on the amount of space you take in the plaza or building. For example, if you have a third of the space in a strip center, then you would pay a third of the taxes, insurance, and common area maintenance, usually referred to as triple net, for that center.

In many cases, it is much harder to raise money for clubs in rental spaces. As described in Chapter 5, once you put in your leasehold improvements, such as mirrors and locker rooms, they then become the property of the landlord, and anything attached to the walls or floor becomes his property if you decide to leave. Even if the landlord lets you take down those things, just how much would a used locker room—or worse, a used toilet bowl—be worth?

This fact makes it harder to raise money from banks or investors for these types of projects, especially if the project becomes larger, because if the owner fails in his new business, no physical assets are available for the lender or investors to go after that can be sold to pay off the remaining debt or initial investment. For this reason, owners who go for rental space and borrow money often have to put up a lot more collateral to get started as compared to buying or building your own place.

Collateral is defined as physical assets that have value and that are pledged against the loan. If you would fail, these assets are taken by the bank and sold to recover the money that they loaned you. Examples of assets that bankers like include equity positions in your home, CDs, and stocks, or other property that the bank would have an easy time liquidating.

Good bankers are by nature conservative, and most banks try to get at least 80 percent collateral against the money you borrow; they also expect you to have a certain amount of working capital that you bring to the table so you at least have a little risk in the project yourself. If you have investors who are cosigning for you, they have to pledge assets that are of value and can be liquidated to cover the loan in case of your failure in the business.

You may find an investor who believes in you and takes a personal interest in your success, called an angel investor, who might put up the money directly for the project and look only for ownership in the business. These types of investors are harder to find, since the return on their investment is often less than they could get for their money if it was placed in more traditional investment opportunities. Often, this angle will be a family member or a client who has prior experience with you and who believes in what you are trying to do.

Another problem with rental-space financing is that banks that loan money to you will want it paid back in a shorter period of time compared to money used to build your own place. For example, if you need $1.5 million to build a 15,000-square-foot club in rental space, you will probably need to have at least $300,000 (20 percent) out of pocket or as money put up by your investors.

The balance of that money, which is $1.2 million, will have to be paid back in a time period equal to your initial lease period with your landlord. For example, if you have an initial lease of seven years, then the payback time for the bank loan will be seven years maximum:

**$1.2 million over 7 years at 8 percent =
monthly payment of $18,703**

This payback schedule is aggressive and does not include the rent for the facility. But if you found the right property and could get a 10-year initial lease (refer to Chapter 5), then your loan might become more realistic:

**$1.2 million over 10 years at 8 percent =
monthly payment of $14,559**

Just a few extra years makes this business plan look much better, because the payment drops substantially compared to the seven-year payback. The goal is to free up cash flow that can be used to develop the business during the early years and then reinvest in the business as it ages.

Rental space may be the only option you have, especially in major metro areas where buying a building or building from the ground up is so expensive. If you are opening a smaller club in the 3,000- to 7,500-square-foot range, for example, rental space is often a great choice because you can get in for a lower total cost, and money for a project that size is easier to get from banks.

Once you move into larger projects, the make-or-break part of the deal will come down to the actual rent factor. A general rule of thumb that might help you evaluate your ability to do rental space, or determine if you need to focus your energies on buying a used club or building from the ground up, can be stated as follows: Most business plans, once the club gets bigger than 10,000 square feet, don't work if the gross rent for the facility goes beyond $18 a square foot.

An exception exists for every rule, but once the total rent climbs beyond that number in most markets, then the business plan has to become much more aggressive in terms of membership pricing.

Gross rent is defined as the combination of your base rent for the space and your triple nets charges, which are usually billed to you monthly as part of your rent. In this example, once the total number goes beyond $18 a square foot, it's hard to make the plan work in most markets. Your rent is determined as follows:

**Square footage x gross rent = annual rent
Annual rent/12 (months) = monthly rent**

For example:

12,000 square feet x $18 gross rent = $216,000 annual rent
$216,000/12 = $18,000 monthly rent

This rule doesn't apply in a number of major metro markets. If you are in Manhattan, San Francisco, parts of Las Vegas, or major metro areas in Hawaii, then you couldn't even find a condemned building for $18 a square foot. In those markets, however, you can often get higher monthly member payments, or use a lower price that chases higher volume, than you can is most suburban areas, which offsets the $18 factor and allows you to break that rule. Opening in these markets, or any major metro area where the rent exceeds that $18 number, also forces you to have at least an extra month of reserve capital when you open since it takes more time to build your revenue stream to cover the more expensive monthly operating expense.

Obviously, if you have to pay $28 a square foot for a basement in Manhattan, but can charge $79 per month per member, then your business plan will probably work. But if you pay $36 a foot for boutique space in a suburban mall for a 12,000-square-foot center and only plan to price your memberships at $39 per month, then the business plan will most likely fail, because the rent factor, along with the bank loan, will be a lot more monthly overhead than the business can handle.

Smaller training centers, especially those that add limited memberships, can handle the higher rent factors due to the expected higher return per member. Those type of facilities need to be where the money is and acquiring space in those areas is always more expensive, but is justified by the higher prices you get compared to a mainstream fitness facility.

Building a Club

A lot of the wealth in America has been made in real estate, and when you consider building a fitness facility from the ground up, you are leaving the world of fitness and getting into the crossover world of real estate investment. If your long-term plan is to build a successful business, sell it, and go do something else, then how to get out is something you should consider before you actually get in. Building your own building and participating in the real estate side might be your best vehicle to achieve your personal financial plan while still giving you an opportunity to be in the fitness business.

In this plan, you are actually investing in a building and property and then using the fitness facility, and maybe other rental space in your new building, to pay for that real estate over time. Think of this scenario as buying a rental house and getting a good tenant. You collect rent each month and then use that money to pay your mortgage and keep the place up. Over time, you gain more equity in your rental house as the mortgage is reduced and you might gain appreciation if houses in that area grow in value. If the tenant is a good one and doesn't miss payments, then the investment becomes passive, since you don't have to do much but collect rent, fix some stuff as needed, and sit back and let your investment grow over time.

Owning a fitness business in your own building is very similar. An investor or a bank loans you money to buy dirt and build a new building or to buy an existing building that fits your needs. Your investor group may own that building as a team and you as the business owner might have a piece of the building as part of the investment team, but you also might own 100 percent of your club/business. Keep in mind that two separate companies will be formed in this scenario: one that owns the building and property and comprises the investment team and another corporation that owns the club, which might just be you as the sole owner.

This practice is done to protect the investors from lawsuits stemming from the club, provide tax advantages for the investment team that owns the property, and keep them free to open other businesses. The simple rule is that most investors, and most bankers through their loans, would rather be in the real estate business than in the gym-owning business, especially if that business fails.

A number of advantages exist for you and your team if you want to build your own building or buy if the market allows:

- It is easier to attract investors who like real estate but don't want to be in the gym business.
- The property serves as the collateral for the bank or investors, keeping your initial cash needs and collateral obligations lower.
- Payback on all loans is much longer, often in the 20- to 25-year range, which results in a much lower monthly payment for the business to handle, thereby freeing up more monthly cash flow.
- Tax advantages related to depreciation, the development of tax trusts, and interest might apply.
- The investors may experience long-term appreciation and wealth-building. At some point, the fitness business might be sold to another owner who buys the business directly and who then pays rent, or the business might even be closed at some point after serving its purpose of paying down the loan over the years and the building converted into offices or some other use.
- Ownership of your building might offer estate planning for those owners who wish to provide wealth for their families in the future.

Most fitness facilities require a minimum amount of land, which is also a consideration for your market. Local codes also add to your land needs, especially in areas such as parking, retention ponds, or green spaces, for example. Your minimum needs, however, will be an acre and a half for almost any type of facility and can go up to 10 to 12 acres if you are considering a tennis facility or a large, multipurpose family complex.

One of the current trends in club design and building is to acquire land on prime streets and then build a retail space on the first floor and place the club upstairs, or toward the back of the plaza if keeping the project to a single story is more desirable in that area, so that the new business is surrounded by other retail space closer to the street and is in a more desirable location for commercial retail.

This type of space has not been open to fitness owners in recent years because of the cost of buying prime lots on the best roads in your market. The cost of the land itself in many suburban markets has risen so dramatically that a typical business plan for a center that has main street frontage won't work because the cost of the land forces the monthly operating expense to a number higher than the club can generate and cover.

Developing a building that offers prime retail space at street level with the club above it, though, allows the club owner to build his center upstairs in what would be considered secondary space, offset the cost of the gym's rent by making a profit on the retail space, and still have the advantage of having his club visible on a main thoroughfare. Investors are again more likely to want to put money into a project that has multiple sources of revenue, such as rents, which further offsets the risk of just being dependent on the club itself to pay all of the rent. This type of venture, featuring the combination of retail space and a working club, provides more attractive bait to get your investors involved.

An important thing to learn at this point is that a fitness business is a destination business, which means that the consumer will leave his house and head directly to the club as his targeted destination. This same consumer will then support all the businesses that surround the fitness facility once he is there, rather than drive all over town running errands after his workout. This point should come up often with your investors and bankers, and especially with your landlord, if you are renting space rather than buying.

All of the small businesses that are located next to a fitness center usually thrive because they live off the constant traffic that a club generates day after day. Landlords often like to have a fitness center in smaller plazas because the other tenants are more likely to stay in business longer and pay rent longer to the owner. The term for this type of business is an <u>anchor tenant</u>. When you present your plan to investors and bankers, knowing the role the club plays in relationship to other businesses in the area, especially if those businesses also rent from your partnership, is important.

Buying a Used Club

Buying a used club isn't glamorous or sexy, but it is often an efficient way to get into the business. Few owners lie awake at night dreaming of taking over someone else's nightmare, which is probably why most potential owners don't consider buying a used club when they are first trying to get into the business.

An emotional element is also in play. New owners, especially those who have not yet been in the business, often believe that their new gym—designed their way and with their ideas—will draw thousands of members (a variation on the famous line from the movie *Field of Dreams*: "Build it and they will come").

One of the advantages of buying a used club, especially if it has been in business for a few years or longer, is that you start with members and cash flow. The obstacle here is that many potential owners don't want to buy someone else's dream. Used clubs often are run down and have poor equipment, and, truthfully, many aren't worth buying, but there are gems hidden in the rock pile, and used clubs are often safer and can be acquired much more cheaply than starting from scratch with no members while still becoming financially leveraged to your maximum threshold as you start a brand new and unproven business.

Potential owners are often like the buyers on television who are looking for a new home. Inexperienced buyers, or perhaps first-time buyers, always say things such as, "I just don't like the colors in this house, let's take it off the list." These people are so naïve that they don't realize that if they own it, they can paint it any color they like and change things to fit their tastes. You're not looking to buy perfect, you're looking to buy potential.

Buying used means you are often buying someone else's mistakes, and those mistakes can often easily be corrected. The key to buying used is to look past the existing mess and examine the potential that lies beneath. Many potential owners just can't force themselves to do this, however, because the present club they are considering doesn't match the dream they have had in their head for the last five years.

Any small business is difficult, and fitness businesses, along with restaurants, might even be more difficult to run successfully than other types of small businesses. You will have staff issues, marketing challenges, competition that is aggressive, and a number of other factors that make rising to the top possible, but not always easy. Your ideas of service, how you will train people, and your concept of the perfect club built for the perfect member are important, but the bottom-line concern is as follows: Does your business plan make sense financially, and can you give yourself an edge to increase your chances of success in this new venture? Then, once you are open, is this new business sustainable over time?

Used clubs can often help a new owner get into business with a lot less money, since the outgoing owner might be willing to finance you in and himself out. This means that you might be able to start more cheaply and keep a certain amount of your start-up capital for additional reserve. For example, an owner who has been in business for a number of years might want out and might be willing to let you buy the business with about 20 percent down and then carry the note himself for five to seven years. Selling a business takes time and a seller in a hurry might want to carry the note himself to get it done quickly. The problem with used clubs is that the current owner often wants more for the club than it is worth, and the buyer seldom knows what it might really be worth.

The used club's listed sale price is often based upon emotional components such as repaying parents, paying off some debt, and getting enough money together to start again doing something else—and maybe buying a new car. Offerings (the listing sheet the realtor or club owner will provide defining the price and what it includes) for used clubs are seldom actually based upon what the club might really be worth but at least provide a starting point for your negotiations.

Before buying a used facility, have your attorney send out a letter in your desired market to all existing clubs. This letter should state that he represents an experienced investor looking for a fitness business and/or property for sale. All responses should be sent to his office and you should not be listed by name, especially if you are known in the area. You may get a handful of responses and most will be high dollar, as everyone dreams of finding a naïve person willing to overpay for a business. Ignore the price at this point and just try to find out who might be interested in selling. Obviously, you should only do this if you are seriously interested in buying a club in that market.

You can also contact local business brokers for any listings in the area for clubs. The broker may know of a business that is for sale but not listed formally. Many owners are willing to sell but don't want to let their members or potential members know because rumors of a club for sale might stop future membership sales if anyone thinks the club is in trouble. It is important to note that, almost without fail, every listing a broker might have concerning a fitness business will be overpriced by as much as 50 percent, and many used clubs are not worth buying at all due to bad location, bad concept (such as a small, dated circuit club), or a lease that is too high for the business and that can't be changed. Again, you are looking for the gem hidden in the rock pile and it may be out there in your market.

If you get any interest, you need to take the next step and get an offering sheet from the owner, which lists the price and what's included. Never offer first; always respond to an offering sheet. Don't get too concerned about the price being too high, which is to be expected. Next, you may be asked to sign a confidentiality agreement that protects the seller. These agreements in theory keep you from getting all his numbers and then opening across the street from him because you know he is weak.

Once you get access to his financial information, you can do your research and then make an offer based upon what the business is really worth and the desired financing. The business's approximate value is based upon this formula:

Business value = [(EBITDA + owner's compensation) x 3.5] – debt

EBITDA stands for earnings before interest, taxes, depreciation, and amortization. This value looks scary, but all it defines is how much the owner made in profit before he incurred interest expense, paid taxes, took his depreciation allowance, and adjusted for amortization. EBIT, in other words, is your pre-tax net before you get taxed. Depreciation is a noncash expense that shows up on the statements, making the earnings look less than they really are because you will actually have that money to use when you buy that business. Amortization can be defined as things such as the money you pay up front to buy a franchise or intellectual property, which is seldom part of a fitness facility sale.

You must also add back the owner's compensation, because once that owner is gone, whatever he took out each month stays for you to use. Owner's compensation goes beyond salary and can include cell phones, health insurance, travel expense, car payments and expenses, and anything else he runs through his business. Do not, however, make any adjustments if the owner tells you he is taking out actual cash each month. You cannot verify that number, nor should you try. Taking cash directly out lowers the value of the business and is a bad business move when it comes to the IRS as well.

Once you come up with a total number using the information provided in this section, you then need to apply a multiplier. Multiplying earnings is a way to determine how many years it would take to pay back the purchase price. For example, if you had an EBITDA/owner's compensation number of $150,000 and multiplied by three, then the business would be worth about $450,000. In other words, it would take you three years at the current earnings rate of $150,000 to pay for your business.

Every type of business has a multiplier attached to it, but most are offered in ranges rather than actual set numbers. Restaurants, for example, often have a multiplier range of 4 to 8. Picking the right number is the art form of business pricing, but it can be made easier when it comes to buying a club.

Many sellers list their club in the 7 to 8 range because a few of the big-name club groups have sold in that range during past years when the investment markets were at their peak. The buyers for those groups, however, weren't just buying clubs; they were buying a concept that they felt could be turned into a national, or even international, brand.

For example, how much would Starbucks® have been worth if you bought the entire company when it only had 20 units? Would you buy the profits of just 20 stores or would you pay much more for an idea that could be turned into 10,000 units? Stay focused when you buy your club. If you are buying a single club, or perhaps two to three units, you are not buying the next big concept because it has not yet been validated. You are simply buying a business that you intend to operate yourself. In other words, don't pay for a future that doesn't exist—only pay for the reality in front of you at the moment.

Independent clubs usually sell in the 3 to 5 range when it comes down to the actual sale, and the majority of clubs sold during the last 20 years or so have probably averaged an actual number of 3.5. If you're buying, you start at 2, and if you're selling, you start at 7 to 8 and get talked down. Where you get into trouble buying someone else's business is paying more than the club is worth because you have no realistic anchor point in your negotiations.

Think of the multiplier 3 as being for a club that has worn leaseholds (old paint, worn-out locker rooms, ripped carpet, or bad mechanicals), dated equipment (stuff that is at least four years old), and declining member numbers and needs a lot of work to be turned around. Think of 5 as being for a club that you could walk into tomorrow and start making money without having to change a whole lot. The more you have to invest initially to revive the business, such as replacing a lot of equipment or blowing out the locker rooms, the lower price you want to offer to the seller, who probably knows how bad his business really is and doesn't want to, or can't, spend the money himself to fix his business.

Ablestock.com

Buying a Club That Is Losing Money

If no earnings/profits exist, meaning the club is just paying its bills or losing money, then you are just buying the physical assets of the business. Cash flow may be present, however, and that still has value as an asset of the business even though it isn't enough to provide a profit. For example, a club owner might be losing money monthly but still have a monthly check from his member payments (net receivable check) of approximately $20,000.

You can approach this business in several ways to get a working value for your offer. First, you can multiply the net-receivable check times 12 (12 months). In this example, $20,000 times 12 months is $240,000. This working number is a rough idea of what this business might really be worth. This number would include all equipment and assets, and then you deduct the debt of the business. In other words, if the seller owes $100,000, then this debt would have to be paid off as part of the purchase price or if you assume the debt, the price would be adjusted by $100,000.

For example, an owner is offering a 12,000-square-foot club for $400,000. The club's expenses are $60,000 and the owner is depositing about $55,000 per month. He isn't getting killed, but his ship is sinking slowly. He floats the business by catching up once in awhile during a good month, skips his salary because his wife has a job, or runs a consistent 30 to 60 days behind on his bills. The equipment is at least five years old, the club needs repairs, and the owner is motivated to sell. He does, however, have a net check from his members of $20,000 per month. What is this club really worth, since it isn't profitable but it does have a few assets?

All you are buying in this case is the cash flow from the member payments and some used equipment that needs updating (five years is the max point for most equipment, especially cardio) and the $240,000 figure is probably close to what this business is really worth, though an emotional seller may not let go of his business for this number. Sellers suffer from emotional issues too. This business was their dream and they are going to lose it, and many owners will ride the business to the bottom before taking a reasonable offer to get out.

You are looking for three things when it comes to asset purchase that might increase the value of this business. First of all, do you have the right to perpetuate the business with the lease and at what price? Businesses that have leases due to expire soon and without fixed options aren't worth much, if anything at all. Don't buy the club unless you have a letter signed by the landlord giving you the right to take over the lease or stating the terms of your new lease. If the lease has solid options, and is below the market value, then this business is worth more because it would be hard to duplicate this space at the price the current owner is paying.

Secondly, how much is the monthly EFT draft from member payments and can you verify the $20,000 in this example? Don't take anyone's word for what they are drafting each month from current members, and don't believe the financial statements without verifying this number for yourself. If you and your financial team cannot verify this number, then run—don't walk, run—away from this project. Sellers have been known to pad this number because they know that this is the only real asset they have to sell. If you can't verify a 12-month income stream from the member payments, do not buy this club.

This caveat is especially important if the owner is collecting his own memberships, which leaves room for a lot of misleading on his part. This receivable base, or cash flow, from member payments is worth more if a reputable, third-party financial service company is collecting the money. These companies, such as ASF International out of Denver, Colorado, often collect and service the memberships from thousands of clubs of all sizes and are reputable due to their size and years in business. If you are considering buying a club that has its receivable base serviced from a company like this, do your due diligence and go visit the company on site so you fully understand how the system works and how the income stream arrives because this is the major asset you are buying in the transaction.

The third issue of an asset purchase concerns the club's equipment and what is usable in the club. Owners in trouble almost always list their used equipment too high. Shop the vendors and find out how much it would cost to completely outfit the club with new equipment and then compare that number with what you are being asked to pay for the used stuff. If the owner in this example took care of his equipment, and you could get another year out of it without having to replace everything, the club might have more value beyond the quick reference number of $240,000.

If no cash flow exists to speak of, meaning that the owner has cashed out most of the members or doesn't have many paying monthly, then the sale becomes nothing but a hard asset sale, which creates the following question: What is the liquidation value of this business?

In this example, if his monthly receivable check was only a few thousand dollars, or the actual amount each month was hard to verify, then you would ignore this factor and make an offer for the used equipment (most used equipment with this age might be worth about 20 percent on the dollar of what he paid for it), the right to take over the lease, and whatever else he might be selling, such as desks and computers, which aren't really worth much used. In extreme cases, you might just assume the debt; get the owner out of the lease with the landlord and he walks away.

Other Hints for Buying a Used Business

Get a realtor involved and find out if any new clubs are coming into the market that the seller is not telling you about. Also, check with the city and see if anything is changing with the road leading to the business. One owner bought a club and then found out that all the traffic was being diverted for two years to another road while the city widened the current street, effectively putting him out of business.

Check and see if the loans and leases are assumable. You can often just take over the bills of the failing owner and he will walk, but first find out exactly what is owed and if it can be assumed. The ideal situation is for you to take over payments but leave everything in the old owner's name.

You seldom if ever buy the seller's corporation, because you would then assume all future liabilities such as lawsuits and tax obligations. Most purchases of clubs are just asset sales based upon buying the assets of the corporation and not the actual legal corporation. Get an accountant and attorney involved in this process from the start, and get professional help to value the business and make sure you are missing nothing. Sign nothing unless your team has covered you legally. Especially, do not fall for the, "Well, I have several other buyers in the game and I can sell it to them quickly." Sometimes, you do have to move quickly, especially if he is close to closing, but do nothing unless your financial team has been involved and have covered your moves.

Real estate is always handled separately. Avoid lumping the business and property together and get separate prices on each. Lumping the two will cloud your judgment and often lead to paying more than the individual parts are worth. Real estate is usually valued by using local appraisers, but the bad news is that if it is an older property, such as an old racquet facility, some appraisers value low because they consider the building single-use and, therefore, of little value on the open market unless another gym person buys it.

If you are seeking bank financing, your banker might insist on using the bank's appraiser, which again might work against you by lowering the value, which might make getting financing more difficult. Gap financing, meaning that the seller gives you a note he holds for the difference between what he wants and what the bank will finance, may be an option if you, and your appraiser and real estate expert, think the building might be of higher value over time than the bank will lend initially.

Another issue with property is that in hot real estate markets, the building might be worth more money than the business can support, which forces a higher mortgage than the business can handle each month. In other words, it may be a great business with great cash flow and still not be able to carry a note for the building, which is worth more torn down or converted into retail space than it would be as a fitness business.

Get a local real estate expert involved if real estate is part of the deal. You will also probably need a strong real estate attorney as well. Also, make sure the real estate agent is working for you. If he is the listing agent, he might be nice and supportive, but he really works for the seller, which is not in your best interests. Get your own expert and make sure he works for you.

Terms are everything when you buy a used business. Try to buy with as little as 10 percent down and payments over five to seven years, if possible. More sophisticated sellers will want at least 20 percent down, but the length of the note can stay in the five- to seven-year range. The business might be worth more at the time of sale if you can get favorable terms, such as a low down payment or a balloon later when the business is healthy.

Before you buy, insist on a 30-day discovery period, which gives you time to tear into all the financial records of the business. Don't put a lot of value on the financial statements, since they are easy to adjust to make the business look better. If you are buying a single unit, go in and reconstruct the business from the checkbook and bank statements and find out what the seller is really paying to run the place and go back for one full year. Bank statements are also worth in-depth study. Sellers will sometimes pad their business before selling by redepositing money over and over again, which looks good on paper but will be obvious when you go through the bank statements. List all the vendors, define who gets what, and look for any unusual transactions with the deposits.

One important thing to remember about buying a used business is that if a club has members and has been in business for a few years, something is right about that location. In other words, the location might be better than the current owner, and you are buying a business that can be run more effectively. Starting new clubs is more exciting, but the day you open, you start with zero members as compared to buying a used club and walking in with members in place and with money already coming in each day.

Keep in mind that buying used means you are buying someone else's mistakes. He might have been weak as a businessperson, undercapitalized, or struggling with marriage issues or other serious concerns that killed the business. When you buy used, you are often buying at a discount because the other guy couldn't run it, and that reflects a better deal to you financially. His mistakes do not have to be your mistakes. More talented owners have been buying the mistakes of less talented owners since the industry began. The key is knowing what you can do differently to correct the mistakes and turn the business around.

One key consideration, however, is that if you buy a club that is performing from an owner that is leaving because of age, marital issues, or health reasons, run your new business as he did for at least 60 days before you change anything. He was obviously doing something right, and although you may not agree with his systems, find out what he is doing that makes money and slowly change the business to fit you and your business model.

Many used clubs, however, aren't worth buying because of the price, location, or how they were built. There are always a few, however, that exist in almost every area that are worth considering if they can be bought for the right price and with the right terms. Do your homework and get a proper value on the business before you make an offer. Don't get emotional and be prepared to walk away if the seller simply won't come off a bad price. Learn this point: walk if the deal doesn't make sense or if you have to force it to work. Emotional buyers are buyers that always overpay for the asset.

One final point about buying used is that while it might not be glamorous, it often saves money and lowers risk. The seller may not be a great operator, but if he has been in business at that location for a number of years and has members, then he has validated the site. Buying an older business that needs fixing up but has 1,000 members is often much more cost effective than building a new business that opens with no members. Unfortunately, most start-up people can't get past the excitement of having something shiny and new to play with that was built with their own hands.

The Key Concept in This Chapter

All three options—renting, building, and buying used—have their strengths and weaknesses. Your choice has to fit the market, your budget, and your ability to raise money.

Don't be afraid to start at a lower level. If you can't get a plan together to open that dream 25,000-square-foot club, then maybe buy a used 10,000-square-foot place already in business. If that is too much, maybe open a smaller hybrid-training center that will at least allow you to get into the game.

Additional Resources

McCarthy, J. (2004). *IHRSA's Guide to The Health Club Industry for Lenders & Investors* (2nd ed.). Boston, MA: IHRSA.

This unique reference will be especially valuable to club owners who want to educate their current investors, or who are seeking new investors or refinancing. www.ihrsastore.com

FINDING THE PROPER SITE FOR YOUR NEW BUSINESS

Chapter Four

What makes the right location for a fitness business and would you recognize a good site if you saw it? Should you look at freestanding buildings or could you make it with a mall or strip plaza location? Is it worth the risk to take a reduced rent but be in the back of an industrial park? Or do you just go for it and throw all of your money into a prime location on the best corner of the best street in town?

There are also a number of additional factors that have to be considered before you make your final site selection for your new business. Any one of these factors is worth noting alone, but where the magic comes into the picture is understanding how all of these factors can combine to influence the final success of your new business.

For example, you might find a great site in a plaza that has a Walmart® anchored at the other end. You have great parking, traffic through the plaza all day long, and it looks like a great location for a club, but after three months of negotiation, you find that Walmart has restrictions in their lease that prevent fitness centers from being in the same mall. Why didn't anyone tell you that up front? No one told you because it's your job as a fitness business professional to ask the hard questions going in and to keep your project on track. You should build a team of professionals, such as realtors, accountants, and attorneys, to help you get into your new business, but it is up to you to learn enough to ask your team the right questions.

In another example, you find a site that has great visibility from the road and has great drive-by traffic, but upon doing your due diligence, you find that the city has very strict sign codes that prevent you from signing your location properly. Signage is a key factor that can make or break a location and is something that has to be on your checklist for every site you consider. In this case, you might have to walk away from this location if no one can see you as they drive by or if the consumer you are trying to attract can't tell you're there and doing business.

As you review the factors covered in this chapter, look at how each one affects the others. A good site, defined as one that will give you the best chance of becoming financially successful, would have the strongest combination of all the factors. When you actually begin your trek to find a location, use the points in this chapter as a checklist to help keep you focused and thinking of it as a business rather than letting emotions pull you off your path.

Demographics of the Area

Everyone throws around the word "demographics," but not too many people understand what the word means and how it affects the process of finding a fitness location. Some new owners, for example, only look at the shear number of people in an area. In northern New Jersey, you might have more than 200,000 people living within three to five miles of your club, but just a few hours away, you're in eastern Pennsylvania in a town of only 20,000 people. The key factor for these two sites—either of which might work for you—isn't the shear amount of volume, but it's the combination of the number of people, the rent factor for your new site, and the business concept you are trying to squeeze into that particular market.

A number of ways are available to you and your team to get demographic information about your targeted area. First of all, if you're working with a realtor, he should be able to get you current information about your location. Most realtors subscribe to a number of companies that furnish demographic information, and they should be able to get you info on your site at no cost. Most of the marketing companies that specialize in the fitness industry, such as Susan K. Bailey, usually furnish carrier route radius reports for free and are good starting points for most site analysis.

What are these tools and how do you use them?

Demographic reports, such as those furnished by a realtor, usually provide information about the people who live within a certain radius of your proposed site. To get this information, you submit your targeted street address and then the information is pulled off the computer for all people within a certain distance of your proposed address. Ask for one-, three-, and five-mile rings when you gather your first information. If you are in a rural area, extend your search to seven miles from the proposed site.

It is interesting to note that in a heavily populated suburban area and in a rural area, it still comes down to how far the potential member is willing to drive to get to his fitness facility. It really comes down to time and not distance. For example, it might take the same time to drive two miles in the suburban market as it does to drive seven miles in the rural area. The maximum targeted amount of time most people will drive to get to their fitness facility is about 12 to 20 minutes from their home, depending on the club and its business model.

Demographic reports will tell you how many people are in the area, broken down by ages and distances from the site. Other information, such as household income, race, average home price, and number of kids is also included in most standard reports. This type of report can be very extensive and can sometimes number 300 pages or more. Full reports of this nature often project the population in your proposed area 10 years ahead and can often give you an idea as to how the area might change during the first term of your lease.

Carrier route radius reports (see Figure 4-1) go after the important numbers from a different angle. These reports give you a total of all the mailing addresses by zip code/carrier routes, starting with the site's address and moving out away from the club by distance. This report also gives you the number of multifamily homes, single-family homes, running total for all households in your market, household income, and age information if you desire it. If you use this report, ask for rural route addresses and PO Boxes as well, since they are not always part of the standard package.

Silverton Fitness Carrier Route Report

Zip	Route	City	Home	Apt	Total	Income	Med_HV	Age	%Child	Distance	Accum
97381	C002	SILVERTON	391	64	455	49873	146394	52	28	1 min	455
97381	C001	SILVERTON	411	51	462	62954	156538	54	29	1 min	917
97381	R005	SILVERTON	421	202	623	49141	164151	60	22	2 min	1540
97381	R006	SILVERTON	273	52	325	71861	153947	57	26	2 min	1865
97381	C003	SILVERTON	581	110	691	57456	147126	52	40	3 min	2556
97381	R004	SILVERTON	636	144	780	61410	166667	58	23	3 min	3336
97362	R002	MOUNT ANGEL	354	231	585	59266	131731	57	33	8 min	3921
97381	R002	SILVERTON	385	24	409	75606	183333	55	24	10 min	4330
97362	R001	MOUNT ANGEL	342	130	472	48630	128125	50	36	14 min	4802
97381	R001	SILVERTON	449	4	453	94390	215541	56	22	15 min	5255
97381	R003	SILVERTON	404	6	410	78510	204630	59	23	17 min	5665
97305	R002	SALEM	392	0	392	78888	171528	57	28	17 min	6057
97305	C037	SALEM	590	46	636	63000	137879	57	26	17 min	6693
97303	C038	SALEM	591	100	691	64103	128020	48	37	19 min	7384
97305	C045	SALEM	803	0	803	81558	138830	47	38	20 min	8187
97305	C017	SALEM	522	250	772	30878	135638	67	16	20 min	8959
97303	C026	SALEM	533	46	579	46394	115144	50	30	20 min	9538
97305	R006	SALEM	437	41	478	57815	160185	63	19	21 min	10016
97305	C050	SALEM	695	0	695	43786	114798	46	39	21 min	10711
97305	C003	SALEM	762	15	777	58628	121250	59	20	21 min	11488
97305	C041	SALEM	654	421	1075	32971	115599	53	23	21 min	12563
97301	C066	SALEM	635	367	1002	19669	N/A	47	25	21 min	13565
97301	C076	SALEM	51	196	247	29792	N/A	46	15	21 min	13812
97301	C064	SALEM	387	33	420	29653	N/A	51	19	21 min	14232
97301	C075	SALEM	22	0	22	31875	N/A	45	34	21 min	14254
97303	C009	SALEM	718	100	818	38720	116981	50	35	21 min	15072
97303	C028	SALEM	753	190	943	24755	110489	53	24	21 min	16015
97303	C021	SALEM	393	247	640	30339	112500	50	28	21 min	16655
97381	H062	SILVERTON	277	9	286	79156	214063	53	30	22 min	16941
97071	R002	WOODBURN	397	0	397	78727	217361	53	33	22 min	17338
97317	C012	SALEM	461	2	463	80956	N/A	55	22	22 min	17801
97305	C027	SALEM	742	30	772	77153	132197	58	19	22 min	18573
97305	C031	SALEM	684	142	826	60733	121853	54	22	22 min	19399
97305	C025	SALEM	701	143	844	27048	117518	52	30	22 min	20243
97305	C035	SALEM	594	470	1064	53785	138007	53	24	22 min	21307
97071	C002	WOODBURN	695	128	823	45459	133519	49	28	22 min	22130
97301	C021	SALEM	747	125	872	59152	113205	53	29	22 min	23002
97301	C069	SALEM	372	182	554	27852	N/A	50	29	22 min	23556
97303	C010	SALEM	591	94	685	50525	120536	57	23	22 min	24241
97301	C067	SALEM	470	25	495	28750	N/A	48	27	22 min	24736
97303	C040	SALEM	532	143	675	59120	121058	51	24	22 min	25411
97301	C068	SALEM	355	227	582	29653	N/A	48	22	22 min	25993
97305	C043	SALEM	786	513	1299	38265	121318	51	27	23 min	27292
97301	C015	SALEM	678	286	964	39502	114274	53	24	23 min	28256
97301	C032	SALEM	391	496	887	30745	112500	57	23	23 min	29143
97301	C019	SALEM	179	165	344	56261	117672	66	11	23 min	29487
97305	C002	SALEM	376	812	1188	21081	106667	42	28	23 min	30675
97301	C072	SALEM	712	31	743	40870	N/A	51	26	23 min	31418
97303	C042	SALEM	703	0	703	96554	141880	51	29	23 min	32121
97301	C061	SALEM	629	74	703	27695	N/A	50	19	23 min	32824
97301	C063	SALEM	537	61	598	33257	N/A	49	25	23 min	33422
97303	C011	SALEM	547	2	549	61987	121824	56	26	23 min	33971
97301	C073	SALEM	433	16	449	24152	N/A	48	21	23 min	34420
97026	R002	GERVAIS	286	4	290	54336	123750	45	34	24 min	34710
97038	R003	MOLALLA	457	0	457	66613	225000	56	25	24 min	35167
97305	C029	SALEM	951	0	951	44568	123818	50	31	24 min	36118
97305	C005	SALEM	462	0	462	60499	128956	59	23	24 min	36580
97071	C012	WOODBURN	402	250	652	34607	127907	55	24	24 min	37232
97303	C012	SALEM	599	474	1073	62273	161520	54	22	24 min	38305
97301	C070	SALEM	443	2	445	47366	N/A	52	20	24 min	38750
97071	R003	WOODBURN	286	134	420	56108	155625	53	23	25 min	39170
97305	R018	SALEM	90	0	90	74209	162500	51	23	25 min	39260
97071	C004	WOODBURN	458	31	489	50409	130970	53	35	25 min	39749
97305	C033	SALEM	251	0	251	26636	113095	56	18	25 min	40000
		Grand Total	31859	8141	40000						

Figure 4-1. Carrier route radius report

Carrier route reports usually don't list the total number of people, but rather the total of households, with mailing addresses. You may estimate the number of people by taking the combined total at any distance and multiplying it by 2.2 people per household, which gives you a working number. If you are in an area that is growing, request a new report every six months since there might be a significant number of new addresses, reflecting new potential members, that have been added since you last checked.

Much of the information in these reports may seem confusing at first, but you can focus on just a few things, including the following:

- Household income
- Multifamily vs. single-family homes
- Ages
- The total number of people

The higher the household income, the more likely someone is to join a club. It is generally recommended that you concentrate on trying to market to the top 60 percent of the people in your area as designated by their household income.

Affluence is the largest predictor of whether someone will join a club, but keep in mind that this is situational and is relative to your target market. For example, the top 60 percent of people in a community in rural Oklahoma by affluence will look a lot different than the top 60 percent of a town in central Connecticut.

The important thing to note, however, is that the top 60 percent in any market will most likely be the people who will become part of a new fitness business in that town. Income is relative and the top 60 percent in any market reflects the more affluent people in that city and those who are probably more highly educated, take better care of themselves, and are more interested in pursuing lifetime fitness.

If you are going for the upscale market that is typical of a hybrid training facility or women's-only club with a spa, then focus on the top 40 to 50 percent by affluence in your area and specialize even more closely on those who are the most qualified to buy your services.. Focusing in this way is simpler than it sounds. If you are using the carrier route radius report, run the entire area once to see what's there and then rerun dropping the lowest 30 percent by household income. The marginal 10 percent is good to reach out to occasionally, or if you are operating a family facility.

In a perfect fitness world, you would want a ratio of two-thirds multifamily homes and one-third single-family homes. In this scenario, you gain the turnover from the condos and townhouses but also have a certain degree of stability from the single-family residences. In most areas, multifamily units, especially apartments, turn over at about a 33 percent rate per year, while single-family homes only turn over approximately once every seven years. Density is also an issue with single-family homes in the nicer neighborhoods. A lot of money may reside in a subdivision, but only 250 homes may be scattered across a very big area.

The aging trend of your area is also important if you are going to specialize in the upscale market or if you're looking for kids. This number is more readily available on a standard demographic report and not found on a carrier route radius report. The area's population is usually broken down into categories, such as 25 to 34 and 35 to 44. If you were trying to build a club based on the 30 to 50 group, you would simply look at the total percentages those ages represent in relationship to the rest of the population. You should also include the group just below and the two groups above your market in most cases. Remember, your target market represents approximately 80 percent of your membership and that likes attract likes. Groups that are a little younger or just slightly older than your target market are potential members as well and should not be left out of your marketing efforts.

You can find research showing that the higher the average household income, the more likely someone is to join a health club. *IHRSA's Guide to the Health Club Industry for Lenders and Investors*, by John McCarthy, is a must-have book when you submit your business plan to the banks or to your investors. This book lists research from American Sports Data citing that those folks with household incomes of $50,000 to $74,999 join clubs at the 17.2 per hundred rate, while those people in the over-$100,000 category of household income join clubs at the rate of 24.4 per hundred. Also note that those people in the $25,000 to $49,999 range joined fitness clubs at a rate of 11.7 per hundred.

Another important point to remember is that average income usually matches all the other important factors of the area. Rent, taxes, insurances, wages, and average income all blend together to define an area. Seldom does one of these factors emerge apart from the others, which would force a business owner to drastically adjust the business plan in some unusual way.

For example, a town in the Midwest might have an average income of $35,000. Entry-level employees start at $7 to $8 per hour and the owner expects to open her club with a $39-per-month average price. After looking for several months for space of about 10,000 square feet, however, she narrows her choice to a spot she likes with a gross rent of $18 per square foot. All the other spaces in town were in the $9 to $12 per square foot range.

This site is unusual in this town and it would have to have some unusual attributes for it to work. Is it an exceptional location with tremendous walk-in potential? Can she build a smaller, more elite facility and use less space, thereby saving build-out cost and rent? Is this boutique space in a very elite part of town that would allow her to charge $49 to $59 per month per member? Since the rent factor doesn't match the rest of her business plan, she would somehow have to alter her business plan to make this site pay off over time or walk away from that location.

Another factor in site selection is that the site and finish have to match the average income. San Francisco, for example, has a very high average income—over $70,000 in most parts of the city. But if you pay $36 per month per square foot in rent and then build a typical white-walled, low-finish box gym that you might find as standard in the Midwest or South reflecting an economical $35 per square foot finish, you won't be competitive in the market and won't last too long. Your club has to reflect the local standard and who the member will be that will be using it.

Visibility

Visibility means that the facility can be seen and instantly recognized for what it is. If a site can be seen easily from the street or intersection, then it has good visibility. If it is easily recognizable as a fitness center because of its front windows or great signage, then the value of that site and the business that location can generate has increased.

Visibility is important because being seen lowers your marketing costs over time. If a site has great visibility from the street, then you are much more likely to get walk-in traffic as opposed to a site that is set at the back of a plaza with no view from the street. Such a location gets little in the way of, "Wow, a new fitness center. I think I'll stop by."

The debate regarding visibility is whether you should pursue a freestanding building, meaning one that would have nothing in the building but your business or that you would share with other people that you rent space to. For example, part of your total business plan might be to rent part of your space to someone such as a chiropractor. This model contrasts with a strip-mall site, which might have a number of other tenants taking their own space as part of a large plaza or mall and you become one of many in the plaza.

Freestanding means that the building stands alone, but it does not necessarily mean that the gym is the only business in the building. Most old Blockbuster® buildings, for example, were freestanding but a few had small tenants in the end positions. Strip-mall sites mean that you share a multi-tenant building with a large number of other businesses. In this case, you might be one of five different businesses in a strip mall, which might simply mean one building in either a straight line or L-shape that holds more than one business.

Advantages and disadvantages exist for both types of sites. In a freestanding building where you are the only occupant, you don't have the advantage of drawing potential members from your business neighbors. An advantage of a freestanding business is that it will usually add to the visibility factor since people driving by will only see one business instead of a plaza with many different signs and logos. Freestanding businesses are also often easier to see by a drive-by if they are near the roadway, which is an advantage that a plaza space usually doesn't have since most plazas are set back from the road to allow for parking and access off of the street. However, a big negative for most freestanding businesses is lack of parking, especially in the buildings that are less than 20,000 square feet.

Parking

A normal building facility will need about 13 spaces per thousand square feet during its busiest months of the year, which are normally February and March. For example, a 10,000-square-foot building would need 130 parking places during its absolute busiest months. Keep in mind that 13 per thousand is a perfect-world scenario and few of us live there, but it is worth knowing this number as you start your business site selection as a base reference.

The minimum you need before the members start to hate you, and what is often required as basic code in most cities, is 9 to 10 per thousand, or 90 to 100 spaces in this example, and some city codes go as low as eight per thousand but that is rare. This is a mandatory addition for your location checklist. Before you sign any lease or formally commit to any space, contact the city and check the parking requirements for a fitness facility at your proposed location.

Parking becomes a judgment call if it isn't regulated by code. Most cities, though, have a minimum parking requirement necessary for a fitness-type of business and won't allow you to open if you don't meet that requirement.

In this case, the term "judgment call" has to relate to your anticipated business. For example, a 15,000-square-foot site in Texas was allowed to open with only 80 parking places as a coed fitness center. The city granted the permit, but the club owner suffered because it wasn't enough spaces to meet his members' needs during prime time. Realistically, how long do you think people will continue to circle the lot after a long day at work waiting for someone to leave the club? It only takes a few frustrated laps and the member is gone. This particular owner sold the club cheaply and the next owner turned it into a women's-only club, which has parking requirements that are spread more evenly through the day due to a more varied schedule when women attend the club. The new owner was successful in that location.

You can also help the situation by eliminating as many barriers in your lots to open parking as you can. The members, minus barriers such as parking islands, too many curbs, unneeded landscaping or those old-style concrete barriers at the front of each space, will find their own way and you'll be surprised how creative they can be if you have any open space not lined or limited by hazards.

Know When the Money Arrives

A typical club makes about 65 percent of its total sales between 4:00 and 9:00 p.m., Monday through Thursday nights, and between 8:00 a.m. and 1:00 p.m. on Saturday. These periods are called prime time. They might be an hour later for your club depending on the market. If you own a women's-only club, you normally have two prime times, with your first being 8:00 to 11:00 each morning through the week.

The newer version of training clubs that are dependent on more group experiences and less one-on-one will have conventional parking issues during prime times as well but will also have a more steady flow of traffic throughout the day with the bulk of their other clients. If your model is based upon boot camps and group personal training, you will need more space than you think, and you need to review the 10 to 13 per thousand square feet rule stated previously.

Knowing your prime time is important because your neighbors in the plaza might influence your site choice. If your neighbors run 9:00 a.m. to 5:00 p.m. businesses, and you have an after-5:00 p.m. prime time, then you pick up a lot more parking when your neighbors close for the day. If you share a plaza with a sports bar, however, or some other late-evening business, then you might have parking problems in the evening since you are both full at the same time. One club owner in Michigan, for example, fought with his landlord for years over the fact that the landlord let a bingo parlor open in the same plaza, which drew hundreds of senior citizens from 4:00 to 7:00 p.m. five nights a week, taking most of the club's parking during its busiest hours.

Signing

The ability to sign a facility is often the key factor for making your final decision about a proposed site. A site with low street visibility, but with a great street sign, can become a strong location and the owner can usually pay less rent for a secondary site.

The problem with signage is that codes vary greatly from city to city, and from mall to mall around the country. The problem occurs when the landlord gives you permission to install signs for your club, you then sign the lease, but the city refuses to allow the sign due to its codes. The occasional not-quite-ethical landlord will apply this trick since it makes him look good by giving you permission and he might get lucky and you won't check with the city. Keep in mind that it is your responsibility to check before committing to a lease; and once you sign, you are in the deal with limited, if any, outs. Check all signage rules with the landlord, plaza manager, and the city before you sign the final lease; get everything in writing from the landlord as part of your lease and make sure you get permission from the city in writing as well.

Signage is one of those things that can make or break a small business, but is often taken for granted. Everyone just assumes that if you own a business and pay rent then you can put up a sign. But if you get lost in the middle of a strip mall and have nothing but a small frontage sign, your business will not do as well as one where the signage is clear and distinct. If people can't find you, they can't spend money with you, and a weak location with poor signage is almost impossible to overcome.

Accessibility

A site may have a great sign, nice visibility, tons of nice cars whipping by on the main road just in front of the club, but the location still might not work if the site is not accessible. Accessibility refers to how easy is it to get to the location once you've seen it. Customers hate to be inconvenienced and if they can't leave work and easily pull into your club's parking lot, they will find an alternative to your business. You might have strong visibility from the main road that gets his attention, but if he has to drive several miles to the next exit and then take a frontage road to the location, then your walk-in, impulse traffic will suffer accordingly.

The rules are simple: Can the consumer pull into your location from several different points? Is the club on a road that has a central island that prevents someone in the opposite lane from turning across the mid-strip and directly into your center?

Test your potential accessibility by trying to get into the center from several different angles during prime traffic hours. If you get frustrated or have a hard time, then your members will too, and your potential members may not even stop at all.

One final point is being on the correct side of road during the right time of day. Most clubs have more traffic after work, so you might want to consider being on the going-home side of the road. For example, assume you're standing in front of your site and a steady stream of traffic is in front of your club. You'd get excited. But you also might come back at night, however, and all that traffic is on the other side of the road with little access to your location without going through a lot of lights or crossing over at an intersection farther up the road. The early traffic was going to work and the return traffic is on the other side of the barrier without simple access to your club.

Another very important issue is the perception of safety for your members. Old commercial centers, for example, often have outdated outside lighting that doesn't really illuminate the parking lot well. Some members will find this intimidating at night and not feel safe entering or leaving the club, and that lighting issue will cost you memberships over time.

Also, be aware of the dual personalities of some neighborhoods. Some locations look good during the day, but at night they turn into areas you would not want to venture into without a police escort. Do your homework and spend time during all key time frames of the day and find out the true personality of your location before you commit.

Other Thoughts

If you aren't from the area, spend more time looking than you might otherwise, and consider moving to that area for a few months before you make your final decision. What looks good during your first visit may not look so good later when you realize that you are in the wrong part of town.

For example, an owner opened a club on a busy street in what appeared to be a good part of town. The problem was, however, that the street was on the wrong side of a major street that divided the town. It was an old southern town and the locals simply thought that the neighborhood near the new club wasn't "a good neighborhood," and everyone from the other side of the major thoroughfare refused to venture beyond that point. It was a good building, but it was about two blocks away from being a good location and the club suffered from the negative image of that area of town.

Also, research the secondary points most new owners miss, such as current and future traffic patterns in front of your business (available from the local department of transportation), get traffic counts for your street (20,000 or more per day is strong), determine if you are on a commuter route, look into any major construction that might be beginning in your area, and most importantly, drive the neighborhoods near your business site until you can't stand it anymore to see how hard or easy it would be for your members to get to you.

Another point to remember is that "if it ain't in writing, then it ain't real"—poor English, but good advice. Signs, parking promises by the landlord, agreements with neighbors, and anything else that affects your site has to be in writing as part of your lease or it may not happen. Get it in writing or don't count on it happening.

You also need to look for natural barriers affecting the site. On paper you might have a great location, but things such as train lines, bridges, rivers, industrial parks, bad parts of town, or other concerns affect the people who live there and prevent them from coming to your site. Endlessly drive your location day and night and see if certain natural boundaries exist that might limit membership.

The Key Concept in This Chapter

Location, location, location! Everyone has heard this old adage and it is still relevant today. The second part of this adage that only comes with experience is that failure or success in this business could be determined by being where you are versus being just one block over. Rushing your decision, forcing your business plan into a site because it is the only one on the market, and not getting opinions about the market from real estate experts are all reasons that lead to being in a location that will hurt your business. Take your time and make sure you and your team find the best location you can for your new business.

Good locations are driven by demographics, but the ultimate success of your business will be measured by a combination of factors. When you consider a site, consider everything that might keep a potential member from coming through your door and look for anything that might enhance the location and help you grow over time, such as great parking. Get the location right and the rest of your business plan will be much easier.

UNDERSTANDING THE BASICS OF LEASING SPACE

Jupiterimages

Chapter Five

Trial and error is not the way to learn about getting a lease for your new business. Even if you are using a local real estate professional, whom you should, you need to be prepared to guide your team into getting the best lease possible by understanding the unique needs of a fitness business.

The first point when it comes to leases is that everything is negotiable except your name, meaning that you should enter into negotiations with the thought that nothing is firm and almost anything can be discussed and negotiated before the final documents are drawn. Most landlords, or their agents, expect to deal and customize within reason to your requests, and most will normally approach the game prepared to discuss every point if needed. Rookies, on the other hand, just accept the first offer as is, which is seldom the best financially, nor does the first offer reflect the major issues you need to incorporate into the lease to protect the business.

Being prepared is a must at this stage. Landlords are weighing risk versus reward when it comes to anyone renting their space. Most landlords start a negotiation with this thought: Has this person offered a thought-out business plan for this new business that is sustainable over time or at some point will he have to throw you out, which means you are behind in your rent and had to be evicted, costing him time, money, and stress?

Experienced landlords usually have a decent sense of their clients and it doesn't take long to separate the ones who have a plan and a chance to make it over time from the endless list of undercapitalized dreamers who are unprepared to run a business and who will fail, costing the landlord time, resources, and money. Being prepared is not just a bluff to get into the deal; it is the professional way to approach a person who you might end up having a relationship with as your landlord for years into the future.

Good business people know what they want and are prepared to discuss numbers when they get to the actual negotiation point. You can be more casual when you are first gathering information to build a business plan, but when it comes down to making the deal, landlords are much more likely to work with you if you know your numbers, what you want from them specifically, what you will do to the space, and if you can demonstrate an ability to pay the lease and any additional costs over time.

Once you analyze potential sites and have narrowed your choices down to just one, you are ready to start the negotiation process. At this point you should have already hooked up with an agent. The most important rule concerning agents is to find out whom the agent is working for in the end. It's common to see a sign, meet a nice, helpful agent, and then start the deal process. The bad news is that the agent on the sign may be working for the landlord and might not be guiding you toward what's best for you and your business.

When you first start looking, it's best to get an agent who represents you and who specializes in commercial real estate. In small towns, many agents handle both commercial and residential properties, but it is always better to find someone who spends most of their time in the commercial world. Putting together a commercial deal with a landlord is a lot different than a residential specialist helping a young couple find financing for their new townhouse. Whenever possible, find an agent that works for you and who has been involved in commercial real estate for a few years.

You will also need to get an attorney who does commercial leases as well. Find one before you start the process so you won't be hesitant to call and get help with the process as your progress. Never sign a lease unless your attorney has read it first. For example, you may sign off on changes during a meeting but the new lease you are handed doesn't accurately reflect those changes or mistakes that have been made in the preparation of the lease. Check again before you sign and let an experienced set of eyes double check one last time.

Before looking at the basics of a lease, know that you should never break this one important rule: Never start the negotiations without first receiving an offering sheet from the landlord or his agent. Offering sheets are usually one-page sheets that list the asking price, size, and other particulars concerning your site of interest. Some agents, knowing that you are a rookie, will not give you a sheet and just tell you to make an offer. Most offers generated this way are significantly higher than what is being asked. Leaving it up to you to start the process is much more desirable for the agent because rookies are emotional or inexperienced and usually bring higher numbers to the table, resulting in higher commissions for the agent.

Once you get an offering sheet, you may make a counter offer, which is the proper form of response. Most offering sheets are simple affairs and the real process starts when you lay out your first counter offer, listing everything you want from the landlord, including the rent numbers you submit. Remember, the offering sheet is the landlord's first offer and unless you are living in an unbelievably hot real estate market where you take it or leave it, the offering sheet is nothing more than a tool to give a general price and structure to the deal to start the negotiations between the two parties.

The Basics of the Lease

The ultimate goal is to sign a lease structured to allow your business to grow over an extended period of time, and then be able to sell your business to the next person, who will have the right to perpetuate the business in that location into the future. One of the most important elements of any lease is the right to perpetuate the business at a location that has proven to be successful, at a fair rent at or below market value, into the future, which is normally established as fixed option periods that extend your base lease. When you decide to sell your business, a good lease and the right to project the business into the future at a known lease factor can add a great deal of value to your sale.

Knowing what you want going in makes the negotiation a much easier thing, but you must also think about getting out of your business at some point and selling it to the next person. You should never, ever get into a business without a plan to get out. Most new owners just plan to build a business that will be worth a lot of money and then sell it to someone at some point. Every decision you make in your new business should somehow enhance the future sale price by clearly defining the key factors that would affect a sale at a later date.

For example, most physical plants (the heating and air, carpets, locker rooms, paint, lighting, etc.) need to be updated about every five years because they simply wear out from member usage. Recapitalizing your business and selling it a year or two after a remodel might be perfect timing because the debt is reasonable and the club looks fresh and new for the potential buyer. It is sort of like a home seller who invests in a kitchen remodel to drive up the total sale price of his house.

A good lease, especially with options that clearly state the right to extend the lease at or below market value, adds value to the buyer in the future but has to be thought out thoroughly going in to your deal, giving you a better chance of getting out at a profit later. Again, always think about getting out before you get in to any deal.

Review the following key terms, which you need to know before you get into the lease process. Knowing these terms will help you understand the information being thrown at you, as well as make sure that you don't miss anything of importance. You do not need to be an expert with leases, but you do need to be able to read and understand what you are getting into with your new business. Many rookies make the mistake of simply handing the paperwork to their attorney without understanding what it really says. You're not the expert here, but you are the one who is dependent on the lease to protect your business so you do need to at least master the key elements common in almost every commercial lease.

Base rent. Base rent is the asking price for the space itself and does not include the extra charges you will have to pay for the space, such as your prorated share of the real estate taxes for the property, common area maintenance (CAM), such as maintaining the parking lots and perhaps snow removal, and insurance that protects the owners from loss and liability.

If you are the only tenant in the building on a freestanding property, you are responsible for all these things yourself, but the numbers are usually smaller and scaled to the size of the property itself. If you are in a plaza with other tenants, you share the cost of these things with the other businesses according to the percentage of total space you take up. For example, if your business is one-third of the property in the plaza, you will pay one-third of the property taxes, common area maintenance, and insurance.

When you get your first offering sheet from the agent, the number listed is usually the base rent. The agent/landlord lists that number because it is always smaller than the base rent and the other extra charges combined. Base rent is a component of gross rent, which is the actual total amount of money you will pay for your space.

Triple net. Triple net is the actual working name of the combination of taxes, insurance, and CAM. If you are in a strip mall or other type of mall where multiple tenants are present, you will pay your pro rata share of the combination of these charges incurred by the landlord for the entire property. If you rent a freestanding building, you get to pay all these charges and each bill is usually passed directly to you.

If you are in a freestanding building, you can often save money by doing your own exterior maintenance on the property. Beware of the word "CAM." Many agents throw this word around as a synonym for triple net, which is incorrect because CAM is usually a smaller number than you will really have to pay when taxes, maintenance, and insurances are combined. CAM refers simply to the maintenance the landlord does to keep the plaza up and open for business, such as snow removal, landscaping, exterior lighting, and lot upkeep, and does not include taxes and insurance for the plaza, which are always extra. Be sure you understand what the agent means and don't hesitate to ask if you are confused.

Triple net charges should be paid monthly along with your rent. Do not, and this is important for inexperienced owners, go for having the triple net billed as quarterly fees, because the bills can get really big, especially during snow-removal months in the north. Also, ask for verification of the bills that the landlord incurs. Most landlords will mark the bills up 20 percent before splitting up the charges among the tenants and some fees can be reduced if you question your bills.

The important side note is that if you have to write a check, always get verification of what you are getting billed for each month. If you can't figure it out, get the bill to your accountant or attorney. Many new business owners, in all businesses and not just the fitness industry, are very passive about money and just assume the landlord is always right. Your realistic approach to small business that protects you over time is to assume that the landlord is always wrong and that you have to verify everything yourself. This approach is safer for you and makes you a smarter businessperson.

Gross rent. Gross rent is the combination of the base rent for the space and the triple net charges. This combined number is the actual rent you will pay each month for your space. Consider the following example:

- Your base rent for your space is $10 per square foot (annual basis).
- Your triple net charges (taxes, insurance, and CAM) are $3.50 per square foot.
- Your gross rent would be $13.50 per square foot for the space.

Rent can be figured monthly or annually, depending on the region of the country where you live. To find the annual rent, multiply the gross rent per square foot by the square footage. Then divide that number by 12 to find the monthly rent cost as follows:

(square footage x gross rent) ÷ 12 = your rent payment

For example:

**(12,000 square feet x $13.50) ÷ 12 =
13,500 per month rent**

This example is figured on an annual basis. Monthly rents are a little more unusual and you won't see them expressed in that form often anymore except in the Northeast, but it is good to know how they work as well. For example, an offering sheet might list $0.90 for the space as gross rent. This number represents the amount you would pay per month, not annually. To calculate this number, simply multiply $0.90 by your square footage to find your monthly rent payment. To find your annual rent payment, multiply that product by 12.

For example:

$0.90 x 12,000 square feet = $10,800 monthly payment

Therefore:

$10,800 x 12 months = $129,600 annual rent

Vanilla box. Vanilla box is one of the great nonsense terms in real estate that is often defined, or it often seems "made-up" on the spot, by the real estate person or owner standing in front of you; who usually gives you the version that best supports what he owns and how much he is trying to get you to pay that day. Vanilla box normally means that your space will be delivered to you as a shell with one bathroom (which meets local codes so that the work people can go to the bathroom), a bare concrete floor, cheap lights with an open ceiling, electrical to one box on the wall, and a basic heating and air conditioning unit normally underpowered for the needs of running a typical fitness center. The walls might be taped drywall, or they might even just be studs.

If you are trying to rent a space that had a previous tenant in a different type of business, you or the landlord will have to do demolition, which means that the space has to be restored to vanilla box condition prior to you accepting it. All this means is that the last tenant's stuff that was attached to the walls needs to be cleaned out, leaving you a basic box where you can start building your club to your needs and taste. The costs related to the demolition process vary, but in most markets it will cost between $2 and $4 per square foot to take it back to the point where you can begin.

It is very important that you get an exact description of what vanilla box means to the landlord because surprises are expensive. One gym owner was taken aback when he assumed possession of his space, after signing the lease, only to find that he didn't have any heating and air conditioning, which was his responsibility to install according to the landlord's definition of what vanilla box meant.

Consumer price index. The Consumer Price Index (CPI) is a government-derived number published every year that indicates how much more money it would take to have the same buying power today compared to the base year of 1967. For example, a year's increase for the CPI might be 1.5 percent, meaning that if a landlord wanted to get the same value for his money, he would have to increase your rent by 1.5 percent. In other words, he needs 1.5 percent more of your money to achieve the same value or buying power. CPI is important in lease negotiations because it is often the universally accepted number used to determine increases in rent, either by the year or during the options periods.

Build-out/tenant improvements. Build-out, or tenant improvements (TI), is what it takes to finish the space, aside from the equipment and operational items such as desks, inventory, or music systems. Standard tenant improvements include wall coverings, lighting, floor covering, finished plumbing, and the physical structure of the locker rooms but usually not the lockers.

Assume nothing when it comes to tenant improvements. When working with your landlord or your own builders, specify exactly what you are asking for and back it up with some type of detailed drawings or other support materials such as itemized checklists.

If you are using an architect, make sure you understand what you are getting for your investment at every phase of the build-out. More than one new owner has been surprised to find out that his interpretation of finish didn't include things such as lockers or mirrors. Know what you want and know what you are paying for and always remember that you are the one writing the checks so there are no dumb questions.

The Actual Lease

The lease itself can be a simple document that is easy to read and understand, or it might be a 100-page nightmare meant to make lawyers everywhere wealthy. The type of lease depends on the property manager or landlord and often the area of the country where you hope to open. Most leases, however, are what are called boilerplates, an old term meaning that most of the clauses in the lease come from software that is used over and over again and covers standard issues common to most leases. A basic lease in our business should contain the components covered in the following sections.

Those interested in opening training facilities need to understand that the rules of leasing apply to you as well. Just because you are opening a smaller space does not mean that you do not need a lease to protect you or that your lease would not include the same protection and coverages mentioned in this chapter. Trainers often get into trouble because they don't believe that the rules of good business apply to them as well.

The initial lease period is for five years.

Five years is the standard period of time for your initial lease period and is the period you will most often see on a landlord's offering sheet. You can use the length of the initial period as a tool to barter for something else later in the process.

For example, most landlords take your lease to the banks and leverage its value against other projects he might want to do. Buildings that have space occupied by solid tenants are worth about 40 percent more than a building that is empty when it comes to getting that building financed or borrowing money against a property. Bankers are less likely to loan money against a building that is empty because the owner has to carry the mortgage out of his personal cash flow without the aid of monthly rent from a tenant.

That same building with a proven tenant, defined as a tenant that is paying or has the ability to pay over time, such as a national tenant in the Starbucks class, is considered an asset that is capable of generating positive cash flow for the owner of the building and is something the bank will lend against or be more willing to finance. The 40 percent number is typical in commercial real estate in most markets but can fluctuate in major metro areas. The individual strength of the landlord and how leveraged he might be in other projects is also a factor.

Using the base period as a bartering tool is simple. Assume that the landlord balks at your request for three five-year option periods. You might counter with an offer to extend your initial lease period to seven years, or even 10 if the space is prime and the terms are favorable, in exchange for getting your options in the future at favorable terms. You win because you gain the options and the landlord wins because he secured his space with a tenant he believes is solid and able to pay the rent for 7 to 10 years.

Option periods are for five years each and you should normally ask for three five-year options.

Three five-year option periods are becoming somewhat obsolete in the more aggressive real estate markets, but it is still a concept worth asking for in your negotiations. These periods give you the right to perpetuate your business, at a known rate, making it easier to budget and worth more when you sell later. Fewer landlords are giving these extended option periods, however, believing that they restrict the total return they can generate over time by selling their future too cheap now. In a tough economy, for example, a landlord might take a beating now to just get space rented and then try to get a better deal from you in five years when the market recovers. This landlord does not want to be tied to a bunch of options that restrict his ability to press for a higher rent in the near future.

Remember that three options are better than two and two is better than one. Ask for three and settle for less if you have to, but remember that you have to have the right to project your business into the future at a known rate to be safe and to add value when you decide to sell it.

Consider what happens if you don't get an option. You are three years into your first lease period of five years but you don't have a defined fixed price or fixed percentage option period with your landlord. Your business is growing and you are on your way to becoming successful in that location.

Instead of a defined option where you know early what you will be paying five years from now, you have something called market value in your lease. This means that the landlord will renew you if you want to go forward, but he will wait until the very end of year five to give you the number. The landlord looks at your business, realizes that you are trapped by your own success at that location, and decides to raise your rent by 20 percent. He has the right to do so since you signed an option clause that states you are subject to a market value, which really means the landlord will make up a number based upon the situation at hand during the last days of your initial lease.

Never assume that this number will ever go down. Always assume you are going to get hammered at the end by the landlord, which means you never sign a lease without a clearly defined option clause that states what you will pay and how that figure is derived. Are all landlords crooks and are they trying to hurt you? No, of course not, but they have no responsibility to make business decisions in your behalf and it is your responsibility to protect your own investment.

Option periods are based upon CPI and you should ask for a cap of 3 percent.

As mentioned several times already, it is important to have a known rent in the future. Fitness facilities need a constant flow of reinvestment capital to stay competitive, which usually comes from long-term (7- to 10-year) loans from your bank. You do not want to become trapped by market value lease options.

As an example, if it is a hot real estate market, your rent might go from $10 a square foot to $14 overnight. This overnight increase is extremely hard to plan for in a fitness business's working business plan. By tying your option period increase to CPI and capping the increase at 3 percent, you can adjust your membership price increases and bank capitalization accordingly. In other words, you know in advance that your business can handle that bank loan comfortably over the seven-year period, instead of worrying that a severe market value bump might destroy your profitability and ability to repay your obligations.

If the landlord balks at CPI, then counter with a maximum fixed increase of 2.5 percent per year during the option periods, but if you have to, settle for 3 percent. A fitness business can survive quite well with a fixed increase of 2.5 percent per year or 12.5 percent over every five-year period and can even adjust to a 3 percent annual increase if needed, but you and your business will struggle if you are forced to adapt to an increase any higher than 3 percent per year during your options.

Ask for three months of free rent, including no triple net charges, for build-out time.

It is hard to ask a landlord for six months of free rent, which is what we really want here rather than the standard three that works for retail but doesn't help us as much as we would like for a fitness business. Most agents or property managers are automatically wired to give a traditional three-month period. They know you will ask for free time because every tenant asks and it is a standard move for almost every landlord to routinely grant the time but most seldom offer or grant more time than the three months.

To break this auto-response habit and make the first year of operation more favorable to your business, you have to bring a different negotiation strategy to the table. Try this strategy, which breaks your desired free-rent period into two distinct areas and has had a high probability of working over the years with many landlords all around the country:

- The first request made to your landlord or his agent is for a three-month period allowing you to finish your build-out prior to the official opening of your club. Three months is not enough in most cases to do your build-out, but it is reasonable to most landlords. Most landlords are used to building out retail and often don't have a lot of experience with fitness facilities. Large, mainstream clubs can often take six months or longer to build out in rental space and your individual negotiations have to reflect the depth of your project. If you are spending millions in someone else's space, you can and should get extended build-out times. New generation training clubs, on the other hand, can often easily get done in a few months, especially if the locker rooms are kept simple. Get your architect involved with sketches and drawings to demonstrate the differences and the time need to complete the project.

- The second part of the strategy is to ask for an additional three months free rent, including no triple net charges, starting from the date of certificate of occupancy (CO), which is issued by the local permit people and states that you have met all building requirements and that you can immediately open for business. In other words, we are asking for three months free rent prior to actually opening your business so you can get the place built and then you are asking for an additional three months after getting permission from the city to start working people out in order to give your business time to get healthy without the pressure of paying rent too soon.

Your new business needs time to get healthy and it has a growth phase of its own. Having no rent, or reduced rent, during the first three months to a year allows your new business to slowly acquire a membership base and the associated cash flow that goes along with increased member traffic. The perfect combination would be a total of six months with no rent and then reduced rent for the remainder of the first year that slowly escalates toward the actual rent number as the club steadily grows and can handle increased rent. This situation, coupled with two to three months of reserve capital, would make you hard to beat in any market and greatly increase your odds of success.

Ask for a build-out allowance from the landlord of at least one-third of the build-out costs.

Depending on the strength of your financial statements, the size of the landlord's pockets, and the time the space has been on the market, you can ask the landlord to participate in the build-out to some degree. If your financial statements are strong, the landlord might put money into the project to get you into the deal, because having a strong tenant increases the value of his property and strong financial statements are an indication that you have a higher likelihood of paying his rent. If your statements aren't as strong, he might put some money into your project in the way of build-out, but he then might expect you to pay a portion of that investment (terms and amounts can be negotiated) back over the initial lease term, which stated above is usually about five years.

Even if you are going into the project somewhat weak, which, frankly, most young fitness professionals do, many landlords will put some money into the deal that you will have to pay back as part of your rent over the initial term of the lease. In any case, ask for at least $15 to $20 per square foot in build-out allowance from the landlord and then negotiate from that point.

Another option might exist if the targeted property has been sitting vacant for a while and the landlord won't, or can't, put any money into something that hasn't generated him any income in awhile. In this case, you might ask for the $15 to $20 per square foot, and if the landlord declines, you might counter with the dollar equivalent in free rent during the first year. In other words, the landlord might not want to put money into a project he has been carrying for a long time without any monthly return, but since he is already sitting empty in your location, and perhaps in others in the same plaza or area, getting a new tenant might make it easier to fill the rest of the idle space since the perception of something happening might attract others who were hesitant to go first.

Do not be afraid to ask. Many inexperienced potential owners are nervous about asking for something free or for something that the landlord didn't offer because they fear they will look dumb. All the things listed in this section are fairly standard requests by someone with a little experience, and don't hesitate to ask for a lot and settle for a little less. You still won if you get anything, and every dollar that you save during the first year or two of your lease, you can invest into building your business and making it stronger.

Ask for exclusions that limit the landlord from bringing competing businesses into your plaza.

If you are in a strip plaza or mall, it makes sense to ask the landlord not to take other businesses that might drain away portions of your business. Exclusions are often done as addendums to the lease and your list might include weight-loss clinics, supplement stores, stand-alone juice bars, day spas, and the stores

iStockphoto/Thinkstock

that sell light commercial fitness equipment usually used in-home but that also sell kettlebells and other stuff that directly takes people out of your club.

Always include other fitness businesses in this list, which may seem obvious but it is something that most new owners forget. Landlords who are not familiar with the fitness business might not see any harm putting a small, women's-only business in a plaza alongside a regular, coed fitness facility, thinking that they are totally different and shouldn't affect each other. Be reasonable here. If you are only going to sell a few supplements, then don't fight giving the landlord the right to add a national supplement store to his mall. But if you are a training facility, for example, and getting a majority of your clients on supplements is part of your business plan, then don't hesitate to fight harder for something that could potentially damage you over time.

Ask for the right to sublet space within your facility to other businesses, such as chiropractors, physical therapists, or other businesses that can benefit from associating with you.

These types of small businesses pay you rent directly rather than renting their own space from the landlord, thereby reducing your overall rent and helping your business grow through their clients. People that own these businesses are looking for daily traffic comprised of people who might be more likely to support their type of business than the typical traffic a mall might generate. For example, a sports specific physical therapist would most likely do well in the lobby of a typical fitness center that has a few thousand active members who occasionally bang themselves up playing and practicing their sports.

Some landlords object to this practice since they are being cut out of the income stream and because you can most likely charge more for this smaller space than they are charging you for the club resulting in additional positive cash flow for yourself and your business. If you have interest or space and want to pursue this in your business plan, you must make sure you have the right to sublet space within your facility at your discretion and that the money paid in rent from your tenant goes directly to you and not the landlord. This is usually nothing more than a simple clause that your attorney can generate and have added to your lease.

Ask for the right to assign the lease without a lot of legal hassle in case you sell the business to someone else.

You may someday want to sell your business and get out but you need to anticipate that now and cover it in your lease today so you have more options open to you in the future. Most of the boilerplate leases have a very generic clause about the landlord not withholding the option to assign that is always framed with the words, "within reason." This little catch phrase allows the landlord to withhold the lease from your buyer if he feels there is a reason, although that reason might seem weak to you and unfair.

For example, your lease might have the, "will not withhold within reason" clause and you go through a divorce and just need to get away from the business for a period of time. Your manager says she will buy you out, you present the deal to the your landlord and you wait to close the deal and take some time off.

The bad news in this case is that you have a strong lease with below market value terms compared to what rents are going for in your area now and your landlord says no, you can't sell it to her. In essence, he refuses the transfer of the lease effectively killing the deal. Instead, he wants her to sign a fresh lease with a higher rent reflecting the current market. By doing this, he in fact took away a lot of the value in your business and probably cost you the sale if the buyer has a good attorney or agent that tells her it is now a bad deal for her.

You want to strengthen your options in the future by having your attorney draw up a clause that you submit as part of the lease-approval process. The clause is simple and states that if you find a qualified buyer, you will want the right to get out without undue landlord interference and that the lease is transferable to a new buyer under the same terms and conditions.

Ask for the option to buy the property, if applicable, between the second and fifth year.

Even if you are in a strip mall and every dime you have is going into the project, you should still ask for an option to buy the plaza within the initial term of your lease. At some point, you will want to own your building. Also, during your journey in small business you might make good money early, find a banker who believes in you, or find that special investor. Think big and always ask for the right to buy the building in the future. Try to establish a predetermined price that will hold during those first five years that is fair to you and fair to the landlord. Usually, the landlord will agree to a fixed price for two years and then a 3 percent escalator on the total price of the property each year after the first two.

Ask for a clear, written addendum to your lease stating your signage rights.

Find out your legal rights to sign your business and get them in writing as part of your lease. Check with the city and any other jurisdiction, such as the plaza management, that might infringe upon your ability to properly sign your business. Even if the landlord says yes, find out what the city and everyone else who has a say will really let you do and get those rules in writing as well. Assume that nothing is real if it is not in writing and a handshake deal is no deal at all; it's just the way to take the first step before you put everything else in writing so everyone understands what everyone else has said.

Ask for a written understanding of your parking needs from the landlord or plaza management.

It is always good to address your parking needs up-front rather than try to deal with the issue when it becomes a problem and your landlord and members are already upset with you. Parking is especially an issue if a number of small businesses are open near you later in the evening that might suffer due to your parking needs during your prime time in the early evening. Define in writing where your customers can park so that no one is surprised later on, and make sure everyone understands the expected busy times where you will have the highest impact on the rest of the parking surrounding your business.

Ask for a written plan on sound proofing your location if you are in a strip-mall location.

Fitness businesses produce sound that most landlords are not accustomed to with their other tenants and this sound can annoy your neighbors if not addressed before you open. The remedies are easy during the build-out stage where sound barriers can be cheaply added but sound proofing becomes much more difficult once the club is open and your walls are covered and your ceiling is in. The landlord should pay for any additional sound insulation that is needed as part of the package, since it affects your business and the ones adjacent to it.

Use rent averaging.

Rent averaging means that you will give the landlord the agreed upon rent number, but you don't necessarily give it to him as he wants it and how he wants it. Your new fitness business will need every advantage it can get during your first year. It takes time to add memberships each month; build your marketing and accumulate cash flow in the form of increasing monthly income from the added new members and for the business to catch on in the neighborhood. Rent averaging reduces your load during the first year or two but still allows the landlord to get his asking price at some point in the near future. For example, a landlord might ask for the following rent during the first five years:

- Year 1: $10
- Year 2: $10.50
- Year 3: $11
- Year 4: $11.50
- Year 5: $12

The average of these five years is $11 per square foot. To give your business an extra edge during the first year, you might offer the following rent structure:

- Year 1: $8.50
- Year 2: $9.50
- Year 3: $10.50
- Year 4: $11.50
- Year 5: $12.50

The average of these five years is $10.50, a little under the average the landlord was seeking, but still within the negotiation range. Most importantly, the landlord gets what he wants, a strong number during the fifth year going into the first option period. You also get what you want, which is reduced rent during your first years that allows your business to get healthy at a safe and steady pace.

Dealing with personal guarantees is a fact of business.

Landlords want you to guarantee everything, especially if you haven't been in business prior to opening this one. You want, however, the ability to get into other projects in the coming years, which is limited at times by the number of things you are personally guaranteeing you will cover if things go badly. Banks are afraid of people that have too many personal guarantees. For example, if you cosign on your brother's car to help him get out of a jam, the bank assumes that at some point this will be your obligation. You hope for the best with your brother but the bank makes its income from assuming the worst.

Guarantees are not unusual and, in fact, are a normal part of doing business. How you handle the guarantee, however, is what sets you apart from most rookies.

In many cases, you may offer an addendum to the landlord that states you will personally guarantee the lease as requested, but after two years you then have a chance to either re-sign corporately or eliminate the guarantee altogether. The terms of this addendum state that if you pay your rent according to schedule and as promised, and meet all of your other obligations to the landlord in the payment of any additional fees, then the lease can be modified based upon your performance.

If this is your first business, it is good business to pay your rent five days early each month. Do not be the person that has the money in the bank but is slow getting it to the landlord each month. If you have it, pay it early and develop that reliability in the landlord's eyes. You will undoubtedly need him later to help you with an issue, so take care of him early in your relationship.

Personal guarantees are not to be taken lightly. If you are a new business owner, you will most likely have to guarantee the lease personally. If you are the investor, you most likely will have to sign the lease and guarantee at least the initial term, because you are the money person. Understand what you are signing and review the ramifications of this agreement in your state by getting your attorney involved before you sign anything. Some landlords will work with you and let you drop the guarantee if you perform according to the lease. You should always try to include this addendum as part of your negotiations.

The Key Concept in This Chapter

The lease determines your rent factor and is the core item in building your business plan. Understanding how leases work will help you get the best deal you can for your area and business. Find an agent that you like and work with him over the long run. Also, remember that everything is negotiable and that you can go back to the table and retry different deals along the way that will give your business the best chance for success. Be patient, be thorough, and leave the emotion at home.

STEPS AND DECISIONS FOR YOUR NEW BUSINESS

Hemera/Thinkstock

Chapter Six

There are a number of other decisions beyond leases that will need to be made before you can launch your new business, such as choosing the correct legal entity or deciding if you want to consider a franchise. Begin by first reviewing the steps of opening your business and then address the individual issues separately by building the ones pertinent to you into your business plan. These tasks should be done roughly in the order listed, but your attorney and accountant may take you through them in a different order.

The Steps of Opening Your New Business

The following sections present a general checklist. Your local professionals should add to this list as they see fit to protect you from costly mistakes early in the game.

The important point to remember at this stage of planning is that every business is different in that the person who opens it is an individual and brings his own personality and style to the process. Your uniqueness will be reflected in the business, as will the uniqueness of the area, the factors of the local economy, and a number of other concerns that separate you from every other fitness businesses in the area and the country.

On the other hand, good business is good business and most fitness facilities that make money usually play by the same rules. You will still have to master marketing, learn the basics of salesmanship and follow-up, learn to acquire, motivate, and train good staff, and figure out how to read your financial statements and manage the money you expect to make.

For example, many rookie owners are surprised at the skill and systems it takes to actually get a client into a membership agreement and then have a high probability of collecting that membership over time. Successful clubs understand the complexity of this system, but most rookies just don't know what they don't know and many insist on doing things their way rather than studying and applying proven business systems.

There is an old quote that many first-time owners, or existing facility owners that are wanting to open another unit but who don't want to repeat the mistakes they made opening their first one, could learn: "There is an exception to every rule—but it is probably not you."

There are a number of facilities located around the country that break all the rules and still manage to make money, proving the adage that sometimes lucky is better than good. The owners of these facilities manage to break almost every simple business rule and still make money despite themselves.

Often, these kinds of owners are the guys speaking at a national convention sharing their business secrets. One notable owner, for instance, often spoke at his national franchise meeting each year sharing all of his proven techniques. His ideas were dated and mostly ineffective, but if you own the only facility in town of 400,000, no matter what you do will work. There were simply no other choices if you wanted to join a club in his area, and he did make a lot of money for a number of years. Was he a good businessperson? No. Was he lucky? Yes, in a big way. But lucky doesn't make you a great teacher for others who are trying to get into the business.

When competition arrived, however, he lost the club within two years. When times got tough, it was proven that he never really learned how to make money; he was just the right guy at the right time in the right town who opened his club before anyone else found the area. Competition proved that he didn't really know the business at all and that, in reality, he wasn't the exception he believed he was.

What you can learn from his situation is to never believe that you are the exception to the rules of probability. Increase your odds by mastering all the needed aspects of owning and operating a financially successful fitness business and rely on your newly acquired skill rather than hoping you are the lucky exception to all proven rules of business.

Do your homework and spend some money learning from the successful owners and operators.

One of the funniest things you will ever hear a potential owner say is that he can't afford to attend a workshop because he is putting all his money into his new business. If you are putting everything in your life on the line to open a new business, budget a few thousand dollars to go learn how money is made. Following are a few ideas to help you start your preopening thought process.

- Research the industry, and your area, before deciding on the exact nature of your business. Spend your time focusing on clubs that are financially successful and can prove it, instead of just copying other businesses in your area. Many new owners make the mistake of just trying to create a new and improved version of what already exists in the area, instead of trying to develop something that better fits the target market and the owner's concept of business.
- Attend seminars, such as those offered by IHRSA or the National Fitness Business Alliance, and also consider mentoring programs offered by successful club owners that have proven business plans and who are willing to share these ideas for a reasonable cost over a day or two.

Use these seminars and mentors to gather realistic information that you will need to build your first business plan, such as the cost of equipment, rent factors in your area, build-out cost, needed reserve capital, and marketing. These are common numbers that are easily accessible once you start to get a focus as to the type and size of your potential business. The ultimate rookie mistake here is to build a business plan that is absolutely perfect. Many first-time owners build the best-case scenario and then continually make it even better as they adjust their numbers higher and higher to cover all the money they find they will need to spend each month in leases, debt, and operating expenses.

As mentioned in Chapter 2, the reality is that you need to build three business plans: the best case, which you throw away; the middle case, which is realistic and shows some loss and pain, and also the one you use for the banks and investors; and the worst case, which you use to actually run your business.

The worst-case plan reflects how bad it can get and then what it takes for you to still make it. This version is the one you keep in your briefcase to keep the reality always in front of you. In other words, hope for the best but plan for the worst and you will be fine.

- Don't forget to budget for an attorney and accountant early in the process. Small business is often a team approach and you need professionals to back you up along the way. Remember, however, that you need to learn enough to run your own business. Your team of professionals should provide advice, as needed, pertaining to their services and make sure that you stay out of trouble, but they are not there to run your business for you. Count on them for help and guidance, but you are the one that has to learn how to make your own business decisions.

- Visit banks and begin to establish relationships with bankers who work with small businesses. Don't present your anticipated plan, but simply tell them what you are trying to do and find out what they need from you in general. Most bankers will ask for a business plan but only give a formal presentation when your business plan is ready and professional.

- Build your business plan and get your money in line for the type of business you plan to open. If you have investors, get their share escrowed or at least get a legal letter of intent before signing leases and legal obligations based upon money being available in the future from someone else. This is an important note. It is not unusual for a potential owner to get a verbal commitment from an investor and then six months later, when you are ready to go and need the money, he doesn't have it because of a divorce or other issues in his own life. The same rule discussed for leases applies to investors: if it isn't in writing, it isn't real money.

Hire an accountant and an attorney who understand small businesses and who have set up and advised other small businesses.

Once you are ready to move beyond the thinking/planning stage and into the getting-it-done phase, you will need to establish the structure of your business. The first step is to get an accountant to help you set up accounts, prepare for tax issues, explore legal entities, and help you avoid other legal issues with the state, county, and city that might prevent you from opening at a later date.

You will also need to set up your company's structure and file with the state. You need an attorney for this who can work with you and your accountant to make sure what you do is legal and that it will give you the best tax advantage in the future.

- Get advice regarding the best legal entity for you, your investors, and where you are in your life financially.
- Start keeping all receipts for your accountant on researching and opening your new business. All this preparation is considered start-up expense and is tax deductible.
- Get tax advice immediately rather than waiting until the end of the tax year. Good tax advice happens before revenue is generated and prior to the

business actually getting started. You want guidance from your accountant as you grow and make decisions, but you do not want to wait until the end of the year and hear your accountant say, "I wish we would have done that differently earlier, we could have saved you a lot of money."

- Get help on building a professional filing system right away, especially concerning all start-up expenses. It may seem like a low priority but you will be in business for years, and learning to manage records early will save you time and money later when you need to access previous documents. For example, most insurance people ask that you save liability waivers off-site in locked storage for 15 years, and most accountants ask that you never throw away any tax return as long as you are in business. Get help early and follow it closely. If you're a natural slob who loses everything, pay someone early to make sure your business is better organized than one old stuffed file cabinet in your office where nothing can be found. Trainers, if it is important enough to save, store it at home in a locked file cabinet and not in a general desk in an open space shared by all your trainers and clients. For example, liability waivers should be saved offsite for 15 years and you should update with every client every year. Another example are the employee files, which should be protected offsite at all times since most trainers have offices in their clubs that are open to most of the staff and even the members. It is safer to store these files outside your business than to risk leaving a file cabinet open and allowing access to files that could get you sued, such as an employee who takes a quick glance at the file of another employee to get a personal address or phone number. You failed to protect the privacy of an employee and could be in big trouble here.

iStockphoto/Thinkstock

Create the legal form and name of your business.

Make sure to research your chosen business name with your attorney before committing to it. You will also probably choose a name for your corporate structure and then a DBA (doing business as) name for your business. Your business may take one of the following legal forms:

- Sole proprietor (If it is just you or you and your spouse/significant other.)
- Partnership/limited partnership (Might be recommended for a small entity with just two partners.)
- S corporation (Your accountant might recommend if you are making a little more money or have other businesses, and it is a common tool.)
- C corporation (You will seldom, if ever, use this form and you should get a second opinion if your accountant recommends this entity to you.)
- Limited liability corporation (or company) (LLC) (If there are partners involved, you will often explore this entity, but make sure there is a partnership agreement/management agreement in place.)

File the appropriate forms for your state. (This step is why your accountant and attorney are important.)

- Fill out all legal forms required by your state.
- File your Federal Employee Identification Number (tax ID) and all other tax forms necessary for your city, state, and business type.
- Check to see if any environmental permits need to be filed.
- Complete all city and state filings as needed.
- Be sure to file all city and county permits as required and in a timely fashion.

Consider the following issues with your attorney and accountant if they haven't yet been discussed.

If you are creating a new corporation of some type

Most of you reading this book will probably have no idea what some of this jargon means, which is standard for any person getting into business for the first time. Don't worry; this is routine legal work that every small company has to do to get started. Make sure you complete these steps as well as follow the supporting advice of your attorney, such as having an annual meeting with him, which is declared a stockholder's meeting. It may seem ridiculous but by going through the steps and following the rules, you will avoid many legal issues later if you get sued or have other problems.

- Have your attorney prepare your articles of incorporation.
- Have your attorney draft your shareholder documents.
- Prepare your board of director documents with your attorney and accountant.
- Get your minute book, corporate seal, and stock certificates.
- File the proper C or S documents with the IRS.

If you are an LLC

- Get a partnership agreement in place (see the section later in this chapter that further explains this document).
- Determine who will be the managing partner and define that role.
- Determine who will be the limited partners and define their roles.
- Create job descriptions for each partner who will be working in the business.
- Establish who has the right to make the final decision if all partners don't agree.
- File all paperwork with the state and the IRS in a timely fashion.

If you are a partnership

- File the appropriate tax forms with the state and the IRS.
- Get a rock-solid partnership agreement in place (this also applies to the LLC option as well) that defines buyout options, what happens in case of divorce or death of a partner, the right to disagree through a third-party arbitrator, and whatever else your attorney needs to do to protect you if your partnership goes bad. Do this before you start moving money around. Do this even if there is just you and your long-term best friend who is opening with you. Do this even if you never in your wildest dreams ever imagine there could be a problem amongst your partners. There will be a problem at some point and this will keep the company going and may save a few friendships as well.

Complete the following general tasks.

- Open bank accounts (again, you need your accountant to set this up correctly and to explain the rules of how to use a business checking account).
- Start getting tax advice for each major decision, such as buying versus leasing equipment or entering into a lease for space.
- Work with your accountant if you need to generate any type of early payroll. There is an important side note for you to learn, and that is to always pay your payroll taxes for each payroll period. Don't kid yourself into thinking you can catch up on the next payroll period if you skip one to save money. Pay as directed by your accountant and get into the habit of running a clean business from the start. Another point that might seem small is to only pay employees on the 15th and the last day of the month. Do not pay every two weeks since you will have two months a year with three payrolls, which is a budgeting and cash flow nightmare for most owners.
- Contact an insurance agent and find out what coverage you might need before you open. This point is especially important since most new owners have little idea of what coverages, and the associated costs, they need to run a business. Once you have access to your space, you will need insurance immediately and do not put it off until you actually open. You will also most likely need to find an industry specialist that does nothing but fitness businesses. Most local insurance guys just don't have the range of products it takes to fully protect a fitness business at a reasonable cost.

Complete the following tasks pertaining to your first employees.

- Create job descriptions. The first step, however, is to define who will be working in the business by task. Most new owners hire employees like they are shopping at a grocery store: "I need one of those, and I'll take two of those." This comes from visiting other clubs and just hiring duplicates of the people you see working in these places. Your first thoughts should be very simple. Who is going to be responsible for signing up new members (you have to have a dedicated person no matter how small you are)? Who is going to specialize in doing the back shop work such as payroll and advertising? Who is going to be your head trainer and what will her role be in the business? An important note is that everyone on the team can't share all these jobs, which is how most fitness businesses start. Marketing? We'll all get together and do that as a team. Break your company down into segments defined by individual responsibility and you will then be able to write a job description.

- Get some basic human resources (HR) help and education, including legal hiring practices, legal applications, and interview processes. There are specialists in your area that can help you with this and you will need help in this area. The rules of hiring and firing are clearly stated and easy to follow if you have taken the time to learn them first. Don't neglect this as something to be learned at a later date once you have time. If you have an employee, then you need to follow the rules and protect yourself and your business from lawsuits.

- Start every employee with a nonsolicitation agreement. Most states don't allow enforcement of noncompete agreements anymore. Noncompetes state that if you leave me as an employee, you can't work within a certain distance from the club for a certain time period. Most judges are simply reluctant to tell someone they can't work and feed their families. Nonsolicitation agreements, however, state that you can work, but you can't take my membership information, solicit the members, try to hire my staff, or, in other words, go after the membership and employee assets of my business. These agreements do often stand up in front of a judge and you should have every single employee, which includes counter people, childcare workers, and janitors sign one. Your local attorney can easily put together a simple agreement for you to use and this should be in place when you hire your first person on the team.

- Get your tax ID.

- Keep secure payroll records. Payroll records are private information. These files need to be locked up in a secure place with no access except by those who absolutely have to see what is in an employee's file.

- Get an employee manual in place before you open. These manuals clearly state all of your policies, which can't be enforced if the staff person hasn't seen them or has a chance to ask questions. For example, it is hard to enforce a dress policy if you haven't clearly stated it in writing and given the employee a chance to read and sign it first.

Legal Entities

Legal entities are important to you for two reasons: the right one provides the maximum legal protection in case you get sued and secondly the right entity gives the maximum tax advantages to both you and the partners in your business. The following information is a *brief tour* of the legal tools you have at your disposal that describes each entity and explains what it can do for your business. As always, get some professional guidance from a local attorney and tax accountant before making your final decision.

Sole proprietorship

This option is the least sophisticated of all of your choices, both for tax purposes and regarding start-up expense. A sole proprietor is just you, and your spouse if applicable. Being a sole proprietor means that you conduct business as you and that no other tax entities are in place.

The issue to consider with your attorney is liability. As a sole proprietor, you have total responsibility for all tax issues and legal issues that arise from your business, because all income from your business is passed through to you personally.

A sole proprietorship might, however, be your choice if you want to open a small facility, such as a training studio, without partners and without any very complicated financing in place. Another thing to note about this type of business is that they are sometimes harder to sell because it is harder to determine the assets of the business versus things you own personally. Also, if you die the business usually ceases to exist. But if you only want one, small studio and plan to work it yourself, your discussion with your tax person should begin with a sole proprietorship.

Partnerships

Partnerships are confusing to most new small business owners. "Hey," you exclaim at the gym during a set, "You're my friend and workout partner and I want to open a new gym, so let's become partners and do it together."

Forming a partnership can be easy and most start as a relationship between two like-minded individuals that love fitness and want to pursue it as a lifestyle. Getting out of the business, however, is always the most difficult part. Starting the relationship, and the partnership, correctly with clearly stated responsibilities, ways to get out, a simple valuation formula that everyone agrees to upfront to be used if one partner wants out, what happens in death or divorce amongst the partners, and perhaps even an agreement as to how you will disagree with each other in the future should all be part of any relationship involving two or more partners.

First, in a partnership each partner has unlimited responsibility for all of the business's debts and legal issues. Another way to look at this issue is that once you're in, all the stuff you own personally, such as your house, can be taken to pay for any debt the partnership racks up while in existence.

Blind partnerships, or those that a couple of people form with a little legal help and without a partnership agreement in place, usually fail. Such failure is expensive. Go into your partnership expecting the worst to happen and cover yourself in advance and you will never be surprised by a lawyer telling you that your house is now the property of the local bank.

The following tips about partnerships should be discussed with your attorney:

- Use your attorney to do the partnership. You will read in the newspaper and find endless solicitations online that you can do this on your own cheaply without the help or expense of an attorney, but get a lawyer involved from the beginning and listen to the advice you are getting that is pertinent to you and your personal situation.

- Draft a detailed partnership agreement (refer to Chapter 9) and be sure to cover how to end the partnership by buying each other out based upon predetermined formulas.

- Make sure only one person has the right to make the final decision if you disagree. The business has to operate each day and it can't wait for partners to come to an agreement. Someone has to be the adult and make the final decision as needed on a daily basis. Most rookies assume that everyone will simply sit down and discuss everything every day, but the normal course of business prevents this. In reality, there is almost always one person that either has more money on the table, or more business sense, and this is the person that usually gets to make the final decisions. There are compromises, of course, such as giving a partner the right to make daily decisions as needed except those requiring the spending of a certain amount of money. For example, a small club might have a managing partner that can get things done as needed except that she can't make a personal decision that involves spending $5,000 or more, which is something that has to be voted on by the team.

- Ask your attorney about selling your interest to someone else. Selling an interest in a partnership is usually difficult because the other partners have to agree to the sale. This point, too, can be discussed and written into the partnership agreement in advance so when the occasion arises, there is already a written legal guide to solve the issue.

- Designate from the outset who in the partnership has the right to make the decisions when it comes to entering into any type of legal commitments, such as signing a lease for a new printer. Legally, any partner can usually go crazy and sign for stuff, but you should put restrictions on this practice through your partnership agreement and restrict the ability to enter into agreements to just one person or, again, any agreement that requires a certain amount of money or higher has to be a team event.

One final note is that most general partnerships are not based upon percentage of ownership. For example, if you own 80 percent of the partnership and two other people own the rest, you are all equal despite the percentages. Have your attorney explain this issue to you up front.

Another version of the general partnership, called a limited partnership, requires more stringent legal controls. Again, talk to your professional advisers before embarking on this voyage. This type of entity does not offer many real advantages, but most new owners and their sidekicks almost always end up discussing a limited partnership when first getting started. Explore this issue carefully, because a limited partnership has many pitfalls and offers little to gain in the long run.

S corporations and C corporations

Most people opening their first small business will be better off with an S corporation versus going after a traditional C corporation. When a new owner puts together a business, he almost always speaks in terms of the C corporation, which is what you see in many of the old movies about business. The confusion comes when the new owner says, "It's okay, I will own 51 percent of the stock and I will make the decisions."

An S corporation essentially splits the difference between a partnership and a C corporation. The real difference, however, among these entities is the tax aspect, which is the important issue to explore with your tax professional.

With C corporations, the issue of double taxation is always present, meaning that you pay taxes as the corporation on profit made and then you are taxed again when you take any money out personally. S corporations, on the other hand, have different tax rules. In this case, profits and losses are passed through to the owners based upon their pro rata share of the company. This explanation is simplistic and, again, you need to ask your tax person about the issues and how they affect you and your new business.

Selling an S corporation is also a lot easier than selling a C corporation due to the tax implications of the double taxation. C corporations are an older tool and are not a good choice for most small businesses. C corporations are normally avoided by most people owning a simple fitness business, and it is rare that a modern tax professional would suggest this form for most new small business owners.

C corporations do have one advantage to explore with your team, which is the limitation of liability for the partners. Simply put, if you get sued, the corporation acts as a shield that can prevent the person suing you from going for anything beyond the assets owned by the corporation itself.

A limitation on the liability for debt you are responsible for personally also exists with this type of corporation. If you would have to bankrupt the corporation, for example, the corporate shareholders are not liable for any of the corporation's debts. Landlords and bankers know about this situation, of course, which is why you usually have to sign personally, not corporately, when you enter into a lease or bank loan.

Assuming that you have decent insurance, which is one of the first and most important decisions you need to make, the protection provided by this entity isn't as important as it used to be. The other legal entities, if your attorney sets them up correctly, can provide a certain degree of protection as well but it is still dependent on a solid foundation of insurance.

A common mistake made by many first-time fitness business owners who buy property as part of their first business is putting the building and the business into the same corporation. Always, without exception, have separate corporations for your property and for your business. Setting up your company this way is another step to provide more protection in case you are sued since your newly acquired assets are not all lumped together in one company.

Limited Liability Companies (LLC)

The LLC is a relatively new option open to small business owners and is now legal in all states. The LLC has several advantages worth exploring with your tax person. First of all, the personal liability for the members is limited. Secondly, the tax benefits flow through to the individuals involved in the LLC.

You will need to establish an operating agreement (similar to a partnership/management agreement) as part of your set-up with this entity. Rules governing this agreement may vary from state-to-state, so make sure you spend time researching them going into the set-up and make sure you do have an operating agreement in place, since most states use a default agreement if you don't establish one yourself. The LLC is the best choice for most small businesses, which is why it should be the starting point of your discussion with your tax professional.

Franchising

Franchising isn't for everyone, but it may be for you. When you buy a franchise, you supposedly buy a proven business system developed by someone who is selling this system to others. To use this system, or franchise, you pay a fee up-front in most cases and then either a flat fee or a percentage each month to the franchisor.

Franchisors usually provide help with site selection, market research, advertising, business training for the owner, staff development, and other business aspects that a new owner would have to develop on his own if he were to open a business without the help of the franchisor. You are also buying the name recognition, national branding, and ability to sell products that are developed through the efforts of the franchise rather than incurring the cost of developing these things for yourself.

The most important rule if you are considering a franchise is to do your homework. Visit a large number of existing units and talk to owners. If you get a negative pattern, walk away and try another option.

Ask the following questions regarding any franchisor with whom you are considering working:

- How long has the franchisor been in business?
- How many units are currently opened (not just territories sold)?
- Is the company growing and adding new units or is it stale and merely replacing the ones lost each month?
- What is the growth pattern for the company? Is the total number of units in the field shrinking or growing over the last five years?
- What kind of reputation does the brand name have in the market?
- Is the product/concept unique and defensible over time or would it be easily duplicated by someone else? This point is important in the fitness industry, especially since many of the franchises that have appeared during the last few decades proved to be easy to duplicate by others.
- Who owns the franchise and what are their backgrounds? Were they successful in the type of business they are trying to sell you or just successful in the franchise business?
- Does the franchisor own any company stores and how are they doing?
- Are there any lawsuits pending by franchisees? How many have occurred during the past five years? Have your attorney research this in the states where the franchise has the highest number of units and also in the home state where the franchise is based.
- What are the exact franchise fees and how are they determined? What are they used for by the franchise? Does a percentage go toward national marketing or branding?
- Do you have to participate in certain programs each month, such as a national marketing campaign, that will add a lot of additional cost to your business?
- How much training will you get as an owner? How much help can you expect once you open? What kind of help can you get if your business doesn't do well? These particular questions are important to ask other franchise owners operating in that system. Most franchise companies will give you a list of their true believers, which is usually based upon a limited number of operators who are extremely loyal to the franchise. If you are checking out a franchise, call a number of random units around the country that aren't on the list and ask these questions.
- Does the franchise charge extra for onsite visits? Are any other "extra" charges to be expected?
- How do you/can you get out of the franchise if you don't like it and how long are you committed to pay?
- What is the failure rate for the existing franchisees?
- How is your territory as a franchisee established? Is it protected? Check this out with other franchisees. This point is often one of the most highly contested issues within a franchise organization.
- Is the length of the initial franchise agreement negotiable?

- What happens if you want to sell your franchise or sell your territory?
- Does it cost more to stay on as a franchise after the initial period?
- What happens if you want to open another different type of fitness business in the same area but with a different name?
- If you die, what happens to the franchise?
- If you are comparing several franchisors, make sure you get down to the actual cost factor per franchise. Some of the cost factors aren't always clear, so make sure you are comparing actual costs across the board.

IHRSA, through its magazine *Club Business International*, publishes a guide each spring listing all of the franchises operating in the fitness business. This guide lists what each one does, along with the number of franchises, contact information, and other facts that will help you begin your investigation, and gives you an overview of how each one fits into the fitness world. Reviewing this list is a great first step, but once you move toward making a decision be sure to get a professional accountant and attorney involved.

Leasing Versus Buying Equipment

Whether to lease or buy equipment is another frequently asked question that comes up early for new owners, especially when an individual is considering his first large equipment purchase. Leasing is often a better option for fitness business owners who have limited capital when they start.

For example, if you have decent credit, you can often get a line of equipment for your new club, which can run as high as a half-million dollars or more, for as little as 10 to 20 percent down, and sometimes even less. On the other hand, if you purchase $300,000 worth of equipment, it would take $300,000 to place the order. You wouldn't have any monthly payments if you pay cash, but you would need to have a large sum of free cash to get your equipment.

If you leased, you might put 10 percent down, and then have payments for three to five years on the balance of the lease. Your payment for three years at 7 percent interest would be about $8,300 per month, or $5,300 a month over five years. Interest and term could vary, but if you can, you should consider leasing your stuff for five years. In this case, your only out-of-pocket expense would be the down payment. You will have monthly debt, but you don't have to come up with $300,000 to get your equipment package.

You might also check with your accountant to see if you can deduct your lease payments as a business expense on your taxes. If you can do this, it lowers your net cost of the lease.

Leasing also allows you to deal with the fact that fitness equipment, especially cardio equipment, will wear out in approximately four or five years. It might break down more quickly if you don't maintain it, or it could last longer if you really take care of it, but four to five years is the average, with five for cardio being the very upper limit, and you will need to replace it somewhere in that time frame. If you lease, you trade in the old equipment and just pick up a new lease. It is important to remember that if you have gotten that far, your business has been handling the payment anyway and simply extending the lease with approximately the same payment into the future probably won't be that painful.

Some advantages exist to buying equipment. You own the asset outright and won't have any payments. Some tax advantages are worth exploring with your professional if you are considering buying the equipment under another corporate name and leasing it back to yourself. This option might also be something to explore with an investor as well.

Buying outside your company and leasing back to yourself might also allow you to charge yourself a higher interest rate and payment, thereby letting you take more money out of your business. This situation might apply if you have partners who don't want to put the money up directly for the equipment or if the business is profitable and you and your accountant are looking for possible ways to get more out of it with limited taxes. Again, explore these questions with your tax professional before actually committing to a set path.

You might also be able to negotiate for a much larger discount if you pay for the order up-front. Equipment people are like other businesses that have seasonal highs and lows in that most would welcome a large order paid for all at once and would deal a little to make it happen.

It is important to note that the fitness business is starting to change its course. Clubs built in the 1990s were often nothing more than fields of equipment lined up in neat rows by brand or by body part. Machines ruled and to be competitive, you had to have a variety of equipment representing most of the popular brands. This scene has dramatically changed during the last number of years.

In today's market, your equipment list would probably look a lot different than one from 1995. For example, cardio would still be one of your biggest purchases. When it comes to cardio equipment, the decision is whether you want televisions or just basic units. Many owners follow the law of "simple is better" and avoid the televisions, going for more units instead. When it comes to cardio, in most cases, more is an advantage and you are often better with more units and less investment in the entertainment factor that can be handled more cheaply with other solutions.

There is also another shift toward functional equipment rather than traditional fixed plane circuit equipment. Most owners are finding that functional types of equipment allow for more variety, more versatility, and fewer units. You will still have a standard line of fixed plane, as of now, but in the future, the more functional the better.

Understanding depreciation

The value of your equipment lessens each year and the equipment will eventually wear out. The name of this process is depreciation, which is a term used by your accountant to write off the value of that asset over time. Another term for this process that you might read about is capital allowances, which is a way of allowing you to write off the cost of capital against the taxable profits of your business.

Before you make any major purchase of any type, consult your accountant to make sure you are covering future tax ramifications before you buy. It is easier to make decisions before you purchase or lease than it is to try to cover your tracks later.

Purchasing fitness equipment

The following information is derived from an IHRSA report on buying equipment.

Each year, the process of obtaining fitness equipment becomes a bit more complicated. New categories, additions to existing lines, more sophisticated features, and new companies all can make the selection of a piece of equipment that much more trying and time-consuming. Obviously, every club has different needs. However, whether you're filling an empty room with new equipment or simply updating your current inventory, you should ask some basic questions when making your purchase.

Questions to ask yourself

- What market segments are you targeting? Beyond traditional cardiovascular and resistance-training equipment, lines exist that cater to specialized populations such as women, children, seniors, bodybuilders, and postinjury rehab patients.
- What kind of space do you have? Nobody wants to work out on a crowded cardio floor. A general rule of thumb states that 46 square feet of floor space is needed per station. When working with special populations, such as members in wheelchairs, that number may need to be higher. Another way to look at this is: Can you plan to keep your cardio units about eight inches to a foot apart on the floor with a three-foot safety zone behind each one if needed?
- What are your power constraints? Certain machines, such as treadmills, have large motors and therefore require a lot of power. Some elliptical machines don't have motors, which is a useful feature if adequate power isn't available.
- What are your staffing and programming capabilities? Make sure you have (or can hire) the appropriate staff to provide programming for the machines you purchase.
- What is your budget? The answer to this question may determine whether you lease or buy, and whether you opt for new or refurbished items. As the level of equipment sophistication increases, so does the cost of buying new.

Questions for vendors

- How long have you been in business? New companies may be eager to please and offer attractive pricing incentives, while more established companies may have proven track records and be worth the extra money.
- Are you financially stable? You obviously want to avoid buying equipment from a company that is about to go out of business. Imagine trying to get parts or service from a manufacturer that no longer exists!
- What's your warranty? Each part of a machine (e.g., frames, belts, chains, upholstery) may be covered under a different warranty, and for a different length of time. Be sure you understand all terms of warranties.
- How long is your typical downtime? That is, how long does it take to fix or replace an item that isn't working properly?
- How complicated is it to service the equipment? Most manufacturers will train your staff to make routine repairs. Some offer a certified technician-training program and may reimburse you for the hours your maintenance person spends on repairs.

Questions for anyone but the vendor

- What's their service record like? To find out what type of service a company really provides, call the clubs on its reference list and ask pointed questions. If you know of other clubs that have the type of equipment you are considering buying, call them too. Ask to speak to the maintenance staff. You want to know what the service will be like after your check clears.
- What was the installation like? Did the delivery process go smoothly? Did the manufacturer take care to get the equipment through the doors, around the corners, and up the stairs without gouging walls and tearing the carpet? Was installation as painless as possible for members? Once installed, was the equipment thoroughly tested, and was your staff thoroughly trained on safety, operation, and routine maintenance and repairs?
- What do members say about the equipment? Are they getting results? If members find the equipment ugly, intimidating, awkward, confusing, or uncomfortable, it won't be used. Instead, it will serve as a constant reminder that you could have done something more constructive with your money and space.

Other equipment thoughts

The trend now that will just get stronger during the next few decades, is the move toward outfitting clubs with more functional equipment, such as kettlebells, sleds, turf areas and training lanes, suspension training and equipment, and other equipment that hasn't ever been seen in most clubs. Your advantage is that most of this equipment needed to fill a typical fitness facility can be purchased for the approximate price of a single treadmill. This is why, in many cases, you will see the next generation of club centered on the hybrid training facilities that are about 3,000 to 12,000 square feet. They are simply easier and cheaper to open than a mainstream fitness club from the 1990s and are often much more profitable.

Following is a list that reflects the trend in fitness facilities toward functional. This list shows the equipment in the order you would buy it.

- Cardio, cardio cardio. Cardio is still important and even small training clubs start with a decent line. Your two biggest purchases will be treadmills and ellipticals, followed by step machines. Stay with the basics. It is also recommended that you don't buy cardio with televisions attached. Go simple and avoid that cost, and use the money you saved to buy more cardio.

- Functional machines. These are rising in importance because of their flexibility as a training tool. These are better known as the cable machines that allow the trainers/members to do so many more training moves on a single piece of equipment.

- Functional tools. These are your kettlebells, medicine balls, balance toys, suspension training, and 50-foot ropes.

- Most clubs in this decade and going further will still have a limited line of fixed plane, single-joint equipment, but you will have far less than a club that opened 10 years ago. The functional machines give you more options, and you will get more use out of that line than conventional equipment. For example, if you buy a functional chest machine, you can often do 30 or more exercise versus buying a fixed plane piece for the same cost that limits you to one exercise. The member is changing and what you put into your club has to as well.

Remember, you are buying equipment for your members. If they like it, if they can figure it out, and if they can use it safely, then positive results are practically guaranteed.

The Key Concept in This Chapter

This chapter is wide-ranging and is devoted to some of the business concerns you need to address as you move forward with your project. As noted, there are many more questions presented here for you to ask your tax and legal professional than specific answers.

How you set up your business and the decisions you make concerning your tax ramifications are more individualized than most people think. How much money you have, if partners are involved, if you already own other businesses or if you plan to open one or 100 additional units, are all questions that can only be answered by you and your professional team.

Study this chapter carefully and share it with your team. If your business is set up by a professional and you begin with the right legal vehicle, you are much more likely to avoid any serious downfalls, such as partner disputes or tax issues, later on when you are making money. And most importantly, understand that getting in right makes it so much easier to get out profitably later in your career.

DEVELOPING A BUSINESS PLAN

Comstock

Chapter Seven

If you want money from a banker or investor, or even an astute family member who might be willing to give you the start you are looking for in life, you're going to have to write a business plan that clearly and concisely makes your case for borrowing money. You should consider writing two types of plans for your first business project. First, a *prospectus plan* is the tool you would use with investors and bankers. This tool is usually approximately 15 to 20 pages long and is what a banker is asking for when he requests a business plan.

The development plan is a tool to help you define your business. This document clearly defines each aspect of your business in detail to ensure that you miss nothing during the project's development and to help you understand all of the components necessary to build this type of business. These plans might be anywhere from 75 to 150 pages in length, and this type of plan is not what a banker wants to see.

The mistake rookie owners often make is that they spend more time building the plan than they do trying to raise money. Writing the perfect 150-page development plan and detailing every nuance, from an anticipated class schedule to the type of amenities in the locker room, is a good exercise in thinking through all the details it takes to create a fitness business, but the last thing a busy banker or investor really wants on his desk is an endless pile of paper representing the smallest details of your proposed business.

Prospectus plans are short and to the point, and they concisely explain such items as an overview of the project: who is involved, the cost, a pro forma (a financial projection that shows how the business will perform over a set time, such as two years), and maybe some demographic information.

The development plan, on the other hand, gets into concepts such as the structure of your group program, people needed per department, a 12-month marketing plan, sales training structure, the tools needed to support the sales department, proposed hours, and other details that help a new owner focus on all aspects of the new business. This plan is for you to create to keep you on track; however, you might be the only person who ever reads it. The simple idea to keep in mind is that you write the prospectus plan to raise money, and you write the development plan to translate your dreams into a realistic business concept.

Bankers and loan officers are normally serious people who do their best to loan money to people who are prepared for banks and business in general. According to conversations with a number of loan specialists, only 4 out of 10 people who come in for money have a prospectus/business plan, and out of those four, only one can actually sit down and defend the numbers in his plan. In other words, the person asking for money usually didn't even build his own plan, leaving it to his accountant or a friend to develop it for him and then can't explain or defend the numbers he anticipates achieving in his own business when asked by the person he is trying to borrow money from.

The Prospectus

The prospectus is a brief history of the universe in 20 pages or less. This universe is the world of your new fitness business, and your prospectus briefly answers all of the major questions in something that can be read in one quick sitting by a busy banker or investor. Experienced business people want a quick look to see if you have a solid idea. If they want more information beyond this first look, they will ask more questions, but this plan is the necessary first step toward raising money and interest in your project.

The prospectus presented in this chapter was originally based on the Small Business Association (SBA) loan application and has since been modified over the years. This particular model has done quite well with banks and investors and is a proven tool for raising money. Business plans do not have to be creative to work. Good plans are conservative financial instruments that briefly define your concept and how it will work financially over time.

As a side note, the Small Business Administration works with banks to guarantee loans for small businesses. Several types of loans are available through the SBA, such as a 504 designed for an owner who wishes to purchase physical assets including a building, and the 7A loan, designed for owners who aren't buying property.

These programs do change from political administration to political administration and were hotly debated and modified during the later part of the 2000-2010 decade. Research these programs and then discuss the details with a knowledgeable banker who can guide you in the necessary steps needed to obtain this type of loan. You should seek out a bank in your area that specializes in SBA loans as part of your research. Some banks loan and do everything they can to get this type of business, and others are less interested and less knowledgeable.

Depending on your loan needs, size of the project, investors, total assets, and a variety of other factors, your chosen banker will guide you down the path where you are most likely to get the right loan package for you. If the bank is aggressive, it might want to do a straightforward conventional loan, or if the bank is a specialist in SBA loans, your bank person may take you a different path. Remember that all banks have their own unique personalities and specialties, and you will most likely need to interview several before you find the right fit for your project.

The information in this chapter is just offered as a guideline. If you have not written a successful business plan prior to your new project, you must have an experienced financial person to guide you. This might be an accountant who specializes in business loan preparation or perhaps a financial person who just specializes in small business in general. Interview a number of people and then commit to the one who will give you the help and guidance you may need to get your plan written and approved.

The heart of every business plan of this type is the projection, which is where you demonstrate to the loan officer or investor how the business will perform over time. Solid projections can be constructed for a two-year period, but some lenders occasionally want five-year projections, which are at best very weak attempts to project the business environment too far into the future.

If you have a choice, limit the projections to two years. The projection section is the core of the plan and is where most potential owners fail in their attempt to raise money. Most of the rest of the prospectus plan can be written following templates that illustrate what you need to add and where it needs to go, but the projections are more difficult and that is where your financial advisor can best help you prepare your plan.

A prospectus should include the following components:

- Cover page (Packaging is important. If the plan looks sloppy to the investor, then he will think the data itself must be weak.)
- Overview of the project/executive summary (This is a short, tight introduction to what the project is and what your are trying to accomplish with this plan.)
- Estimated costs of the proposed gym (Includes the total project cost supported by a breakdown of the components.)
- Proposed financing (Where are you going to get the money for this?)
- Projections and monthly operating expenses (Does this business work on paper?)
- Bank and investor considerations (You have to demonstrate the ability to repay the bank or you also have to clearly define what is in it for the investor.)
- Operating team for the club (Who are the players and why can they run a successful business?)
- Summary of the project (Put it together in one to two tight pages.)

The prospectus presented in this chapter was designed for an actual club for an owner who was a manager in a business but wanted to open his own club. This owner already had partners in place and he had established a banker relationship that could handle conventional financing as well as SBA loans, and had worked with a realtor to get the real numbers on the property. This plan is the basis of what he used to present to the bank with his final application.

If you are seeking money, find a banker who understands both conventional financing through the bank itself and who can also help you with SBA. If you have experience and a track record, most banks will take your loan through conventional financing, although this decision will vary from bank to bank. You can get further information on the SBA's website (www.sba.gov).

You should also explore Certified Development Companies (CDC), which specialize in helping people package their loans for the SBA. These companies often have local inside knowledge and are a good place to start your education because their employees have a lot of experience in helping new owners package themselves for banks and for the loan process and often know what banks in the area want and need to make the loans.

To find the CDC nearest you, explore the National Association of Development Companies, which can be found at http://www.nadco.org/.

An explanation of each component of the prospectus is provided, followed by an actual example that includes actual working numbers. The projection section is based upon just one look at the business and is offered here as just a typical example of what this tool might look like. Do not merely copy this example. Get your local financial expert to do the recommended three versions of the plan: best case, middle case, and worst case.

All names, including the club, are fictional in this plan, but the plan itself was written to help a young owner get financing for his first extended training center with memberships and was actually presented to a bank. This plan was accepted, but the owner eventually changed his goal and acquired another property that had become available nearer to where he wanted to open. He was previously operating a small training facility but did gain valuable experience from his years in business.

You can also learn from his experience. Many rookie owners and businesspeople make decisions without having the proper information at hand. These decisions are often based upon playing both sides of the conversation in your head. For example, you might be putting together an offering sheet for a landlord, but you're stuck because you are saying to yourself: "Well, if I ask for this build-out, I know he won't want to go that high, so I you should offer this number instead."

The mistake in doing that is that you are trying to anticipate everything he might say or do, which you can't because you are basing everything on your perspective and experience and not his. Instead, simply submit your offer and then react to what he comes back with in his response. You can't play both sides of the conversation, and although it helps to think about what he might do or want, you are better off to just submit and react instead of being frozen, trying to figure out exactly what he is thinking and what he might do.

In this example, the young owner gathered information, made a proposal, but then chose another property when he had done his homework. The lesson is that he gathered real information for his team and then made the decision based upon reality, not speculation or emotion.

Cover page

The cover page simply gives a quick look at what is inside. It should list the proposed business name, the owners, the date of submission, and contact information for each owner.

Overview of the project/executive summary

The overview section is a one- to two-page overview of the entire project, giving your prospective investors or the loan officer the overall picture of the project. The overview should state what the project is, where the business will be located, who will run it, why that area was chosen, and how long it will take to open the business from concept to completion. It also helps to offer one or two sentences as to what void your business might be filling in the marketplace.

You might also find that this section is referred to as an executive summary in more formal business-plan templates. The goal is the same no matter what you call it: Give the reader a brief, tightly written picture of your project in just a few pages. As a side note, you can find dozens of business plans online that can offer a wide array of what a finished plan might look like at the time of submission. It is good to study the writing and style of the successful ones and contrast them with the ones that are illustrations of what not to do in your own plan.

Estimating costs of the proposed gym

The next section is the projected expense section for the entire project. This section would present an overview of the entire project as well as the breakdowns of the individual components. The following components are included in this section:
- Cost of the entire project
- Land costs, if any
- Building costs/the outside shell of the building
- Site preparation
- Build-out for the interior

- Equipment costs
- Reserve capital
- A general category for the miscellaneous items, such as computers, music systems, licenses, etc.
- Marketing costs for the presale period and for the first 90 days of operation
- Architectural fees

Proposed financing

This section should discuss where exactly the money is coming from for the project. You should have an initial idea of where you are seeking financing and should do your initial bank investigation before submitting a prospectus plan to anyone for review. Your bank plan should reflect a specific loan amount and payback for accuracy. This can be changed bank to bank if needed to reflect different terms and investor considerations that might arise.

If partners are involved, their participation should be discussed in this section as well. How the partners will participate financially, how or if they will participate in the day-to-day operations of the gym, and how your partners will be repaid are all items that should be detailed in this section.

Partners sometimes scare bankers because most plans allude to them being in the game but they seldom define their role, initial investment, or long-term support in the project. Detail what your partners will do in the business and how much they are contributing financially. Bankers and other investors will ask for information on your partners if needed and you can also expect that everyone investing will at some point be asked to sign for the loans you are seeking.

Projections and monthly operating expenses

Projections are the heart of the prospectus since this tool demonstrates the ability to repay the lender or the investor. Most projections should be kept to two years, since the ability to project beyond that time frame becomes somewhat hypothetical and most modern bankers don't have much interest beyond that initial two-year period. In some cases, though, you might be asked to submit a three-year projection or longer.

It helps to be aware of the following common flaws in projections that usually get the loan rejected immediately. Remember, one of the most important things you have to master is to be able to fully explain and defend your numbers to your investors and your banker.

Flaw #1: The projections are not realistic or are too good to be true.

Projections that show no negative cash flow in the business, especially during the first year, are just too good to be true and the banker knows this from his experience with hundreds of other small businesses. Lenders expect a loss in the beginning and they are more concerned about your ability and awareness to plan for a reserve than to unrealistically expect no loss at all.

Build a best-case projection, a conservative middle case, and a worst case. Throw the best case away, give the middle case to your banker, and run your club off the worst case. This is an old adage but it is based upon a lot of truth and reality when it comes to running a small business.

The worst case is perhaps the most important model because you want to know how bad it can get and still work. Small business is a tough job and there will be good days and not-so-good business days. Another old adage, mentioned often in this book, is, "Hope for the best but plan for the worst." Having tough times is a normal part of owning your own business, and it helps to know how bad it can get in your business before you get into trouble.

Don't make the mistake of submitting your best-case numbers to the bank or investors. It's nice to dream, but it's safer to submit a conservative set of projections (the conservative middle) to your banker.

For example, one young owner lost several months of prime business because his wife was in a car wreck during the first month he was open. He held the club together, but the strain of taking care of his kids and seeing to his wife disrupted his focus. He made some revenue during that time period but the numbers were less than he had planned for during that time period, but he knew from his worst-case plan that he could still make it and keep going if he at least maintained those worst-case numbers. He returned to the business with full focus in about three months and was able to get the business back on track. Knowing where the bottom was allowed him to keep going without panicking and making bigger mistakes by doing crazy sales or business-threatening promotions.

Flaw #2: You can't defend the numbers.

You're not a numbers person, so you have your accountant build your projections. When questioned, you have no idea where he got those numbers and you sit in front of the banker looking at your own numbers with surprise. This scenario makes bankers nervous and is not going to get you a loan. Be able to defend every line and understand how the money will arrive in your new business. If you can't explain the numbers, you most likely won't be able to make them happen in the business either. Practice with your accountant. Go over every line and ask what each number means and how it was derived. If you can't explain it, you can't make it.

Flaw #3: You have no personal reserves.

If you have to take money out of the business from the first day it is opened, the banker knows that your plan is weak. Show a personal reserve of at least six months to let your business get healthy. It is sort of old-school silly, but think of your business as a new baby. The baby needs time to grow, get healthy, and then stand on its own. Your new business is the same. It needs time to grow and get healthy, but if you have to take serious money out too soon for personal support, the business will have a hard time getting established.

Flaw #4: Your projection is not adjusted for the seasons or for the natural flow in the business.

A straight-line projection might be one of the most common mistakes a new owner could make. Straight line means that all your numbers are exactly the same each month and never deviate due to the time of year or the natural flow of the business. Adjust for the seasons and the naturally busy or slow times of the year and show that you understand when money will arrive and when the slower months will occur.

For example, sales for most clubs pick up in late January, followed by a strong period from February to May. Summers are a little slower and then business resumes in the fall after the September holiday and continue strong until Thanksgiving. But if you live in Florida, you might have a strong summer because it is so hot that many people join clubs for the thought of enjoying the air conditioning during the state's hottest months. Do your research and understand what makes your area unique when it comes to membership sales and the natural flow of the business.

Flaw #5: You fail to use real renewal rates and loss rates.

No one collects all the money from all the members. People quit, get divorced and don't pay, close accounts, and just plain decide not to send you any money. Adjust your plans for losses, and during the second year and beyond, show a normal renewal rate rather than having every member keep going year after year. Use the following basic numbers to get started.

If you are using closed-ended renewals, meaning that you are signing up renewals for one year at a time, show a 40 percent renewal rate. You may do better, but you are building a more conservative case in your business plan. This 40 percent number comes from research and decades of experience and reflects what a typical club will retain in membership in the real world.

Losses with auto renewals will probably be higher. Auto renewal means that at the end of the member's first year, his contract goes away and you just keep drafting his payment from his credit card or bank account. Losses for open-ended memberships, which means the member can now walk away with 30 days notice, will range between 4 to 5 percent per month.

Your target is to retain 60 to 65 percent of all members going into their second year, adjusted for losses. It is also highly recommended that your members sign up for a year at a time rather than going from a commitment to open-ended. This keeps your business safer over time. Following is an example of what a typical month's worth of business might look like a year later. This does hold true for training clubs as well, although your losses are going to range between 2 to 3 percent per month:

- A club signs up 100 new memberships in January of 2011.
- The club loses 10 memberships due to the natural collection losses associated with 12-month contracts. (Losses for 12-month members are

less than 1 percent per month from the total file/show monthly loss rates of at least 1 percent for bad debt or 12 percent per year.)

- The club loses another 12 memberships due to people moving more than 25 miles from the club, meaning that the club has to cancel the membership per state laws. (Most clubs lose about 1 percent per month due to moves outside the club's market area. This could be higher in high-transient areas or lower in more conservative areas where people don't move as often. Show another 1 percent per month in your projections or at least 12 percent per year.)
- The club would have 78 memberships left at the end of 12 months after adjusting for losses.

78 x .60 (targeted retention rate) = 47 members

This club started with 100 memberships and started the second year for this group with 47, reflecting a loss rate of 10 percent based upon its membership tool (12-month memberships) and a loss rate of 12 percent based upon people moving outside the club's market. Consider the following numbers as well:

- If you are using 12-month contracts as your base tool, you will lose a little less than 1 percent per month, or 10 percent annually, assuming that you are using a strong third-party financial-service company. Owners who attempt to collect their own memberships often have a higher loss rate since they are often unprepared to collect money from their members. If you are opening a mainstream fitness facility and intend to collect your own memberships, use 2 to 3 percent per month as a loss rate for 12-month memberships and 4 to 5 percent per month if you are using 24-month memberships.
- You will lose at least 1 percent of your membership per month, or 12 percent annually, to those folks who move more than 25 miles away from the club. The state requires you to cancel those memberships.
- If you are using open-ended memberships, where there is no obligation beyond a month at a time, show 4 to 5 percent per-month loss rates, or 48 to 60 percent annually, although these numbers could be higher in transient or highly competitive markets.
- If you are using auto renewals, meaning that at the end of 12 months your members go from contract to open-ended, use 4 to 5 percent monthly losses going into the second year, or 60 percent annually.

Membership retention is measured on an annual basis. In the typical fitness business, memberships are added and subtracted each month. For example, you may add 20 new members in June but lose 22 that move, fail to pay their membership as promised, or do not renew with your club. It is important to track these each month with a goal of finding out your net gain in membership. Remember, it is important to always seek a positive gain in memberships each month since that gain reflects the health of your business over time. Following is a simple formula to use each month to determine net gain or loss:

- Determine the total number of memberships in the system at the beginning of the month.
- Add any new memberships you sold that month to the starting number.
- Add any reinstated members that might have left in the past but who are re-signing with the club.
- Subtract any members that do not re-sign that month, are cancelled for any reason, or are otherwise taken out of the system.
- The end result is net gain or net loss for the month.

Note that this definition excludes all changes between paying membership categories, such as upgrades and downgrades. We are seeking total memberships in this example, not the total amount of outstanding receivables, although that could be used as your starting point as well. If you use total receivable base instead of total memberships, simply convert all memberships in any category to their dollar amount rather than treating them as just one membership each.

A real working budget

Build a budget that reflects the realistic cost of doing business. You should include a sample month of expenses in your business plan, hitting all of the key categories. Figure 7-1, which is used as a monthly management tool as well to control expenses, lists all of the common expenses for a typical club.

Your accountant can help you define this sheet further. Avoid lumping together too many categories when you first start. For example, many accountants put all the income for the club's profit centers into one lump number. The problem with this is that the club might have five distinct profit sources in the club but four of them are not performing and that fact is being masked by one strong center. Lumping the profit centers together prevents you from seeing the weaknesses of the business rather than dealing with those problems each month.

The sample projection components are divided into four sections: general revenue, income from multiple profit centers, operating expenses, and payroll and related expenses. The book will illustrate a number of different ways to look at these since owners starting a new club range from trainers with 3,000-square-foot facilities to owners looking to open a 60,000-square-foot family club.

Revenue parameters for a sample fitness center in the 17,000-square-foot range

- The membership information reflects a short presale and average sales the owner could expect in that market.
- The 90 percent electronic funds transfer (EFT) refers to 90 percent of the members joining the club and electing to buy some type of membership or payment plan resulting in a contractual obligation for one year. The rule to

Expense	Projected	Actual	+/-
Fixed Expenses			
Rent/mortgage			
Triple net charges			
Yellow pages			
Accounting			
Loan #1			
Loan #2			
Lease #1			
Lease #2			
Other			
Variable Expenses			
Payroll			
Payroll taxes			
Commissions			
Advertising			
Utilities			
Phone			
Printing			
Office supplies			
Cleaning supplies			
Misc. supplies			
Postage			
Nutrition			
Pro shop			
Cooler drinks			
Sports bar/juice bar			
Day spa			
Personal/semi-private training			
Tanning			
Childcare			
Group exercise			
Accrual Expenses			
General liability insurance			
Property insurance			
Workman's compensation			
Repair and maintenance			
Education/training			
License/franchise fees			
Capital improvements			
Legal			
Savings/regular			
Savings/accrual			
Totals			

Figure 7-1. Expense budget management report

keep in mind is the 90/10 rule, which states that at least 90 out of every 100 members should elect to join by paying monthly through some type of membership plan, such as EFT, and 10 percent or less should pay in full. If too many pay in full, it reflects a low cash price or heavy discounting by an owner trying to force more members to pay up front. Your business will be healthier if you build a strong receivable base versus trying to get your membership money up front.

- The 6 percent paid-in-full (PIF) is the percentage of members who paid in full for an annual membership (part of the 10 percent in the 90/10 rule).
- The 4 percent is the percentage of members who took short-term memberships as opposed to an annual membership of some type. The short-term membership is paid all at once and is good for up to three months (part of the 10 percent in the 90/10 rule).
- The EFT membership is new sales cash paid as membership fee down payments on the contractual memberships.
- The PIF membership is the total new sales cash for paid-in-full memberships.
- Daily fee membership is the amount of daily drop-in cash for the month.
- Short-term membership is the total amount of cash generated in short-term memberships for the month.
- Total new revenue is the total of all income for new sales for the month.
- EFT base is the monthly draft, or billing check, that reflects all of the member payments collected against the contractual obligation.
- Total membership sales are the combination of new sales income produced on a daily basis as sales are made and the total of the monthly checks received from the outstanding amount of all the member payments.

Multiple profit center (MPC) parameters

- Clothing and accessories, supplements, drinks, tanning, personal training, group programming, and juice bar reflect the revenue collected for the month from each of the club's profit centers.
- Total MPC sales are the total of all the revenue from all of the club's profit centers.
- Net income reflects the combination of the revenue from the profit centers and from the revenue section that comes from club membership sales.
- Cost of goods sold is the cost of the profit centers to the club.
- Gross profit is the adjusted net income for the club.

Operating expenses

- This section reflects the operating expenses for each of these items in the club.
- Total operating expense reflects the total cost of operating, but not the cost of goods sold or payroll and related expenses.

Payroll and related expenses

- Commission paid is for sales and other bonuses paid to the employees.
- Salary expense is for all employees and includes the owner's compensation if he is taking a normal manager's salary.
- Total payroll and related expense is the total payroll and supporting expenses for the club.
- Total expense is the combined operating and payroll expense for the club.
- Net income is pre-tax net for the month (EBIT).

Bank and investor considerations

This section of the prospectus shows what's in it for the investor and demonstrates your ability to pay back the bank. It is based upon the preceding section of projections that should build in the anticipated bank payment or payments to the investors.

iStockphoto/Thinkstock

Most investors stay away from a business deal that gives them equity only in a gym business. The numbers are too small and they have too many other options with less risk.

A common method of attracting an investor is to offer a combination of equity and return on investment (ROI). For example, an investor might put up $250,000 for 25 percent of a gym that will have a million-dollar start-up cost. This investor would be paid back $125,000 over seven years as ROI, at an aggressive interest rate, and the other $125,000 would stay in the business as part of the investor's equity. This possibility is just a starting point for your negotiations, and your deal with your investors may end up being different, but just remember that your investor wants both equity and return from the deal.

Payment to investors should be included in the projection to demonstrate the ability to repay. Anticipated investor notes should also be discussed to demonstrate that they are built into the club's operating budget and are part of cash-flow needs.

Who will own and operate the business?

This section gives an investor an idea of who is going to run the club and if the team has any experience or the expertise to run this project. If the owner has been successful before, then this is an easy section to complete and is based on a simple resume of the owner's experience and qualifications. If you have not been in the fitness business before, real-life business qualifications are the most important thing, followed by any education or work experience you might have to prepare for owning an expensive fitness business financed by someone else's money.

Summary of the project

The summary section should tie the entire package together. Many loan officers will read the summary first and then start at the beginning to see if the data matches the claims at the end.

To be successful in obtaining a loan, you must be prepared and organized when making your request. You must know exactly how much money you need, why you need it, and how you will pay it back. On top of all of this material, you must convince your lender that you are a good credit risk.

The summary should be used to convey information that gives the lender confidence in the fact that you know your numbers and have researched the project. If they like what they read in the short form, they might want you to gather additional information.

Following is the sample plan and all of its support materials.

Prospectus

Table of contents

1.0 Executive Summary

The proposed project is a new 17,000-square-foot upscale adult fitness and lifestyle enhancement center (functional fitness for adults). This new facility will be located in Sacramento, California.

This upscale adult fitness center will be designed to appeal to the upper 60 percent of the demographics by affluence and will heavily market to those target members who live within a 20-minute drive time of the facility. There are a number of other fitness facilities in the area, but none are targeted toward the more affluent population living in the area.

The club will incorporate an aesthetically pleasing design and a unique training philosophy designed to develop the overall health and fitness of clients as well as helping them be more successful in life's activities such as tennis, running, and biking. In fact, almost any activity someone pursues can be improved with the right functional training and support.

The trainers at The Workout Company will be trained and familiar with using the functional approach with their clients. Tom Johnson, the president of The Workout Company, will direct and monitor all the trainers' workouts to ensure quality and consistency.

The demographics for the Sacramento area show a population of over 264,000. Out of this number, over 77 percent have a household income of over $75,000. According to IHRSA (International Health, Racquet & Sportsclub Association), the largest club trade organization in the world, household income is the number one determiner of someone joining a fitness facility. In fact, over 23 percent of those who have a household income that is $60,000 or more join a fitness club of some type.

IHRSA has provided statistics in *IHRSA's Guide to Membership Retention*, which states that members who are involved in group exercise or group workouts of some type will maintain their memberships over a longer term. As quoted from IHRSA: "Their only connection to the club is the connection that they have to the cold metal machines on which they perform their exercises."

Personal training also leads to lower attrition levels, whereas group personal training from 2 to 10 members can all motivate and provide each other energy and fun during their workouts. Fun and play equates to enjoyment and a reason to want to go to and participate in the club or workout environment. Training fees however are typically flawed. It is common practice for clubs to sell packages in volume and to lower the price as the package increases. This makes no business sense.

Providing three options at the point of sale of what a potential member seeks, such as weight loss, support and guidance, as well as a membership is a key difference from traditional membership sales. In other words, being a solution-based club versus always selling the option of membership only. Sell the solution and they get results, they stay, they are happy.

Selling group personal training, even 1:1 training at the point of sale, adding this onto their membership agreement, will guarantee the member will get ongoing motivation and support. This also, from a business standpoint, is the most important difference from other clubs; it stabilizes the monthly receivable base and grows that number quickly. All memberships are sold on a 12-month, closed-end basis, hence, the monthly receivable will grow and provide a healthy profit, all without having to discount and later to resell a member who simply stopped coming because they were not getting the support and the results which brought them to the club in the first place. A happy member will gladly pay and stay.

1.1 Objectives

The main objectives for The Workout Company are as follows:

1. To open the first and only co-ed gym that will feature lifestyle enhancement training (functional training) in the Sacramento, California area. This new club will incorporate the existing members from the current Workout Company training studio. The Workout Company will be known in the Sacramento area for the best functional and lifestyle changing workouts. The creation of a superior "fitness experience." The club's ambience will be intentionally crafted by applying turnkey systems to all products, services, and amenities offered. This ensures that superior quality is delivered consistently. It will also result in more efficient operations, where results can be measured, and necessary changes can be made promptly to reflect changing tastes or conditions.

2. To acquire 900 memberships by the end of the first year of operation, and to expect 1,300 to 2,000 members by the third year, in which time the membership growth may level off.

3. To offer profit centers that will contribute 40 percent of the projected income, with the personal training segment being the highest contributor.

4. To implement an effective marketing program designed to inform potential consumers in our target market of our unique products, services, and benefits. A successful program will consistently generate sufficient leads, which can be turned into a predictable number of new member sales over time. Business marketing has always been somewhat hit or miss, and a strategic 12-month marketing plan will reduce the risk substantially. The club's marketing plan will be based on marketing strategies that have been tested in the fitness industry in many different markets to insure a higher response rate.

5. To hire, train, and retain knowledgeable/qualified staff and management. By providing members with high quality and caring people, they will feel more comfortable and confident that The Workout Company can meet all their needs. This will lead to higher member satisfaction, longer member retention, and increased customer referral opportunities.

6. Most importantly, to own the building located at 3000 Main Street in Sacramento, while expanding the services and profit centers currently provided by the existing Workout Company training studio.

1.2 Mission

We promise to be the best part of your day, every day.

The mission of The Workout Company is to provide the best programs, staff, and equipment to fully meet the various fitness needs of our members, while generating a profit for the owner and investors. Besides providing an excellent value to our customers, The Workout Company is determined to create an unmatched atmosphere that will add to the enjoyment of every member and employee of the facility.

1.3 Keys to Success

The keys to success for The Workout Company are as follows:

1. *Marketing*: We must continue to grow the name recognition of The Workout Company in the Sacramento area for lifestyle and functional workouts. To achieve this, an advertising budget of up to15 to 20 percent of the projected fixed expenses will be allocated during the 60 days of presales and for the first 90 days after the location is open. The national average of a monthly marketing budget for a typical fitness facility is usually 8 to 10 percent of their fixed expenses. Using a noted advertising agency in the fitness industry, Susan K. Bailey Advertising, we can be assured the quality and marketing will target our desired market. The marketing should capture 3.5 of the demographics within a three-mile radius for the membership base within the twenty-fifth month of it becoming a mature business.

2. *Atmosphere of the facility*: By creating an unmatched upscale atmosphere through the use of the newest equipment, facility design, and high-energy colors, the new club will reach out to our upscale target population demographics. To achieve this goal, noted fitness industry architect Rudy Fabiano (www.fabianodesigns.com), who has designed more than 400 clubs, will consult on the latest trends in the industry for style and overall concept packaging. These important concepts will make this facility stand out from any other competitor in the area, providing strong product differentiation. The design of the facility will be a key factor to the success of the business. Each section of the gym will be designed strategically with revenue-producing areas being placed in high-traffic paths. This strategic placement increases the impulse buying psychology of the member. Also, the colors, lighting, contours, and lines of the facility will be designed to create feelings of warmth and comfort. This is one of the most important factors in a business the customer will visit at least several times a week.

3. *Knowledgeable/qualified staff*: The Workout Company will provide the users of the facility with knowledgeable and qualified staff who show genuine concern for the members. The members should feel comfortable and confident that The Workout Company can meet all their fitness needs.

4. *Location of the facility:* Location is of key importance in the planning stages of developing a health club. Drive-by traffic, population, and

income level are exceptional in this area, thus the reason for choosing to transfer The Workout Company to this new location. This location is also where The Workout Company has been training clients and offering boot camps. This supports the location as easily accessible and that the existing membership base of The Workout Company will continue working out at the new location. Also, a popular bike path is located at this new location, which opens further opportunities in membership growth and specialty training for cycle enthusiasts.

2.0 Company Summary

The Workout Company will be a 17,000-square-foot, co-ed facility in the town of Sacramento. In reference to the competition in the area, and understanding the importance of being unique and owning a niche in the market, the goal is to create a training culture that will make this facility unique in the marketplace. Functional training breaks away from traditional seated, one muscle group, one action at a time workouts that are the standard offering in most mainstream membership-driven facilities.

This new concept offers energy, fun, movement, and quicker results all while members feel like they are playing. Since the workouts are unique and fun-filled, membership retention will increase and word-of-mouth will spread because of the positive impact the training has on the members' lives. This approach contrasts sharply from other area facilities that include the traditional hardcore gyms, the impersonal low-cost/no-service environments, and the one-club-fits-all philosophy found in the traditional health and athletic clubs.

The new facility will expand in services and amenities. There are no other types of workouts or profit centers being offered at the new location, which is an outdated racquetball club. However, The Workout Company will add to this location: weight loss programs, café and juice bar, group personal training, boot camps, personal training, spa, retail, supplements, workout attire, cardiovascular and strength equipment. Expanding the services, as well as adding profit centers, is an important component, as it will provide 40 percent of the projected income. A spa will be leased out for rental income, which will house about 2,000 square feet.

This will be a club like no other. With a high degree of finish and impeccable design and furnishings, the facility will possess a warmth and feeling that is not generally found in the industry. The demographics show a need for an alternative to the typical setting for this area and this concept will flourish in a market starving for growth.

2.1 Company Ownership

Tom and Sarah Johnson will own The Workout Company, Inc. The president will be Tom Johnson. The building will be purchased under an LLC with the Johnsons and Frank Smith, MD as partners.

2.2 Start-up Summary

The start-up requirements for this project total $885,000. Included in this cost is the building purchase, build-out, and repairs. The partners will pay 20 percent down, which will be equally split by both the Johnsons and Smith. A bank loan of $708,000 will be necessary, financed over 10 years at 6 percent, therefore, budgeting a payment of debt service of approximately $5,100 per month.

Start-up Expenses

Building purchase price	$540,000
Build-out cost	$325,000
Equipment	$20,000
Total	**$885,000**

3.0 Market Analysis Summary

According to *IHRSA's Guide to the Health Club Industry for Lenders and Investors*, the fitness industry grew 12.2 percent from 1996 to 2002. Gym membership for ages 35 to 54 increased by 143 percent from 1987 to 2002. Currently, the gym market is steadily growing at about 3 percent per year overall.

These demographics are important to note since they are the primary target markets for The Workout Company. The other area in the demographic study that is important in determining an appropriate location is the average household income. The Sacramento area average is $67,918. There is a strong correlation between household income and health club memberships. Whereas one out of eight members of the general population is a health club member, member penetration rates among some high income segments approaches 30 percent. Conversely, when a household income falls below $25,000, only one out of every 14 people (7.2 percent) is a health club member (*IHRSA's Guide to the Health Club Industry for Lenders and Investors*).

The four factors that matter most in calculating the success rate for gyms are: population density, travel time, household income, and education.

Population density. A location that is densely populated, with the right affluence, is a prime location. The demographics for the Sacramento location show within a five-mile radius a population of 264,000 with an estimated growth potential of 9.8 percent over the next five years.

Travel time. Demographic studies show that upwards of 85 percent of club members come from within a 12-minute travel time (calculated during the prime commute traffic hours for the club) of the facility or an average of a 5- to 10-mile radius.

Household income. There is a strong correlation between household income and health club memberships. One out of eight members of the general population is a health club member. Penetration rate among high-income households approaches 30 percent, whereas in households with income that falls below $25,000, it is only 1:14. The Sacramento demographics show the number of residents with household incomes between $50,000 to $100,000 and over to be 86 percent, and the average income level is over $65,000.

Education attainment. Educational attainment levels are another factor in assessing demand. In general, the higher the education level of people in the community, the higher will be the overall market penetration rates of the clubs serving that market.

To cite a few examples: the overall health club penetration rate among full-time college students is 24 percent; the club penetration rate among men and women with advanced degrees is 25.2 percent; conversely, among men who earn $75,000 or more, but who did not got to college, the penetration rate is 11.6 percent (*IHRSA's Health Club Trend Report*).

Currently, it is estimated that 5.1 percent of the population age 25 and over in this five-mile radius have earned a master's or doctorate degree and 11 percent have earned a bachelor's.

3.1 Market Considerations

The sports and fitness club industry produced over 140 billion dollars in 2006 and is projected to continue its current growth trend according to the latest statistics from IHRSA.

The clubs target market area—a 12- to 15-minute drive time of the location—contains 264,000 people with an average annual income of $65,000.

The club will be able to carry a maximum active membership base of 2,700 members without being overcrowded. Based on average industry statistics, a target market with a population of 264,000 people has the ability to attract 10,000 total members between all of the clubs in the area. This demographic can support eight moderately sized, well-run facilities. There are six main competitors within the club's target market.

Over 59 percent of the population has an average household income of over $50,000 per year; 86 percent of the population is over $100,000 per year. Also, 41 percent of that demographic is between 18 and 55 years of age and 53 percent are between the ages of 35 and 65. Anyone else within the demographic market that falls outside of these parameters has been excluded in our study. This doesn't mean that the club won't attract members outside of these parameters, but they won't comprise the majority. The parameters chosen make up the "worst-case scenario." In the worst-case scenario, calculating only the potential prospects within the target demographic group based on age and income only, there are 132,000 potential prospects.

Utilizing this target market, there are a minimum total of 132,000 to 145,000 available members that could be captured and maintained. Therefore, the demographics show a sufficient market to operate a successful health club.

3.2 Market Segmentation

The facility's primary focus will be the adult upscale market. What will set this facility apart from other competitors in the market are a "hands-on" approach, experienced staff, unique training, and the trendy physical plant. These few things can make a large difference in the member success rate. Member success rate is determined by various factors: Is the member achieving his goals such as losing weight, lowering body fat, becoming healthier, and making positive lifestyle changes?

The higher the member success rate, the higher renewal and member retention rates will follow. Member retention rate is the ability to keep the member. If we do not provide what they need or expect, the member will simply stop coming in or worse, stop paying. When this happens, our business plan requires that we need to replace them, as well as add other members, so our membership growth continues.

The average membership use rate is about five to six months for a typical club, due to the indifference and the inability of most gyms to provide proper training and orientation. By using the Thomas Plummer Company business systems, this number can increase to 15 to 16 months. The Workout Company has a training system, which will be implemented for this adult market, ensuring a higher success rate and a training method that other gyms in the area have not advanced to. Functional training will be the determining factor in member success and retention success for The Workout Company.

The population in the five-mile radius is 264,000. Out of this number, our target demographic numbers for club membership use is 53 percent. A 17,000-square-foot facility, coupled with these demographics, should allow for a penetration rate of 3.5 percent or, in other words, the club should attract a membership base of about 1,700-4,000 members.

4.0 Membership Details

(*Note*: All monthly payments will be collected by an EFT system using ASF International in Denver, the largest service company in the fitness industry.)

The following memberships will be featured:

- **12-month membership**. A closed-ended, 12-month membership paid in 12 installments of $39 per month, with a one-time joiner's fee of $59.
- **18-month membership.** A budget consideration membership, which is a closed-ended membership with 18 payments of $35 per month and a one-time joiner's fee of $59.
- **Group personal training membership.** This membership also includes unlimited group personal training classes. A one-time joiner's fee of $59 and 12 monthly payments of $129 will be the core membership.
- **One-on-one personal training membership.** This membership also includes a personal coach four times a month and unlimited group personal

training classes. A one-time joiner's fee of $59 and 12 monthly payments of $299 with a closed-ended membership.

- **Weight management membership.** This membership is for anyone whose main reason for joining a club is weight management and who wants to concentrate on just weight loss as their primary focus during the first few months they get started. A one-time joiner's fee of $59 and three payments of $199 per month, after which they can continue with a different membership or repeat the diet program.
- **Short-term membership.** A short-term membership is up to three months of membership time for $299.
- **Daily drop-in.** A day pass may be purchased for $20. Members may bring in a guest with a 50 percent discount off the drop-in fee.

All memberships, regardless of type, as well as potential members will be able to participate in a **14-day trial membership** program. This will allow them the opportunity to experience the club and get involved in a very extensive orientation program. This program will include an outline of the products and services provided by the club, as well as fitness testing, weight training, cardiovascular training, and education on nutrition and supplementation.

4.1 Competition

Many times, even when clubs are very close to one another, they may not be head-to-head competition. When clubs differ significantly in terms of price, size, facilities, programs, and, most importantly, target markets, they can appeal to significantly different market segments. The following are existing clubs within a five-mile radius. All clubs listed vary in size, features, and populations. These show that The Workout Company will be unique in its market niche.

- **Anywhere Fitness.** This facility is about two miles from the new proposed facility. This is a 24/7 facility with no service or amenities. This type of facility does not market to our demographic market. These types of clubs appeal to the prospect who simply wants to come and go at anytime and for those who do not need motivation or direction. These types of gyms have high loss rates because the average member needs to be motivated and encouraged to continue his workouts. The monthly membership rate is about $39. Their target market is 18- to 34-year-olds.
- **24-Hour Gym.** If a member is looking for the personal touch, this would not be the type of facility he would join. Upscale facilities like the proposed Workout Company are often more appealing to a higher income demographic member who wants a more intimate environment and more support than the 24-Hour Gym offers. This gym is located about one mile from the new Workout Company location. The target market is young as reflected by the staff they hire. The facility itself is dated and run-down. The monthly membership rate is about $29 per month.
- **The Training Zone.** This is a 10,000-square-foot club located about two miles from the new Workout Company location. This is your typical box gym with no services or amenities. The member's experience is what he can make of it on his own. There are no support or profit centers to help

the member achieve his goals, hence, perhaps a high loss rate in the club would be considered. The membership is about $39 per month.

- **For Woman.** This is a women's-only facility located about one mile from the new Workout Company location. Their main focus is group exercise. They do offer personal training and other profit centers, but those features are secondary to group exercise, which totals about 50 classes per week. Their monthly rate is $39 per month.

- **Personal Fitness.** This is a 3,000 square foot personal training studio. There are about five trainers in this center and they only provide the 1:1 service. The current rate is about $45 per hour for training. No other services or profit centers are offered.

- **New Life Now Fitness.** This is a small group-training center. It is about three miles from the new location. The hours are very limited.

What makes The Workout Company different from the others?

There is a large differentiation between this proposed location and the competition in the area. The difference that stands out most predominantly is the combination of the service, amenities, and profit centers that will be offered. The facility will not only be known for its ongoing boot camps, but known as the "solution" for the members in weight loss, motivation, support, and service. There is no facility in the area that is designed to be a "solution based" type of club for the member by offering all the profit centers revolving around an exemplary customer service plan. The Workout Company will now be that location.

Another point of differentiation is the theme or niche that The Workout Company will be offering, which is upscale adult, functional training (often referred to as lifestyle enhancement training). The unique training approach for the members, along with the equipment that will be used, makes this location stand out from the competition.

The facility itself will be designed for the high-end clientele, with attention to all the small details within the physical plant as well as unsurpassed customer service.

5.0 Management Summary

Tom Johnson will be the **operations manager**. His background includes owning and working in the existing Workout Company training center for the past six years. He also has the vision and knowledge to develop staff and to continue to grow and develop his sports enhancement and customer service philosophies.

Tom will continue his day-to-day operation of The Workout Company, handling scheduling, marketing, and promotions, along with running and developing various programs. Tom was also involved in running My Racquet, the business that currently exists in the facility, for four months during the transition with the banks and the previous owner. During this time, even with a difficult economy and extremely difficult business circumstances, the club was able to turn a profit each month. This demonstrates his incredible skills and his ability to manage, lead, and run a profitable business.

The **sales manager** will be Kristen Moran. This position is one of the most important jobs within the club. Kristen brings a high level of sales and leadership experience. She will be selling and tracking the 14-day trial prospects as well as converting the existing My Racquet membership base onto The Workout Company monthly receivable base.

The **lead nutrition/fitness professional** will be Charles Wrangler, who has worked with Tom in the existing Workout Company training facility. He will be selling training and upgrading memberships as well as developing workouts for the trainers to follow.

Qualified staff has been working with Tom for the past six years in sales and training at his current training studio; however, additional staff will be needed and hired for the desk, membership sales, sports bar, and as personal trainers due to the increase in size. Following is the personnel plan for The Workout Company:

- **Personal trainers:** 5 full-time/part-time
- **Group exercise leaders:** 5 part-time
- **Front desk/customer service:** 3 full-time/part-time
- **Membership sales:** 3 full-time/part-time
- **Weekend manager:** 1 full-time
- **Bookkeeping:** 1 part-time
- **Maintenance/cleaning:** 1 full-time

The staffing equation is critical for the fitness business. Gyms are considered to be a 98 percent intangible commodity. This means the clients are not buying a product, but purchasing an expectation that the gym staff will provide quality services and a good experience.

The prospective members are purchasing the environment and the experience of the staff, which can help these clients achieve their goals in a friendly, clean, and supportive environment. Since members are purchasing a high-end item, and usually leave without a product, the facility needs to sell itself (staff) as the product that can make a difference in their lives, change their lifestyles, and help them achieve the results they are seeking.

Internal and external training on a regular basis for the staff is critical. This helps guarantee the highest level of customer service and fitness knowledge. These standards will make The Workout Company stand out from other gyms, which traditionally do not have the skilled staff needed for the high-end customer. The recommended outsource for staff training and manager/supervisor development is the National Fitness Business Alliance and the Thomas Plummer Company. These companies are the leading educators within the fitness industry. They provide support, consulting, training, and seminars. (The goal of these companies is to help club owners find financial success within the fitness industry.)

Tom Johnson has attended Thomas Plummer's advanced two-day business school. The supervisors of the new facility will also attend these training seminars.

The Management Team

General Manager

Hours: 40 to 50 per week

Description of work: The general manager is ultimately responsible for the club's total revenues. The manager is also responsible for running a club under a fixed, definable budget.

Duties include:

- 40 to 50 percent of all membership sales while the club is under 500 members
- Hiring and firing of staff
- Staff development
- Daily reporting and number analysis
- Payroll
- Working the club's prime hours of revenue
- Budgets and budget controls

Sales Manager

Hours: 32 to 40 per week

Description of work: The sales manager is responsible for the club's entire sales effort.

Duties include:

- 40 to 50 percent of the entire sales goal per month for the club
- Sales training for the entire staff
- All follow-ups for prospects
- Maintenance of the club's support systems and sales material for the club

Lead Customer Service Representative

Hours: 32 to 40 per week

Description of work: The lead customer service representative is in many ways the most important person in the club. He is the prime deliverer of customer service for the club, drives profit center income during prime hours, and is responsible for the training and development of all counter people.

Duties include:

- Working with the manager in charge of the profit center and the general manager to promote front counter profit centers, generate orders, manage inventory, and prepare reporting for the rest of the management team
- Training and supervision of all counter people
- Scheduling for the counter staff and participation in the hiring and evaluating of counter people
- Assisting with sales efforts when necessary

Weekend Supervisor

Hours: 32 to 40 per week

Description of work: The weekend supervisor would work a minimum of 32 hours per week on Saturday, Sunday, and Monday. This job is considered an entry-level management training position. This person takes lead responsibility on the weekend, making sure the club is properly staffed and produces the maximum amount of revenue possible.

Duties include:

- Opening and closing the club on Saturdays
- Closing the club on Sundays
- Being responsible for all sales on those days
- Being in charge of the weekend staff
- Running specials and generating income from the multiple profit centers with the help and direction of the assistant manager in charge of profit centers
- Working non-weekend hours as senior staff person in either sales or in the training function

Lead Nutrition and Fitness Professional

Hours: 32 to 40

Description of work: The lead nutrition and fitness professional is the liaison between the club and dotFIT® and Lone Star nutrition companies. This person would also do personal training. This position is also in charge of developing and maintaining supplement sales in the club.

Duties include:

- Liaison between dotFIT and Lone Star
- Educating and training the staff on supplements and nutrition in the club
- Preparing orders for the manager concerning supplements, support material, and other nutrition/training-related items
- Supervising all trainers

Group Programming and Training Director

Hours: 32 to 40 per week

Description of work: The group programming and training director develops and supports all structured group programming in the club. This position is also responsible for the successful implementation of all specialty classes. The job includes the development of instructors, implementation of the programs, analysis of the schedule, and internal promotion.

Duties include:

- The rollout of each program as it is introduced
- The development of instructors to support the programs
- Schedules and analysis of instructors' classes
- Promotion of special events, such as advanced classes, held to generate additional income in the group program
- Development of semi-private revenue from the group programs and personal training
- Supervision of all activity trainers
- Development of a schedule of quarterly club offerings, portals, and seasonal activities that can be sold to the consumer

6.0 Important Assumptions

Following are the assumptions for the projected profit/loss for the years 2011-2012.

Membership outline

Presales. Memberships sold before the new location is open usually start about 60 to 90 days prior to the club actually opening. A target of 100 memberships is projected to be sold during the presale. This number includes converting some of the existing Workout Company training members on to the receivable base as well as new members. These memberships will be promoted with direct mail pieces and flyers in the daily newspaper produced by Susan K. Bailey Advertising. This presale starts the club's receivable base the first month of operation at $12,000.

Loss rate. These are members who, for some reason, move out of the area, incur a medical disability, or simply do not pay. The loss rate is determined on a 12-month, closed-end membership. For the first year, a rate of .023 percent is applied, followed by the second year of less than .012 percent, and the third year a factor of less than .010 percent was used. Losses drop as the club ages and are slightly higher during the excitement of the presale. *Note*: The loss rate was an 80/20 split for the membership and training EFT receivable adjustment.

New membership breakdown. EFT (electronic funds transfer) will account for 90 percent of the membership payments. The additional 10 percent would include paid-in-full and short-term memberships. The monthly payments or receivable base gives the gym stability with monthly income. Payments are usually credited to the gym's account on the 15th and 30th of the month.

Receivable base. The main membership receivable base is directed from membership payments, which will be billed through an EFT system by ASF International, located in Denver, Colorado, the largest third-party billing company for health clubs. *Note*: The EFT membership average used on the pro forma was $37 (membership price is $39) and the training EFT average was $214.

Sales closing rate. For the first year, this rate is a target of 55 percent as a minimum. There may be higher closing rates on the first year due to the "newness" that entices new members to join, but we wanted to factor in the training factor for staff in the sales steps for the first year to have a comfortable closing rate. After the first year, a closing rate of 60 percent will be used in closing the prospects, since the staff will then have more experience. We are also assuming only a 10 percent close rate on the training membership at the POS. The remaining 90 percent of sales at the POS is membership based.

Renewals. These start in the second year of business. Renewals in the fitness industry average from 40 to 50 percent on an annual basis (this represents the attrition number). A well-run facility that pays attention to member details has a renewal rate of 50 to 60 percent and higher. A factor of 65 percent was used for the renewal percentage due to the training expertise The Workout Company offers. The more attention the member receives, the higher the chance they will want to continue their membership.

Profit Center Ratios

The profit center ratio is tracked and analyzed through a member usage rate. Each time a member comes into the club to exercise, the average revenue generated in each profit center is calculated. Income is based on the number of visits per month. An average of 60 percent of the membership will use the gym at least twice per month. The following formula is used to determine the profit center income:

Drinks. The club will have two drink coolers available for members to choose from during their visits. Each cooler will feature diet soft drinks, a variety of waters, sports drinks, juices, and other popular drinks. The club will average about $0.24 per member visit in drink sales.

Nutrition/weight loss. To add to the member's success, the weight-loss program by dotFIT www.dotfit.com will be a featured profit center. The program is a 12-week weight-loss system, specifically designed for health clubs to offer to their members. The program is turnkey and utilizes grocery store foods, in-between-meal snacks, protein bars, and shakes. The club would average about $0.75 per member visit.

Juice bar/sports bar. The juice bar is the social center of the club and many members enjoy shakes and other beverages before and after a workout. The juice bar will be a licensed bar developed by City Blends, one of the largest companies in the industry providing a total business system for shakes and coffees. The club should expect about $0.75 per member visit in shakes, coffee, and snacks from this profit center. During the summer months, the ratio is lower due to members using the gym less frequently. Beer is also served and is expected to average about $0.85 per member visit.

Personal training. This includes one-on-one personal training sessions, as well as groups and clinic formats. The members pay an additional fee for this service. An average of $3 per member visit is estimated for this profit center. Many of the memberships will package the training directly into the monthly membership rate. However, we will still offer the ability to pay by visit or with a punch pass series.

Specialty programs. This profit center focuses on boot camps and other workouts that have a start and end date as well as a fee associated with it. The monthly income was determined from history of The Workout Company Training Center.

Pro shop. This profit center is usually the smallest from the rest; however, with the brand, logo, and The Workout Company name, it lends itself to having funky designs and logo attire that will appeal to the member population. An average of $0.10 per member visit could be expected.

Cost of goods. A rate of 70 percent for the cost of goods was assumed.

Operating Expenses

Insurance. This is an average quote for a 17,000-square-foot facility, including liability, and contents in the Sacramento area. Prices were quoted from the Association Insurance Company—the largest and most established provider in the industry

Bank loans. The repayment of the loan was determined using an interest rate of 6 percent over a 20-year period.

Expenses. General expenses such as telephone, utilities, janitor, maintenance, supplies, postage, and printing are based on a general average for a facility this size. Some expenses do vary according to the time of year.

Advertising. Advertising will be about 10 percent of expense. For the presale and during the first three months, a higher ratio was used. To market the adult upscale market, The Workout Company brand, logo, and themes will attract that demographic niche.

Rent. The business will rent the building from New Club, LCC. The first three months will be free from rent, to ensure a healthy receivable base before the rent kicks in. Beginning in the fourth month, the rent will be $5,100 per month. The spa will be rented out, which will average about $2,500 per month.

Bank fees. ASF charges about 7 percent of the total receivable base collected. They also assume all collection costs. The services provided in this fee included the software tracking system, POS, and renewals, as well as all the billing aspects for collection.

Payroll

As the facility matures. the average percentage should be about 37 to 42 percent. The first year, the totals may be higher due to staffing requirements needed to attend to the new members. The employer's payroll tax of 7% was also figured into the payroll tax totals.

6.1 Financial Projections

It should take two years for clubs to reach financial maturity, which is where we tend to see a leveling off in membership as well as in the receivable base. This normally happens at around the twenty-fifth month of operation.

Although the future is never certain, the two-year pro forma (Figures 7-2 and 7-3) makes it clear that The Workout Company becomes a confident financial success. It should be noted that conservative, real-world assumptions were used to assess the future potential of the business.

6.2 Sample Monthly Operating Expense

Rent payment	$5,100
Payroll	$20,000
Officers' salary	$4,000
Advertising	$4,500
Utilities	$4,300
Phone/website	$950
Accounting/legal	$700
Printing	$100
Office supplies	$250
Janitorial supplies	$1,100
Postage	$100
Insurance	$1,200
Building tax	$500
Maintenance	$1,000
Repairs	$2,100
Monthly BOE (Base Operating Expense)	**$45,900**

Workout Company - Year 1													
Revenues	yr 1	March	April	May	June	July	Aug	Sept	Oct	Nov	Dec	Jan	Feb
Prospects		300	200	150	150	120	120	150	100	100	75	125	150
Members	100	165	110	82	82	66	66	82	55	55	42	69	82
Renewals													
Loss rate			0.023	0.023	0.023	0.023	0.023	0.023	0.023	0.023	0.023	0.023	0.023
Total members		265	366	438	508	561	613	679	718	756	780	830	892
EFT		132	90	64	64	54	54	64	45	45	35	56	64
EFT training		16	9	8	8	6	6	8	4	4	3	6	8
PIF		17	11	10	10	6	6	10	6	6	4	7	10
Enrollment $		8732	5841	4248	4248	3540	3540	4248	2891	2891	1295	3658	4248
PIF $		7238	5633	3808	3808	2612	2612	3808	2612	2612	1605	2911	3808
Total Revenue		15970	11474	8056	8056	6152	6152	8056	5503	5503	2900	6569	8056
EFT		12008	16614	19970	23252	25522	27755	30712	32060	33421	34161	36285	38917
Total Membership Sales		27978	28088	28026	31308	31674	33907	38768	37563	38924	37061	42854	46973
MPC Sales													
Supplements/diet		833	1136	1359	1577	1741	1903	2108	2229	2347	2421	2577	2769
Drinks		263	363	435	504	557	608	674	713	750	774	824	886
Personal training		3291	4545	5439	6321	6967	7613	8433	9041	9389	9687	10308	11078
Specialty programs		10000	11000	11000	12000	5000	4000	10000	11000	5000	2000	12000	8000
Juice bar		822	1136	1359	1577	1741	1902	2108	2229	2347	2421	2577	2769
Beer		932	1287	1542	1787	1973	2156	2389	2526	2659	2744	2920	3138
Pro shop		109	151	181	210	232	253	281	297	312	322	343	369
Total MPC Sales		16250	19618	21315	23976	18211	18435	25993	28035	22804	20369	31549	29009
Net Income		44228	47706	49341	55284	49885	52342	64761	65598	61728	57430	74403	75982
Costs of Goods Sold		2071	2745	3413	3958	4370	4775	5292	5595	5890	6077	6468	6951
Gross Profit		42157	44961	45928	51326	45515	47567	59469	60003	55838	51353	67935	69031
Operating Expenses													
Advertising		9000	9000	7000	5000	3000	1500	4000	5000	2000	2000	5500	4000
Rent				5100	5100	5100	5100	5100	5100	5100	5100	5100	5100
Accounting/legal		700	700	700	700	700	700	700	700	700	700	700	700
Janitorial		1100	1100	1100	1200	1200	1000	1000	1200	1300	1100	1300	1300
Property tax		500	500	500	500	500	500	500	500	500	500	500	500
Bank fees		840	1162	1397	1627	1786	1942	2149	2244	2339	2391	2539	2724
Repairs/maintenance		1000	1000	1000	1000	1000	1000	1000	1000	1000	1000	1000	1000
Insurance		1200	1200	1200	1200	1200	1200	1200	1200	1200	1200	1200	1200
Telephone		500	500	500	500	500	500	500	500	500	500	500	500
Yellow pages/website		450	450	450	450	450	450	450	450	450	450	450	450
Printing		1200	100	100	100	100	100	100	100	100	100	100	100
Postage		100	100	100	100	100	300	100	100	100	100	300	100
License/fees		300	300	300	300	300	300	300	300	300	300	300	300
Utilities		3300	4100	4100	4700	5000	5200	4700	4200	4200	4500	4500	4200
Office supplies		250	250	250	250	250	250	250	250	250	250	250	250
Total BOE		20440	20462	18697	22727	21186	20042	22049	22844	20039	20191	24239	22424
Payroll Expense													
Officers salary		4000	4000	4000	4000	4000	4000	4000	4000	4000	4000	4000	4000
Salary		17000	17000	17500	17500	18000	15000	16000	19000	20000	21000	25000	25000
Commissions		2000	2200	1600	1600	1300	1300	1600	1100	1100	850	1400	1600
Payroll taxes		1960	1974	1967	1967	1981	1771	1862	2037	2107	2159	2478	2492
Total Payroll Expense		24960	25174	25067	25067	25281	22071	23462	26137	27207	28009	32878	33092
Total Expense													
Rental Income		2500	2500	2500	2500	2500	2500	2500	2500	2500	2500	2500	2500
Before Tax Net													
Running Total													

Figure 7-2. Pro forma (year 1)

Workout Company - Year 2												
Revenues	March	April	May	June	July	Aug	Sept	Oct	Nov	Dec	Jan	Feb
Prospects	135	175	128	150	90	90	200	225	80	100	200	225
Members	81	105	77	90	54	54	120	135	48	60	120	135
Expiring	92	38	32	28	23	23	29	19	19	14	24	28
Renewals	173	72	50	54	43	43	53	36	36	28	45	54
Loss rate	0.012	0.012	0.012	0.012	0.012	0.012	0.012	0.012	0.012	0.012	0.012	0.012
Total members	871	927	961	1010	1029	1048	1126	1229	1244	1303	1384	1474
EFT	66	85	62	73	44	44	98	109	39	50	98	109
EFT training	7	9	8	8	4	4	10	12	4	4	10	12
PIF	8	11	7	9	6	6	12	14	5	6	12	14
Enrollment $	4307	5546	4130	4779	2832	2832	6372	7139	2537	3186	6372	7139
PIF $	3808	5633	2911	3509	2612	2612	5932	7348	1904	2612	5932	7348
Total Revenue	8115	11179	7041	8288	5444	5444	12304	14487	4441	5798	12304	14487
EFT	36570	37872	38945	39953	39673	39393	41471	45856	45899	46096	49013	52627
Total Membership Sales	44685	49051	45986	48241	45117	44837	53775	60343	50340	51894	61317	67114
MPC Sales												
Supplements/diet	2703	2877	2983	3136	3195	3254	3496	3816	3862	4045	4297	4576
Drinks	865	920	954	1003	1022	1041	1118	1221	1236	1294	1374	1464
Personal training	10815	11511	11934	12543	12780	13014	13983	15264	15450	16182	17187	18306
Specialty programs	12000	10000	8500	10000	5000	4500	9000	12000	4500	4500	12000	9000
Juice bar	2703	2877	2983	3136	3195	3254	3496	3816	3862	4045	4297	4576
Beer	3064	3261	3381	3553	3621	3687	3961	4324	4377	4584	4869	5186
Pro shop	360	383	397	418	426	433	466	508	515	539	572	610
Total MPC Sales	32510	31829	31132	33789	29239	29183	35520	40949	33802	35189	44596	43718
Net Income	77195	80880	77118	82030	74356	74020	89295	101292	84142	87083	105913	110832
Costs of Goods Sold	6786	7222	7488	7872	8021	8168	8775	9579	9696	10154	10786	11488
Gross Profit	70409	73658	69630	74158	66335	65852	80520	91713	74446	76929	95127	99344
Operating Expenses												
Advertising	10000	8000	8000	8000	3000	3000	5000	5000	2000	2000	5000	6500
Rent	12000	12000	12000	12000	12000	12000	12000	12000	12000	12000	12000	12000
Accounting/legal	800	800	800	800	800	800	800	800	800	800	800	800
Janitorial	1200	1150	900	1100	950	1100	800	650	900	1200	900	1200
Property tax	500	500	500	500	500	500	500	500	500	500	500	500
Bank fees	2559	2650	2726	2796	2777	2757	2902	3209	3212	3226	3430	3683
Repairs/maintenance	1300	1300	1300	1300	1300	1300	1300	1300	1300	1300	1300	1300
Insurance	1300	1300	1300	1300	1300	1300	1300	1300	1300	1300	1300	1300
Telephone	525	525	525	525	525	525	525	525	525	525	525	525
Yellow pages/website	450	450	450	450	450	450	450	450	450	450	450	450
Printing	100	100	100	100	100	100	100	100	100	100	100	100
Postage	100	100	100	100	100	100	100	100	100	100	100	100
License/fees	300	300	300	300	300	300	300	300	300	300	300	300
Utlities	4400	4500	4300	4400	5000	5200	5300	4800	4500	4100	4000	4000
Office supplies	275	275	275	275	275	275	275	275	275	275	275	275
Total Operating Expense	35809	33950	33576	33946	29377	29707	31652	31309	28262	28176	30980	33033
Payroll Expense												
Officers salary	9000	9000	9000	9000	9000	9000	9000	9000	9000	9000	9000	9000
Salary	19000	18500	18500	17000	16000	15000	19500	21000	20000	19000	22000	22000
Commissions	2025	2625	1925	2250	1350	1350	3000	3375	1200	5000	3000	3375
Payroll taxes	2100	2200	2100	2000	2000	1900	1800	2100	2100	2100	2300	2300
Total Payroll Expense	32125	32325	31525	30250	28350	27250	33300	35475	32300	35100	36300	36675
Total Expense	67934	66275	65101	64196	57727	56957	64952	66784	60562	63276	67280	69708
Rental Income	2200	2200	2200	2200	2200	2200	2200	2200	2200	2200	2200	2200
Before Tax Net	4675	9583	6729	12162	10808	11095	17768	27129	16084	15853	30047	31836
Running Total	-14687	-5104	1625	13787	24595	35690	53458	80587	96671	112524	142571	174407

Figure 7-3. Pro forma (year 2)

7.0 Demographics

Population

- The population in this area is estimated to change from 5,627 to 6,294, resulting in a growth of 11.9 percent between 2000 and the current year. Over the next five years, the population is projected to grow by 8.8 percent.
- The population in the United States is estimated to change from 281,421,906 to 304,141,549, resulting in a growth of 8.1 percent between 2000 and the current year. Over the next five years, the population is projected to grow by 4.9 percent.

Age

- The current year median age for this population is 37.0, while the average age is 39.0. Five years from now, the median age is projected to be 38.5.
- The current year median age for the United States is 36.7, while the average age is 37.5. Five years from now, the median age is projected to be 37.6.

Ethnicity

- Of this area's current year estimated population: 74.4 percent are White alone, 4.0 percent are Black or African American alone, 0.8 percent are American Indian and Alaska Native alone, 2.9 percent are Asian alone, 0.1 percent are Native Hawaiian and other Pacific Islands alone, 13.3 percent are some other race, and 4.5 percent are two or more races.
- For the entire United States: 72.7 percent are White alone, 12.4 percent are Black or African American alone, 0.9 percent are American Indian and Alaska Native alone, 4.4 percent are Asian alone, 0.2 percent are Native Hawaiian and Other Pacific Islands alone, 6.6 percent are some other race, and 2.8 percent are two or more races.
- This area's current estimated Hispanic or Latino population is 27.5 percent, while the United States' current estimated Hispanic or Latino population is 15.2 percent.

Households

- The number of households in this area is estimated to change from 2,492 to 2,753, resulting in an increase of 10.5 percent between 2000 and the current year. Over the next five years, the number of households is projected to increase by 8.3 percent.
- The number of households in the United States is estimated to change from 105,480,101 to 114,694,201, resulting in an increase of 8.7 percent between 2000 and the current year. Over the next five years, the number of households is projected to increase by 5.3 percent.

Income

- The average household income is estimated to be $70,193 for the current year, while the average household income for the United States is estimated to be $67,918 for the same time frame.
- The average household income in this area is projected to increase 12.0 percent over the next five years, from $70,193 to $78,587. The United States is projected to have an 11.7 percent increase in average household income.
- The current year estimated per capita income for this area is $31,084, compared to an estimate of $25,933 for the United States as a whole.

Employment

- For this area, 50.3 percent of the population is estimated to be employed and age 16 and over for the current year. The employment status of this labor force is as follows: 0.0 percent are in the armed forces, 62.3 percent are employed civilians, 4.8 percent are unemployed civilians, and 32.9 percent are not in the labor force.
- For the United States, 47.2 percent of the population is estimated to be employed and age 16 and over for the current year. The employment status of this labor force is as follows: 0.5 percent are in the armed forces, 60.2 percent are employed civilians, 3.6 percent are unemployed civilians, and 35.7 percent are not in the labor force.
- For this area, 50.3 percent of the population is estimated to be employed and age 16 and over for the current year. The occupational classifications are as follows: 16.5 percent are blue collar, 63.8 percent are white collar, and 19.6 percent are service and farm workers.
- For the United States, 47.2 percent of the population is estimated to be employed and age 16 and over for the current year. The occupational classifications are as follows: 23.9 percent are blue collar, 60.1 percent are white collar, and 16.0 percent are service and farm workers.
- For the civilian employed population age 16 and over in this area, it is estimated that they are employed in the following occupational categories: 11.0 percent are in management, business, and financial operations; 27.9 percent are in professional and related occupations; 18.3 percent are in service; 25.8 percent are in sales and office; 0.4 percent are in farming, fishing, and forestry; 8.2 percent are in construction, extraction, and maintenance; and 8.3 percent are in production, transportation, and material moving.
- For the civilian employed population age 16 and over in the United States, it is estimated that they are employed in the following occupational categories: 13.7 percent are in management, business, and financial operations; 20.3 percent are in professional and related occupations; 14.6 percent are in service; 26.7 percent are in sales and office; 0.7 percent are in farming, fishing, and forestry; 9.5 percent are in construction, extraction, and maintenance; and 14.4 percent are in production, transportation, and material moving.

Education

- Currently, it is estimated that 10.3 percent of the population age 25 and over in this area had earned a master's, professional, or doctorate degree and 16.9 percent had earned a bachelor's degree.
- In comparison, for the United States, it is estimated that for the population age 25 and over, 8.9 percent had earned a master's, professional, or doctorate degree, while 15.8 percent had earned a bachelor's degree.

Housing

- Most of the dwellings in this area (55.1 percent) are estimated to be owner-occupied for the current year. For the entire country, the majority of the housing units are owner-occupied (67.1 percent).
- The majority of dwellings in this area are estimated to be structures of one unit detached (61.6 percent) for the current year. In the United States, the majority of dwellings are estimated to be structures of one unit detached (60.8 percent) for the same year.
- For the current year, the majority of housing units in this area (20.8 percent) are estimated to have been built between 1950 and 1959.
- For the current year, the majority of housing units in the United States (16.2 percent) are estimated to have been built between 1970 and 1979.

iStockphoto/Thinkstock

Cap Ex: How Much Is Enough?

Note: The following text is excerpted from an IHRSA publication.

What is cap ex? Cap ex (capital expense) is a broader expense category than "depreciation." Depreciation, technically, is a noncash expense relating to the continually decreasing value of fixed assets by reason of time, wear and tear, and the continually changing nature of every marketplace.

Cap ex is a real expense, a cash expense. It includes depreciation, but it also includes improvements, such as a new yoga studio, additional fitness equipment, a new front desk design, a new software package, an expansion of the parking lot, etc.

What percent of revenue should be allocated to cap ex? A cap ex budget that will keep a club vigorously competitive over a 10-year period does not follow a straight-line formula. One way to budget cap ex is by determining the percentage of revenue that needs to be allocated to this expense on an annual basis. Using the "percentage of revenue" method, and allowing for all the factors relating to wear and tear and essential improvements, a sensible cap ex budget might look as follows:

- Year 1: 0 percent
- Year 2: 3 percent
- Year 3: 4 percent
- Year 4: 10 to 15 percent
- Year 5: 4 percent
- Year 6: 4 percent
- Year 7: 4 percent
- Year 8: 20 to 25 percent
- Year 9: 4 percent
- Year 10: 4 percent

Using this formula, if you take the mean expense for years 4 and 8, the average annual cap ex over a 10-year period would be approximately 6 to 6.5 percent.

Why the spikes in years 4 and 8? Every three to five years, the market takes a significant turn or, put another way, it makes a significant advance. Whenever such advances occur, a cap ex adjustment is required. For example, about five years ago, it became clear that yoga and Pilates were going to become mainstays of the club business. And five years before that, Spinning became a major industry trend. No club can afford to miss these opportunities. Yet, doing them properly requires an investment "spike." If you do not budget these spikes, then change becomes a threat rather than an opportunity.

Then, at least every eight to 10 years, a health club, as is the case with any other retail business, needs a total overhaul so that it can once again become a "brand new" facility. Otherwise, the club will become old, dated, and marginal, and can be severely harmed by any new competitor.

What other methods can be used to calculate cap ex? The "cost per square foot" method has been successfully employed by many clubs. Using this method, and excluding large court areas (tennis, racquetball, squash) from the calculation, a reasonable annual cap ex for most clubs might approximate $2.00 to $2.50 per square foot. Thus, for a 30,000-square-foot club, this method would require an allocation of $60,000 to $75,000 (annual average over a 10-year period).

Do these formulas always work? A key factor in determining cap ex is revenue per square foot. These formulas will work for most clubs that fall in the normal range with respect to revenue per square foot (i.e., $40 to $60 annual revenue/total indoor square feet). However, for clubs that generate significantly greater revenue, adjustments need to be made. The adjustments would be to a lower percentage for clubs using the "percent of revenue" method, and to a higher dollar amount for those using the "cost per square foot" method.

For example, for a club generating $100 per square foot in revenue, the annual cap ex budget might be 4 percent rather than 6 percent of revenues, and, at the same time, it might be $3.75 per square foot rather than $2.50. In any situation, however, market conditions can change rapidly. Whenever this situation occurs, a cap ex plan, no matter how well-conceived, may need to be reevaluated.

What if you budget less? Some very bright people in the industry would argue that annual cap ex can and should be lower. And others who are equally bright who would place it higher. However, the risk of underbudgeting cap ex is greater than the risk of overbudgeting it. The risks of underbudgeting cap ex can be severe. Club members and frontline club personnel are keenly aware when clubs begin to deteriorate. Whenever this happens, a club can rapidly become less competitive with respect to neighboring facilities. You want both your members and your staff to be proud of your facility. And your members notice when they see you continually investing in improvements.

What else should you know? Probably the most important thing about cap ex is not simply what you do, but how well you get the word out. Whenever a club makes improvements, it should have a comprehensive strategy to trumpet those improvements to the local media, current members, prospective members, and the community as a whole. How you leverage cap ex is as important as the money you spend on it.

One final word: Please use these formulas as guidelines, not as rules. Your own sense of what must to be done (on an annual basis, as well as periodically) to make your club as dynamic as possible needs to be your primary guiding principle. The general guidelines specified in this tip are meant to serve as background data for your own, more experiential judgments.

Tips for People Seeking Loans and Investors

- Interview more than one banker if it is your first project. Tell them you would like to submit a loan proposal and ask about various loans and what they like to see in a project.

- You will have to show some type of personal participation. Very seldom can you do an entire project without having some personal money involved. Even investors like to see at least $50,000 on the table. The investors might put up the rest, but they also like to know that you are vested in the project.

- Leave the ball cap at the door. You are there to borrow money, and ties or dresses are considered proper business clothes. You are dealing with very conservative people who like to loan money to other conservative people.

- Contact IHRSA. You should be a member of IHRSA, as is mentioned in the resource guide at the end of the book. This group has many publications that can add to your loan package, such as the *IHRSA Guide to the Health Club Industry for Lenders and Investors* (2nd ed.).

- Get a job in the business first. If you are new to the industry, go get a job in a gym and learn how to sell a membership. If you are not willing to take this step, then don't get in the gym business. Even if you have a lot of money and have been successful somewhere else, learn to sell somebody something in this business before you invest.

- Be prepared. As mentioned previously, very few owners can defend their business plans. Understand how cash flow works and be able to discuss every aspect of the business. Again, if you have never worked in a gym, this discussion will be short, followed by a "no" from the lender.

- Almost everyone started with their family first. It's the rare owner that didn't have some type of family help to get that first gym opened. Consider a family partnership for the first club.

- Investors are more interested in the real estate than they are in owning a gym. Owning your own building often makes more sense to investors, and is better for your long-term future, in most cases, than renting and putting all that money in someone else's space. It is easier to attract investors if they are gaining a passive investment such as a building with a built-in tenant. It is like buying a great rental house and having a tenant that paints the place and even does his own plumbing. He pays rent while you get appreciation. Investors look at the gym business in the same way. They own the real estate, you make the payments, and it becomes a passive appreciation-growing business deal.

- Give up a lot to get your first gym, but make sure you can't get kicked out of your own business. If you have nothing and investors want a large portion of your business to do it, then go for it. Give up 60 percent if you get 40 percent with little of your own money, but make sure your attorney structures the partnership deal so you can't get kicked out of your own business.

- Getting a loan may be as simple as having a cosigner. You may need less cash but a stronger cosigner to get into your first gym. Ask your lender about what it would take to involve a cosigner.

- Look for used gyms. Have a lawyer send a blind letter, meaning that his name is on it, but not yours, to every gym in your target area. The letter states that the lawyer represents a qualified buyer wishing to purchase a gym in the area. You may get no responses or a few outlandish dream deals, but you might also get the real thing. Most used gyms are absurdly overpriced, but start there and see what's in the market. The valuation section in Chapter 3 may help you get a better idea of what a gym is worth.

- Build smaller than you think. Some excellent gyms are 1,300 square feet and make the owners a decent salary and got them into the business. Most first gyms are too much for the market, since the owners had too long to think about building the perfect gym. Start smaller, as you can always expand or build a second unit later. One of the dumbest things heard from even experienced owners is, "I have to build a gym that big. If it's too small it will get too crowded." In other words, you are too successful and the gym is too popular—a tough problem easily remedied by another unit or expansion. Remember that the gym of the future, because of the increasing start-up costs, will be a smaller more-intimate delivery system probably in the 5,000- to 20,000-square-foot range.

The Key Concept in This Chapter

If you want money, you're going have to build a business plan. The model included in this chapter can be your reference point when you first get started. If you want more help beyond what is included in this chapter, turn to the reference section at the end of the book.

Additional Resource

McCarthy, J. (2004). *The IHRSA Guide to Bank Financing*. Boston, MA: IHRSA. www.ihrsastore.com

BUILDING A STRONG RECEIVABLE BASE

iStockphoto/Thinkstock

chapter Eight

Club owners should be seeking long-term stability, the ability to project revenues into the future, the capacity to have cash flow during slight downturns in the business, and most importantly, the ability to increase the worth of the business and sell it in the future at a gain if or when they decide to get out of the business. Only one method can accomplish all of these financial goals, and that is the development of a strong receivable base based on consistent member payments.

As you plan to get into business, or if you are already in business but haven't mastered this concept yet in your existing club, you must first understand just what a receivable base really is and how it affects the financial success of what you do. A receivable base can be understood in several ways, but the simplest way is by thinking of it as how much money you could count on collecting in the future from your current members if you never sold another membership in your club.

Anyone who is opening a training facility also has to pay attention to this as well. In the past, training facilities have been based upon short-term tools, such as packages and sessions, that restrict the ability of the owner to project his business more than a few weeks ahead. This owner who is dependent on just sessions and packages will always be trapped by the need to constantly collect big payments from his clients in order to pay his bills, since this is the only source of income he probably has in the business. He also has an additional issue in that while he does collect money from his clients, he usually spends it today for his expenses but then has to service the client for weeks, or even months, into the future without additional revenue.

This old concept is changing as the more financially successful training companies switch away from short-term tools to longer term commitments for their clients that generate steady monthly income. For example, a training client might sign up for $1,000 a month for 12 months as opposed to just buying a 10-session package.

The key phrases to learn when mastering the concept of a receivable base are "count on" and "future." For a receivable base to exist, an obligation must be present between the member and the club. If no obligation exists, then the club owner has nothing to count on at a later date. He might have cash flow from his member payments if people pay to attend each month without any real obligation, but he doesn't really have stability and money he can project into the future without the obligation that might exist between the club and the member.

For example, an older-style club that sells the majority of its memberships as paid-in-full does not have a receivable base because no revenue can be projected into the future. The owner received cash today, most likely spent the cash today to pay bills, and must sell memberships in the future to have revenue in the future. This is also the way most training clubs actually work. Get it today and spend it today and you have to sell more soon to eat.

This same scenario applies to club owners who build their membership based on open-ended, month-to-month memberships. This membership allows members to come to the club for a month at a time with the ability to come or go as they please without any obligation beyond the current month.

These owners do have cash flow in the form of a monthly check from the total of their member payments, but they don't have a true receivable base because they can't count on revenue in the future. The nature of being month-to-month means that if the entire membership decided to leave tomorrow it could do so by simply calling their banks and canceling the monthly draft if the club was using some form of electronic funds transfer (EFT). EFT is simply the member giving the right to the business to automatically withdraw the member's payment each month from either his credit card or bank account.

This type of club seldom loses its entire membership in one swift shot, but it can often lose 30 to 40 percent of its membership in a 90-day period if a fresh, bright competitor moves across the street. Without obligation, meaning that the member has some type of commitment to pay the club in the future, such as a 12-month contract, the club with open-ended memberships doesn't have the stability that a similar club would have with a strong receivable base and a set commitment term for its memberships.

Another way to look at a receivable base is that the club sells memberships over time, meaning that it adds new members each month that it is open, and the accumulation of the monthly payments each member makes over the length of his contract or commitment to belong to the gym continues to grow, providing stability for the club owner in the form of a monthly cash flow that can be projected into the future.

Chris Clinton

This stable cash flow becomes the club's most valuable asset, because it is something that bankers will recognize and loan against as compared to equipment or the number of members a club claims to have, both of which have little meaning to a bank because they are worthless assets if the club owner should fail.

Consider the following example. A 13,000-square-foot club opens with a $59-per-month membership and a 12-month obligation (annual contract), for a total annual membership of $708. This example ignores any type of one-time membership fee because you are only concerned with the receivable base, not the money a club would get up front for its memberships.

If the club enrolled 90 members a month for 12 months it would have a gross membership of 1,080 at the end of the year. But, in real life, owners never collect all of the money from all of the members. Loss rates are inevitable and need to be subtracted.

Loss rates are discussed in detail later in this chapter, but you can look at the 1,080 members and determine how this number would be affected. First of all, not everyone pays as promised, creating one type of loss rate that will affect the total. By using 12-month contracts, which have the highest chance of being collected, this club would only lose about 10 percent of its membership due to nonpayment.

The club would also lose another 12 percent due to cancellations. This type of cancellation would be due to either a member moving too far from the club, or because of a medical, death, or three-day right of cancellation, which is a cooling off period the members can use to escape any type of retail installment contract, such as a 12-month membership on a contractual basis at a club. The total of these two numbers is 22 percent, which means that a 22 percent adjustment must be made to the members paying the club.

1080 gross members x 0.78 collection rate = 842 members paying at year's end

When these members make their $59 monthly payment, the club would receive a gross check before collection expenses of $49,678. This gross check would be adjusted by about 7 percent, which is the national average for clubs using a sophisticated third-party financial system. These companies specialize in servicing membership contracts for people who own and operate fitness businesses. These companies can, for example, collect the member payments for you, install member-tracking software, chase members who don't pay as promised, and provide data and reporting that help a club owner make more informed decisions.

The power in these companies is that they usually collect more from the same member base than you can do yourself, which is true for many reasons. These companies have the perception of power in the member's mind and many members feel obligated to pay their membership payment when they make their other major payments in their lives, such as a car payment or mortgage.

These companies also specialize in the fitness business and have the systems in place, and know the collection laws, to be able to collect the most money from the members you have in the state where you live and operate. An economy of scale also exists with these companies that a small operator with less than 25 clubs would find hard to duplicate. Therefore, this owner would most likely spend more to collect from the members than it would cost to pay a professional third-party service company to do so.

A degree of vulnerability comes with collecting your own memberships. If an employee dies or a small team quits, your business is at risk because you are dependent on too few people handling your most important asset, which is your club's receivable base.

Therefore, you should always use a third-party financial-service company to handle your memberships. If you do, the net amount to the club after the national average of 7 percent, which includes EFT members (less expensive to the club), as well as those members who decide to write checks each month to pay for their membership (more expensive to the club, but you still need to offer the option), would be calculated as follows:

$49,678 x 0.93 (7% collection fee) = $46,200

This number is an example of what the club might collect monthly from its members' payments. This number also reflects a portion of the total amount of payments the club might collect over a 12-month period since the club is using a 12-month contract as its base membership tool. For example: $46,200 x 12 months = $544,400—the amount the owner might collect from his total receivable base over a year's period of time.

Let's assume this club also has a monthly base operating expense (BOE) of $60,000, which includes all bills the club pays each month, including payroll, taxes, cost of goods, debt service, and any other bills the club has to cover to reach its monthly break-even point. The exception would be if the owner is offsite and has a manager. In this example, the owner's salary, which is paid from the profits of the business, would not be counted as part of the club's BOE since it is not essential for the club to pay to stay in business each month.

The Single Most Important Number to Look at in Your Business

A relationship exists between the monthly BOE and the net amount of the monthly member payments, or receivable check. Once the net check grows to a level where a certain percentage of monthly expense is automatically met each month, the club has then reached a level of stability and maturity that will allow it to better withstand heavy competition as well as any serious downturns in member sales.

Your goal is to achieve 70 percent coverage of your monthly BOE by your net receivable check.

In this example, the club's BOE is $60,000 per month. A 70 percent coverage goal would mean that the club's goal for its net receivable check would be $42,000 per month. The club in this example has a net check of $46,000, which represents a very stable and financially secure business. For example:

$46,000 net check ÷ $60,000 BOE = 76 percent

This percentage of coverage could happen as early as month 13 for a new club and should happen no later than month 25. Existing clubs that are revamping their existing receivable base and pricing structure as discussed in this book should make reaching 70 percent coverage of their BOE by their net monthly receivable check one of the prime goals for their business.

The ultimate goal, of course, is to grow your net receivable check to the point that it covers 100 percent of your monthly expenses. In such a comfortable business world, you receive your check from your third-party financial service company on the first of the month and your club is immediately profitable for the month. Every dollar you make from that point forward is profit. From research conducted by the National Fitness Business Alliance, only about 6 to 9 percent of the clubs in the country reach the goal of 100 percent coverage of their base operating expense. It is, however, *the* goal to strive for in your club business since reaching that level of business sophistication makes you practically bulletproof in the market.

The Difference Between Obligation and Method of Payment

Many owners become confused about the difference of setting an obligation for the member, which is establishing a length of time based upon a contractual obligation, and establishing the member's method of payment, which defines how the member will actually make his payment each month. The actual confusion occurs when owners start to use EFT for collecting their member payments, thinking that this tool will solve all of their collection problems.

Method of payment refers to how the member actually makes his payment each month for his membership. A member may give a club actual cash, write a check, or allow the club to automatically draft (withdraw funds electronically from a checking, savings, or credit card called electronic funds transfer or EFT) each month.

EFT as a method of payment means that the member will, for the sake of convenience, allow the club owner to automatically take the payment each month electronically from one of his bank accounts or credit cards. This arrangement does not infer obligation but merely ease of payment for both parties.

Having 1,000 members on EFT each month does ensure good cash flow. It does not, however, mean that there is any implied obligation between the member and the club. Obligation is just another way of saying contractual agreement and unless the club has established a 12-month contract as a condition for membership, there is no obligation beyond a month at a time. This is the point that gets many owners into trouble. There will always be a certain percentage of members who don't pay each month and EFT will make it a little cleaner, but is does not set a long-term commitment or obligation between the business and the member.

In other words, without first establishing a contract between the member and club that promises payment for a fixed period of time, such as 12 months, the club owner has not developed a strong receivable base by merely enrolling the member on EFT payments. The member can still walk away by simply calling his bank at any time if he has not first signed a contract for obligation.

The rule of thumb is to first establish an obligation (contract) and then let the new member pick his own method of payment. The contract builds a receivable base, which is the main goal of selling club memberships, and the member makes his payments using a method he feels meets his individual needs. The right flow, or order, for a club membership is as follows:

- The club establishes a pricing system that is fair to the member, yet allows the club to collect the most money from the most members while developing a strong receivable base. It is always recommend that you use the lowest entry point needed to attract the widest range of clients without compromising the integrity of the business.
- This pricing system is built upon the 12-month contract, which is a tool that is fair to the member yet highly collectable for the club. These 12-month contracts have approximately a 10 percent national loss rate annually (less than one percent per month) if collected by a strong third-party financial service company. This method establishes obligation first as the foundation of the membership structure.
- Once the new member agrees to the obligation, the club then offers method of payment. For example, the club's monthly price might be $49 per month if the club may automatically deduct the payment from the member's checking account or credit card. If the member wishes to write a check each month instead, something at least half your members will choose if given a choice, the club might charge $54 per month, passing along the slightly higher charge of servicing a check with the third-party financial-service company as opposed to EFT. Most training facilities will not have to offer this option due to the size of their payments and financial sophistication of their clients.
- The club should have established a relationship with a third-party financial-service company (data management company) to be the hired bad person and separate the collection function from the workout function. The third party becomes the power that collects money directly from the member, rather than leaving the owner hoping that a member will pay the club and then having to set up his own collection effort in the club or be forced to use his staff to chase member payments issues each month.

A club really doesn't wield any leverage for collections since the member wants out anyway and a club representative can't really threaten the past due member with anything except banishment from the club. Keep in mind that most collection problems are not just members refusing or unable to pay. Many times the issue is a closed account, expired credit card, divorce, move, or other common problem that is almost mind-numbing to manage for a club staff on a routine basis. You should farm out this service to the professionals and put your energy and time into getting new members and ensuring they get results.

The big question for most new owners is whether EFT has a higher collection rate than just allowing people to simply write checks each month to pay their memberships? The answer is both yes and no.

Overall, EFT payments are collected at an average rate of about 7 to 8 percent higher than using a system that just depends on members writing checks each month. It seems logical that this number should be much higher because the club is automatically collecting the payments directly from the member's account each month, but in reality the difference isn't that great. It also seems that it should be higher because the companies that are EFT processors, as opposed to true third-party financial-service companies, claim that by using EFT you will collect all the money from all the members every month.

Unfortunately, no one collects all the money from all the members each month. No one will ever collect all the money from all the members each month. Anyone that claims to do so doesn't understand the concept of basic loss rates. Each month, you can count on members who don't want to pay, members who can't pay, members who gave you an expired card, members who got divorced and didn't arrange to pay the club, and a myriad of other situations too numerous to mention. The goal is not to collect all the money, which is impossible, but to collect the most money from the most members every month you are in business.

The illusion of EFT is that it is a magical cure for a club's collection woes. EFT is advertised directly at most clubs' weakest part, the back shop business area. A club owner who has tried ineffective systems and is now extremely frustrated is drawn to the illusion of the magic cure being offered by a system that claims to be totally effective in solving the gym owner's biggest headache, which is trying to collect payments due from the members.

For example, many new club owners believe they are too small to use an outside servicing agent for their member's payments. But even if you only add about 10 new members a month, you are big enough, and will benefit from, a strong third-party financial service company.

Many owners also believe that they can easily figure how to set up a collection/service department in the club for themselves, therefore, saving a lot of money by using their sister or mother to collect member payments each month and to service the member accounts that have issues.

Reality strikes when the owners get their first batch of rejected payments due to expired cards, closed accounts, or disputed charges. This negative situation is then followed by the addition of being held hostage by just one employee who handles all of your money. When she is on vacation, you are effectively out of business, or worse yet, you don't really check on her and then realize she doesn't like to make a lot of calls, so those accounts that would have been easy to save, such as the ones with just an expired card, are set aside in a pile and neglected until they are far beyond saving, costing you thousands of dollars a month in losses that should have never occurred.

The realization that you are getting clients but can't collect their payments is the point of terror when most owners panic and look for the magic in ads promising that just one simple solution will end the pain. There is not one simple solution that ends the terror, but it sure sounds good when you hear the pitch for the first time.

These clubs often use EFT as the only method of payment, besides paying cash for the year, setting up an adversarial relationship between a potential member and the club.

According to the major business magazines, only about 50 percent of the people in the country are comfortable with EFT as part of their bill-paying routine. The exceptions are a person's insurances, car payment, and investments, which a slightly higher percentage of people are comfortable using EFT to pay.

Assuming that owners build most of their clubs to appeal to the top 60 percent of the area's demographics, it can probably be estimated that the more financially sophisticated segment of the market is most likely more comfortable with having their accounts automatically drafted. You might then be able to project that at least 60 to 70 percent of your target market is likely to be okay with an EFT system.

That projection still leaves 30 to 40 percent of your market uncomfortable with giving their checking account information or credit card numbers to a club. And if the potential member is not comfortable with giving out that information, then he will most likely not be happy with paying for a membership in full, which is often the only membership alternative a club that forces EFT will give.

Age is also a factor. Training clubs, for example, often appeal to an older, more affluent demographic that has the money to pay but may not be totally comfortable with EFT. These people pay their bills as promised, but they do so using checks as their primary source of payment.

Club owners often say, "I have no problem with EFT at my club. Not a single member that enrolled complained about having to use it." In this case, it's not the members who enrolled that are the problem; the problem is the potential members who never even came into the club because they know they have to use EFT. While this might not be a huge number, the question to ask is how many potential members are you willing to lose because of a situation that should never occur in a service business?

Paying your rent or mortgage payment is a necessity. Making your car payment is something you just have to do. Joining a club is something a person can do without in his life because he is using discretionary money, which is money left over in his life to do with as he pleases after he has paid all his other real-life bills. It seems obvious, but if someone is trying to become a client or member, take the money. Take pennies, take American Express®, take monthly checks, or take a flock of chickens if both parties agree, but avoid creating systems that prevent people from doing business with you.

EFT does have a place in the club business as a method of payment option, but it does not guarantee collections. It just makes collections simpler in some situations, especially if you aren't using a strong third-party collection company in conjunction with your EFT.

Doing It Yourself

Many people in the gym business are in the profession because they were such lousy employees in the real world. In other words, they are somewhat unhirable for most employers, because gym owners, and most of the others who suffer from the entrepreneurial spirit, would rather do things themselves than let people tell them what to do.

Collecting your own memberships is the ultimate example of trying to be in control. The problem with this scenario is that the more you try to do yourself, the less control you really have in your business, because of one of the true maxims in small business:

You can manage more than you can do yourself.

Collecting and servicing your own memberships usually means higher loss rates, little economy of scale (even if you have multiple units, you seldom get to the point where it is cost effective to establish your own billing and collection company), and higher risk, because your most important asset is controlled and managed by too few people. In other words, if you have three units and a small office set up to service your own accounts managed by two or three people, you are only one car wreck away, especially if these people go to lunch together, from being out of business.

You can collect your own memberships, but the effectiveness is seldom adequate. Generally, two key things go wrong when you service your own accounts. First, your effort is concentrated on the good members that would have paid no matter what you did to them and not enough on the problem members who move, close accounts, are chronically late with their payments, get divorced, are overdrawn on their accounts, or any of the multitude of problems associated with trying to collect payments from hundreds of members. Even with an in-house system that forces EFT as the only membership option, you will still have problems with closed accounts and overdrawn accounts. Remember that no one collects all the money from all the members every time.

The second common issue with do-it-yourself collection systems is that the losses are too big too soon. Remember, the national average for the cost of collection with a major third-party financial service company is approximately

iStockphoto/Thinkstock

7 percent of what is collected, not what is billed. Keep in mind that when you do your own collections, you will incur a charge whether you collect the money or not.

This 7 percent number represents the combination of the charges for the servicing and collection of EFT and the slightly higher charges for the servicing and collection of coupon/check payments. Checks are more expensive to service and you will pay slightly more for that option, but you still have to let members have the option to send a check to the third-party company each month.

The situation is similar to small retail stores who refuse to take American Express cards because they will pay about a point-and-a-half difference in processing fees. Let's see, someone is trying to give you money by buying your product or service and you are mad because you don't like the extra charge of about a dollar and a half per hundred dollars the customer is spending with you so you punish the guy trying to do business with you—and yourself by losing a sale—by refusing the card. Again, take the money. Take pennies. Take small farm animals if it means a sale. You are in business to make money and adjust prices and services if needed to make it easy for the consumer to spend money with you.

Owners that collect their own memberships usually do a decent job of servicing and collecting from the members who willingly pay each month. The difficulty arises from the problem members.

Instead of collecting these payments for the 7 percent average, these problem accounts are usually turned over too early in the process by a frustrated owner to an end-of-the-road collection company. Clubs don't normally do well in chasing down and solving member account problems. This work is vastly detailed and it's hard to develop a process that can systematically turn a troubled member account back into a strong, reliable payment. Doing this takes patience, people, and a system—all things the typical club can't handle by using its staff or just one or two collection people.

These "end of the road" companies specialize in hardcore collections on bad accounts and they usually charge somewhere between 33 and 50 percent of what's collected. They can do their job, but the problem is that most of the membership contracts they received as bad accounts would have never been turned over to them in the first place if the club had been using a sophisticated third-party financial-service company.

Third-Party Financial-Service Companies

The name "third-party financial-service company" is in many ways not even a valid name anymore. This type of company has evolved into more of a data-management provider for clubs, since a true third-party company now provides much more to a club than the servicing and collection of member accounts.

The name "third-party" came about because early clubs created the illusion of a strong outside company to collect their payments. It didn't take owners long to figure out that the club would be the last thing to get paid each month by the member, especially when the members realized that the club had no leverage to collect. What was the club going to do, kick the member out? He already wasn't paying and wanted out anyway so the club owner in those days never had the big stick to ensure that he might become a priority payment in the member's life.

In essence, data-management companies become your virtual partner in your business by allowing the club owner to totally concentrate on the production side of the business while the third-party company concentrates on giving you management information and strong cash flow from the memberships the club sells over time. This partnership provides the long-term stability and planning ability a club owner needs to continue to grow a business over the years.

The next step

With the advent of the Internet, the third-party financial-service/data-management companies have evolved yet another step. The logical course is that all your data is held, stored, and maintained in the data-management company's computers and you access all of your account information online through the daily course of business.

Over time, the club owner should gain quicker access and more pertinent information to make club-management decisions. For example, a club owner might be considering a change in her marketing plan. Using just a few simple key strokes on her computer should allow her to access the demographics of her current membership, including where they live, ages, usage in the club, income, email address, average member payment, and other information that would influence the type and amount of marketing a club would need to do to establish a niche or specialization. Other information that becomes available to the owner in this scenario would be the amount spent in profit centers during each member visit, renewal percentages, and daily cash flow from all sources.

Factors That Influence the Strength of Your Receivable Base

Four major factors influence the strength of your receivable base and the total money you will collect over time from your membership base. These four factors, when applied to a single payment, determine the yield an owner can expect from an average membership over a year's period of time.

The owner of any fitness business only has one main purpose: to strengthen and protect his most valuable asset, which is the receivable base. All of these factors can be controlled to some extent and an owner needs to do whatever it takes to minimize the effect each has on the club's total outstanding contracts to be collected. These four factors are as follows:

- Loss rate
- Cancellations made by the club
- Cost of collections and servicing member payments
- Free enhancements added as part of the membership

Loss rate

The term "loss rate" can be understood in a number of ways, but the simplest is to think of it as money you should have collected from the members but didn't because they opted not to pay for some reason. For example, assume a club signed up 100 new members in July of last year. True loss rate would mean that you track those 100 members through their year and determine exactly when they stopped paying on their membership agreements.

This is, by the way, a highly recommended exercise for any owner who wants to gain mastery of the key numbers in his business. True loss rate means you follow a single month's membership for the life of those members. Each month, you look up the core members and record who is still paying and those who left. The ones who left need to be assigned an exit reason. Did he move too far away from the club to stay a member? Did he close his account and just disappear? Was he injured and unable to continue due to a note from his physician?

You can learn a lot about your business by doing this a minimum of one time, and it is recommended that you do it at least twice using two separate groups from two different years you are in business and then follow the members forever as long as they are members in the club. This process will give you exact loss rates and give you an indicator as to when losses might occur in your system.

The club in this example is using 12-month agreements, which should have an annual loss rate of about 10 percent, meaning that 10 people will not pay for some personal financial reason, such as losing a job, but 90 will pay until the end of their membership term. This example also assumes that the club is using a strong third-party financial-service company to service these memberships, giving the owner the maximum power possible to collect the most money from the most members. Do-it-yourself collection efforts often have a higher loss rate because it is virtually impossible for a club to create the systems and duplicate the effort it takes to chase a large number of members over time.

Another way to look at this situation is that the club will lose slightly less than 1 percent of its 100 hundred members each month for 12 months. The reason this scenario gets complicated is that the club is also adding new members every month and there are other reasons that exist why a member may not pay. These reasons are discussed later in this chapter.

"Applied to principal" is another way to consider loss rate. This term means that each month the total outstanding principal to be collected, which is represented by the amount each member has to pay on the remaining balance of his contract with the club (i.e., the obligation), changes. During each month, the club adds new members to its total outstanding receivable base, but it also subtracts from the total outstanding in the form of members who make their last payment but don't renew, those who elect not to pay, members who have a legitimate reason to suspend payment, such as a move or medical reason, and those who pay the balance of their membership in full when it gets down to the last few payments.

Tracking this number allows you to compare what should have been collected from your total outstanding against what is actually collected each month and then allows you to use those totals to figure out the loss. Your goal, obviously, is to gain a positive net position each money, meaning you have added more new accounts, and kept more existing members, than you have lost. Positive growth is an indicator that your net collections will go up for the month, leading to more free cash flow for your business.

The club doesn't have to have a true loss rate or the exact amount applied to principal to stay in business. These are great tools for the more advanced owner who wants the ability to fine-tune his business to the highest degree of efficiency. However, to gain valuable information on protecting and strengthening your receivable base, all you really need is to understand that during each month a certain percentage of contracts will kick out of your system, and then work with this average. Three prime factors directly affect how high or low the loss rate will be:

• The higher the pressure applied to the potential member at the point of sale, the higher the loss rate will be, especially during the first month's payment period.

- There is a loss rate associated with each membership tool the club uses. Theoretically, the longer the membership term, the higher the loss rate will be over time.
- Overpromising by the sales people and then underdelivering by the club will increase the loss rate. (If you lie, or if things don't quite happen the way they were promised, the member will punish you financially.)

High pressure produces high loss rates.

Many normal, and often timid, people just sign a membership agreement to get away from an aggressive salesperson in hopes of getting out of the club alive. Pounding people into submission results in higher loss rates, especially in what's called first-payment defaults. First-payment defaults are people who, after thinking about their sales experience in the club, feel that some slick salesperson talked them into something they didn't really want. They then exact their revenge on the salesperson and the club by defaulting on the first payment of their membership agreement. It doesn't matter if the member writes a check or is set up on EFT, he will find a way to not make that first payment if he feels justified in not paying due to his experience.

Clubs that live by strong first-visit sales closing should track their first-payment defaults, both by the club's total and by individual salesperson. A salesperson that claims an unusually high first-visit closing rate will almost always have the elevated first-payment default number to go along with it. Yes, the salesperson is getting the sales, but the sales numbers he is generating are false because the club can't collect the money from the members.

Normally, a good salesperson in a club will close approximately 30 to 40 percent of their first visits over time and a total of about 60 to 65 percent of all potential members he encounters over a 30-day period if the club is also using a trial membership. A more trained and experienced salesperson might close as high as 50 percent of their first visits in some markets or clubs where there is little competition and the club's sales staff merely takes orders. Many of the sales that occur on the first visit are usually buddy referrals and should have a higher percentage closing rate anyway.

If the sales team is closing at a higher rate than 50 percent or so on a potential member's first visit, then their first-payment defaults should be tracked monthly with the anticipation that the salespeople with the highest number will be losing more payments during the first month. There are some salespeople that can close early and make the person feel good about it that will rack up high numbers without the defaults, but these are much more rare creatures in the fitness world than is claimed.

The key element behind pressure sales is the term "buyer's regret," which means that somebody bought something and then had serious second thoughts immediately after the purchase. For example, you go to the mall to buy sandals and two hours later you're sitting in your living room feeling bad about that entire new outfit you just bought because some salesperson said, "Hey, you would really look good in these shorts and they really go well with those sandals you were looking at." This feeling is buyer's regret, or the "What the hell did I buy this time?" feeling you get while thinking of how you are going to pay for this purchase on your credit card while driving home surrounded by lots of bags.

In most cases, the club actually causes buyer's regret. Too much emphasis is put on the first visit, a habit leftover from the earlier days of the fitness industry. In addition, the use of extreme discounts at the point of sale both adds to high buyer's regret and makes losses higher than they need to be. Making an outrageous deal at the point of sale may get the sale, but the new member heads home with a sour taste in her mouth. Could she have held out and gotten an even better deal? Did the salesperson take advantage of her? What is wrong with the club if they have to pressure a person like that to get members? For every reason there is to make a deal, there are more reasons not to because of the longer-term damage done to the new members and the club's reputation in the community.

Trial memberships take a lot of the buyer's regret out of the picture because the consumer has an actual chance to try before he buys. With trials, the consumer also feels that he is in more control of the buying situation than he does when forced to make a buying decision 20 minutes after visiting a club for the first time. We forget that we are asking for a lot of money, even though it is paid over time, from a potential member and forcing someone to make a buying decision within minutes of his first visit is antiquated technology that belongs back in the dark ages of the fitness industry. In reality, do we really think that someone will drop several hundred dollars or more on impulse in today's heavily competitive marketplace?

True trial memberships, such as a 30-day for $19 or a 21-day risk-free trial, coupled with a strong third-party financial-service company and 12-month contracts, can usually drop a club's loss rate to less than 10 percent annually. Keep in mind this does not include members who move over 25 miles from the club or permanent medical cancellations, which affect the club's total collections but are in addition to the losses being discussed here. Most of this gain occurs because the client felt he actually participated in the buying decision instead of being forced into something he didn't even know he really wanted when he decided to check out a gym on the way home from work. Pressure may get the sale, but it doesn't keep the member over time.

The membership tool the club uses influences the loss rate.

Who collects the member payments and how the memberships are collected are factors in how much money the club will collect from its memberships through its receivable base. Using a strong third-party financial-service company will significantly increase the overall money you collect from your memberships.

The tool you use with the members also plays a role in how collectable your membership agreements are. "Tool" is defined as the agreement and term the club uses to define its relationship with its members. For example, one club might use a 12-month membership agreement, another may use a 24-month agreement, and a third in the same area might use month-to-month, pay-as-you-go memberships. Each tool has its positives and negatives regarding its effect on the club's loss rate.

There is also a strong trend in the training clubs to move away from short-term tools, such as sessions and packages, and move toward using a more professional approach based upon 3- to 12-month EFT membership programs. Training facilities that switch find that they can stabilize their monthly income and gain the advantage of having money coming in when they aren't doing a session.

These clubs have also found that switching away from being too dependent on just one-on-one clients adds another layer of stability to the business. These clubs use offerings such as group personal training where they have one coach and up to 10 to 12 clients together. The clients are offered perhaps 8 to 12 options to attend each week based upon a set schedule and might pay anywhere from $89 to $249 per month for a minimum of a 3- to 12-month commitment, depending on the area and the experience of the owner.

The month-to-month, pay-as-you-go tool was popularized by some of the large chain clubs in the early 1990s. This type of membership means that the club does not establish any type of obligation with the member and is going for mere cash flow. The member can simply pay month-to-month and cancel any time he chooses. Members do appreciate this option, but it is not the best tool to stabilize a business because the losses are so high.

This type of membership was a strong marketing ploy against the clubs that forced long-term memberships, defined at 24 months or longer, upon their members. It made competing in those days somewhat easier since the clubs with the long-term memberships had a difficult time changing over their membership systems Instead of contracts, why not just let the members pay month-to-month and come and go as they please? We went from too far to perhaps too short in a single jump and no one at the time really had an idea of what the loss rates might be with this new system.

Several problems exist for a club with a month-to-month membership. The losses are approximately 3 to 4 percent per month at the very least, or about 36 to 48 percent annually and can often run as high as 5 to 7 percent, depending on the area and competition. If a club has a lot of new competitors and if the owner is letting his club run down a little, the loss rates will be on the higher end of the scale.

For example, if a club owner signs up 100 members in January, by the end of December he will only have between 52 and 64 of those members left. In other words, you could lose half your members over a year's period of time, just through the loss rates associated with this type of membership.

This means that the club owner will become dependent on shear volume at some point to stay in business because he will need to replace all those lost members to maintain the income stream. In other words, at some point, he might be in the position where he loses 100 members and has to sign up another 100 just to break even each month. These numbers really get scary when you get to the point that you need to replace several hundred members or more each month. This type of club needs density and turnover in area residents in its marketplace to survive, but the system does work in certain areas if the supporting factors are there.

This type of membership system that is dependent on volume is also similar to large clubs that price in the $19 range. You are basing your business plan on the ability to constantly replace lost members each month and that ability is limited if there are too many other clubs in the market doing the same thing or if there isn't much density in your five-mile market.

This type of membership seems logical, but is actually not necessarily a good thing for the club. Clubs using month-to-month memberships have to do the same amount of work as clubs using a fixed obligation to sign up a new member, have to run the same if not more marketing because the losses are so high, and have the same start-up cost per new member and the same labor cost to get the new member into the system. In other words, they have the same costs, but much less of a chance to collect money from the membership over a year's period of time due to the higher loss rate.

Month-to-month memberships may work in very high-volume, high-density markets, such as San Francisco, Orlando, or Manhattan, but owners in the rest of the country should be careful using month-to-month memberships as their primary tool because of the excessive loss rates that will trap the owner into a flat growth rate in the third year and beyond.

The recommendation to avoid using month-to-month memberships has an exception. Club owners that feel they need to compete with other clubs in their market that feature month-to-month options can offer the same tool but in a different and much safer format. This type of club would offer month-to-month memberships at a rate of about $8 to $10 more per month than its 12-month contract rate. Given a choice, approximately 80 percent of the members will chose a 12-month option if it is priced $10 lower than the month-to-month option. If the member wants the freedom to truly come and go, such as a person with a second home somewhere, then he can choose that option defined by the month-to-month. If, on the other hand, he intends to support the club year-round, he can then save approximately $120 per year by choosing the annual membership.

For example, if the club sold 12-month memberships for $49 per month, it could offer a month-to-month option for $57 to $59 per month, possibly coupled with a slightly larger membership fee. Using the $8 to $10 spread, approximately 80 percent of the club's new members each month should take the 12-month membership, which provides more stability and lower losses than the month-to-month memberships, thereby giving the club a higher return per member.

This system also works if you are using the $19 pricing model. You could, for example, offer $19 as your primary rate for a 12-month membership and $29 for an open-ended, month-to-month membership option.

Training clubs most likely will not encounter the need for month-to-month as a barrier to sales. Even if you are using the EFT model with training paid for over three months or more, you can control the member's need to come and go by the length of your initial membership agreement with your client.

Overpromising by the sales team and underdelivering by the business increases the loss rate.

Salespeople that promise more than the club can deliver, or enhance the membership with extras that can't always be delivered, also drive up the loss rate for the club. This statement is especially true for a club sales team that promises a lot of free help for the new member to get started and then the trainers, or even the salespeople if they are the ones who have to deliver the workouts, are always too busy and the workouts are short and poor in quality. For example, a large club chain was having the sales team promise free training for every new sale for their first 30 days, but the weak point was that it was the sales team who was going to have to do the training.

There was a lot wrong with this situation. Was the salesperson also a certified, or even basically qualified, trainer? What happened to the new members and their training once a new prospect walked into the club? It is doubtful that a salesperson, whose job depended on getting new sales, would stick with the new member he was supposed to be training if a prospect was standing there waiting to be greeted. And the biggest issue might be that if the salesperson did his job and added 40 to 50 new members that month in the chain box, how many of these could he successfully train for a full 30-day period assuming that the average new client might come in about eight times during the first month?

This system was obviously designed to get new members at any cost and then assume that those that did enroll are expendable. The assumption in this situation is that many of these new members were extremely dissatisfied with their first month's experience and either refused to continue payment or hurt the club in other ways, such as a refusal to refer friends.

General customer service is also an issue. If the new member is promised great service but can't get a towel during her first visit, has to wait to get on a cardio machine, or can't get into a class that is too full, she will take it out on the club by not paying or canceling her membership. Members don't mind paying when they get what they pay for, but they will fight if the promised service is not delivered.

Promise only what you can deliver and don't create scenarios based upon service the club doesn't have the staff or training to deliver. Most losses in this category are preventable, but club owners with aggressive sales staff have to be particularly on guard to prevent a high-pressure salesperson from guaranteeing something the club can't back up.

Cancellations made by the club

Your cancellation policy should be restricted to only what the law allows in your state. Typical state cancellation policies are usually pretty simple and very straightforward. For example, most states require that you cancel the membership of anyone who moves more than 25 miles away from the club.

Most club managers, however, too easily cancel someone who moves instead of following a set policy that reflects a combination of common sense and the state law as it reads. This simple law, for example, is made much too complicated by many club owners. The tough and confusing part for most owners comes when you try to verify the member's move, especially when you don't have a predetermined system in place.

A bad scenario takes place when a young female or a drinking buddy comes into the club and says, "I'm moving and need to cancel." Your young manager, either interested in the young female or going drinking with the friend that night, and lacking a set system that clearly defines his actions to follow, says, "Sure, I'll take care of that." The membership is then cancelled and the club loses a chance to collect the remainder of the contract; revenue that had cost the club a commission to sell as well as marketing expense and set-up costs for the new member.

Two issues are in play in this situation. The club should farm out its cancellations during your first year of business. If you pick a solid, third-party financial-service company, they will be able to set up your cancellations in your club's file.

In this example, the manager should have said, "We actually don't handle the cancellations here at the club. Please call this 800 number and our service company will help you." The service company would then cancel per your instructions and per your state laws. A typical response might be, "Your club and state will allow the cancellation of your membership if you move more than 25 miles away from the club. Please send a copy of your new utility bill once you arrive and you will be cancelled immediately."

Utility bills are the hardest to fake and are good tools to keep the members honest. Again, this situation could have been handled by the service company or by the club itself if it had the right systems in place. If you do choose to handle cancellations at the club level, you then have a chance to try to re-sign the member and get him in the club again, especially since a large number of these casual cancellations are nothing more than members who simply aren't using the club at the time or who have become irritated with the club over some minor detail that is easy to remedy.

Your goal is to keep your cancellations to 1 percent of your total file each month. For example, if you have 1200 members, you should only have 12 or fewer that actually move more than 25 miles or cancel for other legitimate reasons, such as permanent medical disability. Loose managers that are too easy and don't understand the laws of the state they live in can easily hit 3 percent per month in cancellations. Check this number monthly once you open and work hard to keep it near 1 percent.

This example assumes that you are using membership contracts. Month-to-month, pay-as-you-go memberships allow most members to cancel with 30 days notice, which means that your cancellations will be included in your overall loss rates associated with the tool you select for memberships, which was discussed earlier in this chapter. In the case of open-ended memberships, coupled with legitimate moves and medical reasons, the losses will be at least 5 to 7 percent per month and possibly higher.

Some states also allow for a cancellation fee. Remember, cancellation fees are not another profit center, as in, "Hey, we made $200 in cancellation fees today. Yahoo." You had to cancel part of your receivable base to generate those fees and you gave up part of your future to collect a small percentage of what was owed you in total membership dollars. Again, if your state allows you to charge a fee to cancel, and if you have a legitimate cancellation, then go for the money.

Learn to fight for every dollar and make sure you try to save every member who is trying to leave the club. One thing that you should learn early is that most members want to leave over really small matters that usually stem from a perceived customer service issue. For example, a member who has been around for three years has a training appointment and the trainer just doesn't show up or call in to the club. The club team usually just shrugs and tells the member to reschedule at another time. The member leaves really pissed at both the trainer and the club itself because of poor service.

This member will be one of those wanting to cancel that month. He can be saved with a simple apology and a couple of training sessions, which he deserves. Many young owners believe that the members try to abuse the system and hurt the club, but in this case, the member is correct and has a legitimate reason to be mad. He should be compensated for his situation and the club should try to save this person as a member. If he is saved, you now have a friend for life who understands that a mistake was made but that the club did the right thing to take care of a loyal customer.

Cost of collections and servicing member payments

The national average for the cost of collections using a third-party financial-service company is about 7 percent of what is collected. And no, you can't beat that number and efficiently collect your own memberships. You could do it cheaper, but you will never collect the most money from the most members over time.

The question to ask yourself is whether you are getting into the business to build a financially successful fitness business dedicated to helping members and providing a legendary service experience, or are you getting into the business so you can chase people for missed payments, expired credit cards, and closed checking accounts?

Remember the foundational rule of any small business: If it gets in the way of production, farm it out. Do not do your own payroll, because it gets in the way of generating new revenue. Don't do our own accounting, except for basic

QuickBooks®, since it gets in the way of producing new money every day. And don't do your own servicing of your member's payments, because your time is better spent generating new memberships and letting a professional company collect the most money from the most members possible.

You will have extra cost associated with your service company. Some companies charge separately for software and some have extra services available in a menu-driven format, letting you choose the tools that fit your new business. Some companies offer other support tools, such as lead-generation tools, that you might pay extra for if you can use them for your business. Check the cost first and then choose the items you need to be successful.

Also, remember that it is always cheaper to buy proven tools off the shelf than to try to copy and recreate everything because you're cheap. Do it right and use proven tools and always concentrate on the production end of the business as your first priority.

Free enhancements added as part of the membership

Everything has a cost and that cost has to be absorbed into the business somehow. The best example is the owner who likes to give out free coffee in the morning, thinking that he is providing great customer service. The coffee is cheap and the cups are small, and yet he ends up spending approximately $700 to $900 per month to provide an unnecessary and wasteful service that doesn't really please anyone.

Customer service is seldom offering something for free. Besides three or four old guys who are there in the morning, everyone else in the club knows the coffee is lousy and the cups are small because who can afford to give out good stuff in big cups? Instead of being wasteful trying to create the illusion of service, you should offer quality options that actually represent true service. This same club owner could offer quality coffee in 16 to 20 ounce cups for $1.50, along with a special flavored coffee of the week, and thrill his members. If the coffee is good, reasonably priced, and, most importantly, convenient, the club will make some profit while providing excellent customer service.

Watch for the money-losing traps, because these money wasters lower the overall return per member in your business. For example, if an owner also gave out free towels and free childcare, it would cost him about two dollars per month per member in most clubs, which is a lot of money. In addition, he has to lower the value of these items because he is losing money on each of them every time the member uses one of these services.

If you have to give it free, is it really good service for anyone? You know it is not free and, in fact, it costs you a lot of money often to provide a weak service to a very small number of people. Childcare, for example, is only used by about 6 percent of the members in a typical club. That means that about 94 percent of your members aren't using a service that causes you a loss each month to provide. In this case, you might be better to cancel the childcare, and the members using it, and offset the monthly loss. This owner might actually come out ahead by canceling the service freeing him to chase more lucrative parts of the market. If you can charge for it, then charge fair prices, such as $15 to $25 per month for the first child and about $5 less per month for the second, set up on EFT.

Get a good coffee bar and build a legendary childcare room and then charge for it. The towels, especially if you are in a club that charges $49 per month or higher, are something you include for free. But if you are in a club that charges less, offer nice towels and charge customers $1 to $2 to use one during each visit.

Most new owners try to give everything away, thinking it will drive their business, but you'll find that it is hard to maintain quality when giving things away for free. Free childcare almost always comes down to a small room with badly painted walls, a cheap television, and lousy toys. If you're going to offer something, do it well and then charge for the extra quality you are offering the members. Keep in mind that the member will pay for nice things, but you usually can't give cheap stuff away while maintaining any type of quality.

Your goal is to hit zero. In other words, you want to eliminate as many things that lower your return per member as you can and replace them with offerings that the members will pay to support. Profit is the goal and the numbers don't lie. You either directly made money or you didn't. You also need to be aware of the trap, "Well, no one uses childcare, but I know a lot of people signed up because I offer it." Remember, the numbers don't lie and stick with what you can verify, not what you have talked yourself into believing to be true.

Building a Membership Structure

This section provides basic information that you can use to start your thinking process. The information will be divided into mainstream fitness systems with a separate section for those of you looking to open a training/sports performance center. More information about building an effective structure can be found in other Thomas Plummer books and seminars, but this example will help you build your first business plan.

Foundational concepts everyone needs to master no matter what business you own

The core of a membership system is the 12-month membership coupled with a one-time membership fee. Remember that you can't vary from the rules and make adaptations that fit your unique business unless you first understand the concepts and the rules you are varying from in the first place. Good consultants, and good fitness business owners, realize that every business is different, but good business is good business. This means that you can vary your approach to fit you and your marketplace, but that variation must be within the scope of what constitutes good business practices.

For example, every owner will say this at least once before they mature in the business: "That is a good idea, but you know, things are different here and my people just won't really like that." This owner is correct in saying that things are different in his town; and things are different in the north, south, east, and west, in the big cities and the small cities, and in Canada, Bulgaria, and the Far East. But good business principles, once understood, can be applied and adapted to all these markets.

Customer service is a perfect illustration. What we consider good customer service in clubs in North America might be considered forward and rude in the Middle East, and what we consider good uniform choices might be horrible in South America, but the idea of customer service and the idea of professionally dressing your staff is a basic, solid business concept that is important to implement in all small businesses with variations that fit where you live and work.

Keeping this idea in mind, let's look at the foundational concepts behind building a financially success fitness business.

The concept of a set membership time period

New members should pay a one-time membership fee immediately at the time they become members, and their first payment would be due about 30 days from the day they sign the contract/membership agreement. Start your thinking with the idea of all members/clients signing up for time rather than sessions or packages. The time may vary depending on the owner and business, but the core of a financially successful business is building a receivable base, which gives the owner the ability to project his business ahead in time.

The tool we use, as discussed previously, is the 12-month agreement, which has the highest collectability with the lowest loss rates. Training clubs might alter this idea to three months as the base tool and then progress to longer agreements with experience. Most clubs will have some variation of the 12-month as the core and then wrap longer or open-ended memberships around this base.

For example:

$69 one-time membership fee + $59 a month (EFT) for 12 months

The one-time membership fee should be at least equal to one month's dues, but no more than $89 for most clubs. Exceptions exist to that rule, but most clubs will benefit by having at least one membership where someone can start for $89 or less. This rule also applies to trainers. Let your client pay $69 today and then pay $450 a month for a semi-private, small-group experience, using a three-month minimum, for example. It is easy to get started for the person and the club now has established a receivable base of three months worth of payments.

Always keep the first step simple for the new client. There is a lot going on in his head during that first visit. Can I do this? Will I stick to it this time? Will I fail again? Is my wife going to kill me for doing this without talking to her? Keep money out of this equation no matter how much you charge and remember that the monthly payments are more important than what you get down today.

Do not get the first month's dues and the membership fee together. The combination of the two would make it over $89 per month, thus limiting your ability to get the consumer to make an impulse buy. Getting a small chunk today, in this case $69, and then getting the first month's payment about 30 days later is called payment in arrears, and it allows the club owner to build a stronger receivable base because he is getting 12 payments rather than 11. For example, the money could arrive as follows:

- Today's date is November 15, 2011.
- A member who joins today would put down $69 as the one-time membership fee.
- The date the membership begins is November 15, 2011.
- The date of the first payment is December 15, 2011, and the payment amount is $59.
- The date the membership expires is November 15, 2012 (not December 15, 2012) and the final payment of $59 is due that day.

Again, you should always offer the person the choice of writing a check each month. Using EFT is becoming more popular each year, but you still should not force EFT in your club. Give the new member the option to pay a little more to write a check each month (sent to your third-party financial-service company), since you as an owner are usually charged more for processing those checks.

For example:

$69 one-time fee—$59 a month (EFT) for 12 months

or

**$69 one-time fee—$64 a month
(coupon/check system) for 12 months**

The key idea in this concept is to establish an obligation between you and the client. Using membership agreements based upon a set length of time is fair to both the business and the client. Many new business owners are somewhat uncomfortable with this idea but keep in mind that this is really no different than using a retainer with your attorney, who might charge you a fixed fee per month to have access as needed.

Membership agreements are common in mainstream fitness but less common in the training world; however, that is changing rapidly as the new generation of businesspeople/trainers is emerging. In this world, you may talk about sessions and packages but you are really selling time. For example, you might charge a client $149 a month to have the right to attend as many group experience classes a week as she likes.

In this example, the owner might offer 20 or more small group options a week on a schedule set by the club, and the member can come as often as she likes. In reality, you will only train about 9.6 times per month (round off to 10 here) and you want her to come at least eight times per week.

The number eight is magic in the fitness world. Clients who use their facility, or attend training sessions, eight times or more a month are at least 50 percent more likely to stay and keep paying than clients who drop below eight. Based on this fact, it is recommended that most of your programs are priced to give the client unlimited access to the club, because if she trains more often, she will stay and pay longer.

There are a lot of reasons for this statistic but the easy one to grasp is the fact that if this woman is coming to your facility eight times or more per month, she is probably getting results and will most likely stay committed to the club. If she falls to less than eight, in many cases, she is probably not getting any outside fitness either and will stop paying once the progress ends. Keep them in the club eight times or more a month and set your programs to allow for maximum access.

The issue of what to actually charge as your base rate for one person

This debate has changed more in the last three years than it has in the preceding 30 years in the industry. What is the new base rate for one person? Should you go for a higher price, say $49, to establish yourself as the upscale choice in the market? Or should you go for $19 and be the easy to access price in your marketplace, making it a no-brainer for everyone to join. You could also go radical and become a shear volume club with a price for one person of just $9—a price structure that was the rage for a number of years during the first decade of this new era but one that was slowly replaced with an emphasis on the $19 model.

The answer is that all of these choices might be correct, depending on the marketplace, the competition, the owner's philosophy, and the current state of the economy. Your price has to match you, your business plan, and the market where you will operate. Pricing for most new owners is random in most cases or just a reaction to what is already going on in the market. Following are a few ideas to think about and descriptions of what it takes to run each of these business models. Training clubs are excluded in this section and will be discussed later in this chapter, but it is very important for the training people to read this part so you understand what your competitors are trying to accomplish in your marketplace and where the weaknesses are in their systems.

The $9 business model

Welcome to the world of volume membership sales. This model is based upon generating big sales numbers each month and then being able to maintain those numbers year after year. The delivery box in this model might be anywhere from 10,000 square feet to 50,000 and is based upon a passive approach to the membership. This means you would have a heavy cardio presence, such as 100 pieces in 12,000 square feet, a lot of selectorized equipment, limited free weights, and large, clean, but traditionally plain, locker rooms that are at best merely functional in nature.

This model does not usually allow the club to offer group exercise of any type, and it has no childcare, no trainers as employees, and often no real sales people. In this case, the front counter people simply take memberships filled out on clipboards since there is nothing really to sell but the price itself once the person takes a look at your equipment offerings.

In essence, the members are doing nothing more than renting equipment in a supposedly clean and well-equipped club. It has been cited, for example, that 73 percent of most daily visits in a mainstream fitness center are for cardio use and these clubs are designed to do not much more than rent those treadmills for about $9 per month.

When these clubs first came out, it was proclaimed that you could operate one of these for a lot less than mainstream fitness centers with trainers and group exercise people, but that did not prove to be true. These clubs have virtually the same expense as a regular club; however, that expense is not in staffing but in equipment leases, maintenance, marketing, and other payroll.

The strength of these clubs is that they tend to attract big numbers and can often have 10,000 members or more, which sounds impressive; but keep in mind that all those members might not produce that big of a monthly membership receivable base since the memberships are just $9 per month.

There is also the theory that most people will keep paying longer because while they might not be using the club regularly, they intend to come back at some point in the future and besides, it is only $9 anyway, which is nothing and not worth the effort to even cancel it.

This does sound logical and is, in fact, somewhat true in that these members do hang on a little longer than a regular member who is paying $49 and stops using the club. The members do continue to pay for a while past the point of where they stop using the club, but at some point most will stop anyway, no matter what the price because if you are not using it, you will at some point stop paying for it.

You will, however, get a person to make a few extra months of payments, which disguises when the losses actually occur. We have found that a member might average about four extra months worth of payments in comparison with a typical member paying $39 per month or more before he would cancel. These four extra months are significant in the business world and do add up over time, but the reality is that the member will quit at some point in time and losses do occur.

The core concern of this model is that going into your third year, you might add 300 new members that month and you will lose 300. In this plan, this is a good thing since you are now maintaining the numbers you built during your first two years of business, which should have been growth years, allowing you to achieve a decent monthly receivable base.

One of the weaknesses in this model is that it takes a lot of density in the marketplace, coupled with a lot of constant turnover in the people living in the area to make this work. Markets such as Orlando, for example, are perfect for this model. In this market, you have density due to all the attractions in the area and the large number of workers needed, a younger marketplace seeking a lower price option, and a constant turnover as people move into and out of the market looking for work and then moving on after a few years.

This model can work but many people who get into the business don't do so to run this type of club. This model is a numbers game and servicing the member, no matter what any operator of this system will tell you, is not part of the model and the sales it takes to keep replacing lost members will be a factor during your third year. It does work financially in many markets, and for the owner seeking to open a number of clubs in a market that can support this and then sell in a few years, this model might be something to explore. Although another weakness is that if many clubs in the same market chase this same volume, someone will stumble because there is only so much volume available in any given market.

The $19/$39 business model

This model is, in reality, a hybrid of the $9 model. In this business model, you use a low price to attract the largest number of potential members in the market, but you usually offer a full-service club rather than the stripped down version the $9 players normally use.

In the past, the $19 players have also limited the offerings in the club, emulating the lower priced players who cut everything to keep expenses down, but this is changing quickly in the market. Today's $19 players are usually offering a wide selection of services including group exercise, extended training built upon an EFT model rather than merely sessions or packages, and other amenities, such as smoothie bars and weight management.

The price of $39 is also included in this model. In many northern markets, $39 is the equivalent of $19 in other areas of the country. For example, $39 in New Jersey is the equivalent to charging $19 in St. Louis, which has a much lower cost of living than the east.

The $19/$39 model in many ways might be the model of the next decade or longer in the fitness business. Even the more sophisticated owners/operators are lowering their prices to $19 as a way to attract a wider range of potential business that might have never appeared without a lower entry point.

This model does work, and it even works with a full-service component added on, but it works especially well if you use a layered price model on top of the low price entry. Layered pricing means that you might use four to five different price points above the $19 entry point, which are designed around the clubs training options.

These training options should be a mainstream fitness business's highest source of revenue, surpassing the total of the club's membership receivable base. Let's look at a typical mainstream club offering using this model. The price structure of a typical financially successful training club, on the other hand, is really nothing more than this model without the low entry point of $19.

It is important to note, however, that the key to this system in a training club is the ability to attract a wide range of potential clients through the use of a paid trial membership. Prices do not make sense to the typical client who has no experience with your tools and products. Start every new person in your training facility with a 30-day paid trial, giving you time to establish your credibility and expertise before you talk about real money.

- *$19 a month for an individual* using the club. This would be for simple access to the club and include the club's group exercise program.

- *$89 per month for group personal training* in groups of 10 to 12 provided by the club on a set schedule for the month and repeating the same workout, led by a trainer, for the entire month. The key is that you are introducing training to a whole new market in the club. These are normally the clients who would not respond to traditional one-on-one training due to the high cost or because they simply enjoy the group experience more than one-on-one.

  Traditional training for these people is either too expensive, too boring and doesn't meet their needs, or not challenging enough. The traditional model also lacks the group dynamic that is so important to so many members and that is completely eliminated by the traditional one-on-one system. In this system, we are allowing the member, for only $89 a month in this example, to share the cost of the trainer. This means you can have access to a trainer every time you come to the club for only $70 more per month over the $19 entry-level membership.

  In other words, this person can have a trainer every time he comes to the club for only $89 per month (price for a smaller market) and the membership to the club is included. This sounds cheap, but the important points to remember is that the club is using one trainer to service 12 people and that if people attend the club at least eight times or more a month, they will get better results, leading to the person staying longer and paying longer.

  Group personal training, or the group experience, is not group exercise (aerobics). This particular experience is based upon the members having access to a structured, challenging program on an unlimited basis each month. The trainer/coach, in this situation, does not stop the group to teach. Everyone who is in this experience should be cleared in the basics, such as a kettlebell swing or the use of suspension training. This group experience is loud, challenging, and doesn't stop the energy to teach anyone something new. If you are in this, you are working hard. A good coach will probably use two-minute time segments, coupled with one-minute rest periods, to allow him to mix the levels of the participants. Time is a much more efficient way to run these sessions, as opposed to simply using repetitions. In this case, you can easily change a new person's intensity and load to match his level of fitness and experience and still keep him working with a better-conditioned person who might go at a higher weight for a full two minutes.

- *$129 a month for small group/semi-private training* done in groups of two to six. This is a more structured offering for small groups. This is also a teaching format and the coach would use a workout of the day centered on general athletic conditioning to keep his group focused. The club would offer about 20 to 30 slots a week and the clients could come as many times as they like (unlimited access). The price also includes access to the group experience as well as unlimited access to the club, too.

- *$300 a month for limited one-on-one.* You will still have one-on-one in this model, but you should price it with the assumption that you are targeting only about 10 percent or less of your clients for this product. In this $300-per-month example, the client would get four sessions per month ($75 per session) to be used any time during the month, access to the group options, and unlimited use of the club.

  The key is that the commitment for the member is $300 a month for 12 months instead of just buying a package or session. As noted elsewhere, most club owners establish a higher price for training but because they can't sell enough of it at the higher price, they then start discounting for packages. So, instead of $75 an hour, the club might sell five sessions at $250 equaling 10 sessions at $40 each, effectively dropping their return per session to only $40.

  In this model, once you establish the real personal training rate for your club, which is probably about $50 per hour on a national basis, you can then up the price slightly and use that rate as "the" rate, using it as the basis for all one-on-one training. In other words, you don't have to worry about lowering the price to attract more training clients since you have other lower options available that let the client pay less but share the cost of the trainer.

- *$899 to $1,699 for unlimited one-on-one training.* We sometimes forget who the elite clients really are in the clubs, and keep in mind that elite clients exist in mainstream facilities but we seldom have anything of value to sell them. In other words, we don't have enough cool stuff for them to buy.

  In this model, the client gets everything. This price, which is dependent on where in the country you are operating, might range from $899 a month for unlimited training up to $1,699 in this example or up to $2,500 a month and higher if you are in a major metro area.

  These memberships would include everything the client needs to be successful including supplements, powders, water each visit in the club, a recovery shake, and anything else he needs or wants. Build it all in and hope he trains at least 10 times or more a month (retention, retention, retention).

  Clients in this category do not like to be nickel-and-dimed with dozens of small extra charges. Include it all, including assessments and testing, and then work on total support for this client.

The key to remember is that all these prices are layered on top of a low entry price, allowing the club to attract a wide range of members and then placing as many members as possible into a higher priced position. You may show $19 as your base price, but your real average might be much higher.

For example, let's say a mainstream club has a base price of $19 and sells the following seven memberships—all based upon 12-month EFT agreements—on a Monday:

- $19 per month
- $19 per month
- $89 per month
- $300 per month
- $19 per month
- $19 per month
- $19 per month

Do not worry about what the club got up front from each member. Assume it is nothing more than a $69 membership fee. The real point is that the club owner is showing just $19 to get into the club, but he is seeking a higher EFT return per member. What is its real average EFT for the day?

The total of the seven payments is $484. Divide this total by seven and you get a $69 per membership EFT average. In other words, the club can use $19 as the introductory level to admittance, but in reality is generating an actual $69 per membership EFT due to the layered pricing system. This gives this owner a huge advantage over a competitor that is merely chasing volume using $19 and has only $5,000 or so a month from traditional training.

The $49 and higher business model

This model emulates more of the traditional health club model that has been in use for decades. Despite the price, however, this club owner is still chasing volume, but he is doing it at a higher price level. Everyone claims to be different who is in this game, but, in reality, most of the businesses in this class are just expanded versions of what was built all over the world in the 1990s.

iStockphoto/Thinkstock

If you are interested in this type of club, you need to move the business model to another level. If this model is going to work in today's market, it has to be a training-centric club, meaning that you are still trying to develop your training receivable base to a point that it can surpass your membership base. It has been said several times in this book, but, again, you can't just make it on membership volume anymore, especially in this class where the guy down the street is offering the same basic concept for a lot less money. If you pursue a dual income stream, based upon membership as one track and training revenue as the other, with both given equal importance, then this model will work.

This is, by the way, the club that is usually hurt by the introduction of a low-priced club into the marketplace since, in reality, the owner of this business model is doing nothing more than renting treadmills at a higher price. The club may be bigger, brighter, and more up-to-date, but if it has not established an intense training program that gets the maximum members maximum results, then the member will leave quickly in pursuit of the lower price. If you think about it, why would a client that does nothing but use a treadmill for $49 a month not leave for a club down the street that offers the same brand of treadmill at only $19 a month if the client has no other relationship with the business?

If you are going to be a club in this category, you have to change your model dramatically from the 1995 era when this big box craze really went wild. In those days, you could compete in this price range with limited services because almost every competitor was in the same category as you.

Everyone from that era mostly had two or three group rooms, decent locker rooms, a lot of equipment in a large area, and a few amenities such as tanning. Every club in the market was different, but every club was really the same in that prices were comparable and always within about $10 of each other; the equipment was mostly from the same few manufacturers, and the winner in the market was determined by who was the best operator or who had the best location.

During the next decade, you will see fewer of these built due to the start-up cost and due to the expected return on investment. These are big money to build and can often cost over $2,000,000 in rental space and $4,000,000 and higher as a stand-alone, with some of the more extensive facilities in the 100,000-square-foot range starting in the $20,000,000 to $40,000,000 area. The ones that will be developed will most likely have a higher price for a membership and be more of an elite, full-service club that is seeking a stronger differentiation from the low-priced players.

In summary, your price determines your business model. There is no such thing as building a perfect club and then setting a price to match the market. Set your price first that fits you and the market, and then build your concept around that price. Low-priced clubs in the $9 range are limited-service volume clubs. Clubs priced in the $19 range, and especially those being built currently, are becoming more full-serviced but are using a layered pricing system to drive up the return per member. The new generation of higher-priced clubs will have to be beyond full-service with all the amenities seeking differentiation in the market and separation from the low-priced players.

Specialty facilities built for niches have been discussed elsewhere in this book. The pricing structures do work for those if you master the basic elements first. For example, if you open a women's-only facility at 12,000 square feet, then the price structure of either the $19/$39 model works, or if you are in the right area, the $49 and higher full-service model might be for you.

Markets with competitors using open-ended memberships

If you are in an area that has a lot of competitors using the open-ended, month-to-month, pay-as-you-go option, you may need to show one as well. This membership offering should be priced at least $8 to $10 higher than your regular annual membership. It may seem like you will get less from your annuals, but you will actually collect more money from more members over time due to the lower loss rates using annual memberships as compared to the losses associated with open-ended memberships. For example:

$69 membership fee—$69 per month open-ended, pay-as-you-go

or

$69 membership fee—$59 a month for 12 months

It Is not necessary for training facilities to adapt this system, but most mainstream clubs will benefit from this idea in competitive markets. This was discussed previously, but it is a key core concept and needs to be understood in relationship to your other memberships offerings.

Price-sensitive markets

If you are in a price-sensitive market, or in a market that is rapidly becoming one, you might show a lower price for a longer commitment to stay competitive without destroying your higher pricing model. This is especially true for those owners who have been in the business for years but who now need to adjust their price to be more competitive. For example:

$69 membership fee—$59 a month for 12 months

or

$69 membership fee—$49 a month for 18 months
(often called a value membership)

The 18-month membership is a better choice in most markets than the 24-month membership because the 18-month tool has much lower loss rates. The 18-month option usually has loss rates that emulate the 12-month membership, or about 1 percent per month, while the 24-month will often have much higher loss rates in the 3 to 4 percent per month range and, in many cases, as high as 5 to 7 percent.

Multiple people joining your facility

The proper term for two people joining your club together is not "couple rate." The correct term that avoids discrimination is "two people living at the same address." If you offer this type of membership, don't discount severely for two people joining at the same time. A good model is discounting only $5 or so for the second person or no more than 10 percent if you would rather think in those terms. You are also better off writing up two separate memberships and getting each individual's personal financial information dealing with the fact up front that over half of your members will get a divorce anyway. Many people keep their own accounts in a relationship and you will collect more money over time by getting separate memberships at the point of sale.

It is important to note that the old-style operators always insisted on verifying the relationship. For instance, if the club offered a couple's rate, many owners from the past would insist on proving, either by checking last names, or other archaic methods of embarrassing the people in front of you such as looking for wedding rings.

If you offer a discount for two people at the same address, do not waste the energy trying to verify or put your staff in the position that they are forced to discriminate. If two people of any combination of ages, color, or sexual orientation represent themselves for a product you are offering, accept them at their word. You do not want to put your young staff into the situation where they have to be the membership police and ask far too personal questions when not needed. This is a bad situation for the staff, and it is also a form of discrimination since these questions are usually asked to exclude people from a service that you sold to others. If this is an issue for you, check with your attorney and he can help you apply the rules as they exist in your business.

This is a nonexistent issue for training clubs. There should be no valid reason for discounting for a family member in a training club. For example, if a guy becomes a client, why would you feel obligated to discount for his significant other? While the case can be made for not discounting—simply because the facilities are usually smaller and lowering your return-per-member doesn't make sense when you have limited clients and limited space—most of you will do it anyway because the other clubs in the area do it. If this is the case, do not discount more than 10 percent for the second person at the same address.

Short-term memberships (good for up to three months)

Avoid junk memberships or too many options when you own and operate a mainstream fitness facility. The short-term membership combines many of the shorter options clubs tend to develop over time in reaction to the constant exceptions members present through the years. It seems that most owners, over time, just keep adding more options to cover every exception that has ever arisen since they opened the club. For example, an owner has a person who says he is in town for only a month because he is a consultant working at a local company. The club works out a special membership for the guy—a one-month, paid-in-full membership—and that new membership gets added to the pricing sheet. Owners keep adding but never subtract from the list, and over time it just keeps getting longer and longer with a listing for every person who has ever walked into the club.

Keep your list short and tight. The choices here cover most every person through the door. In the previous example, the guy could have purchased a short-term membership, paid a daily fee each time he came to the club, or purchased a punch card. Avoid adding options to fit the individual in order to keep it simple for the sales team.

The short-term membership should be good for up to three months, and has to be paid for all at once. If the consumer bought four of them (totaling one year), he should end up paying approximately $200 more than your regular membership. For example, you could use the following pricing structure:

- Standard membership: $69 + ($59 x 12) = $777
- $777 + $200 = $977
- $977 ÷ 4 = $244 (round up to $249) for a three-month membership

Do not present this as a three-month membership but use the term, "short-term." Do you have a one-month membership? Why yes we do; it is called a short-term membership and it is good for up to three months. This short-term option should allow you to eliminate many of the "garbage" memberships most clubs end up creating out of the fear of losing a person.

Daily fees

Your daily drop-in fee should be at least $15 to $20 in most markets and higher where you can get it. Create a high daily fee, because you want to be able to offer a member's guest a deal, which is usually half the daily fee. If you don't have this option in place, the members often expect you to let their guests in for free. This scenario allows you to still get paid, but the member and his guest are both happy as well, thinking they received a deal to the club. For example, if your daily fee is $15, the member's guest would pay $7.50.

If you have a large percentage of transient guests, such as professionals visiting the area for short periods of time, consider a punch card. It is an old tool, but it is still effective if used in the right markets. For example, you can offer a punch card at a price of 10 visits for $99 to $120 (based upon a daily fee of $15). Put a two-month expiration on these cards if your state allows.

VIP and other membership options

If you live in a resort area, don't cheapen the club by offering a week's membership at a giveaway price. A better way to solve the need for a membership for the tourists is to create the VIP week and offer a T-shirt, a full seven days of workouts, a few bottles of water, and maybe some tanning in a package. Price this package at approximately $69 to $129 for the week, depending upon the market, but don't forget, if you're on vacation, it's all about bringing home the cool shirt.

Many clubs, especially those that are catering to an upscale or older market, are doing away with discounting for older members. Keep in mind that as the population continues to age, at some point most of your members would qualify for the senior discount. Consider going without this discount if you can. If you feel you must do this, keep the discount reasonable and within the 10-percent limit.

Most clubs are also moving away from discounting for cash. Your receivable base is the club's most important asset and you want to do everything you can to grow it as large and as strong as possible. The more effective way to offer a paid-in-full incentive to a potential member who asks is to enhance rather than discount. You can do this by adding several months to the membership (14 for the price of 12 for example) instead of cutting the cost. The club still gets full price, but most importantly, all the members are paying the same price, which protects your integrity in the market.

Sample Price Structure for a Mainstream Fitness Facility

- Basic membership option for an individual:
  - ✓ $69–$59 x 12 months (EFT/direct payment from the member's checking/savings account or from his credit card)
  - ✓ $69–$64 x 12 months (coupon similar to his house payment/check system where he writes a check manually each month)
- If you have strong open-ended competition, add this layer:
  - ✓ $69–$69 per month, open-ended, pay-as-you-go membership
- If you have strong, low-priced competition and have been established at a higher price for any length of time, add this layer:
  - ✓ $69–$49 x 18 months
- Second person at same household:
  - ✓ $89–$99 x 12 (split into two contracts if possible)
- Paid-in-full membership option (this is usually not presented but is available if the client requests it):
  - ✓ Add two months to the membership length but don't discount the price of the membership for cash
- Short-term membership (good for up to three months):
  - ✓ $249 (do not finance/this membership is paid all at once)
- Daily fees:
  - ✓ $15 to $20 per daily visit and as high as $30 in metro areas
- Member/guest:
  - ✓ Half of the daily fee for a member's guest who is not qualified for a trial membership or other current marketing
- Punch cards:
  - ✓ 10 visits at $99 to $120 (with a two-month expiration date)
- VIP week (for use in tourist areas or heavy transit markets):
  - ✓ One full week at $69 to $99, including a T-shirt and assorted stuff

The Key Concept in This Chapter

Your receivable base is everything in your new business. As you conceptualize your business, always start with the financial foundation, which is how the member pays, how much he pays, and who collects the money each month. If you get these things right, you can make a lot of mistakes and stay in business. Get these things wrong and you will find that it is hard to sell your way out of trouble.

Most club owners also make the initial mistake of trying to offer membership options that please everyone, which is a bad habit to get into if you want to be profitable. Remember the old adage:

- Rule #1: The customer is always right.
- Rule #2: See Rule #1.

What most people don't know is that the guy who wrote this adage went out of business about 20 minutes after he hung it on the wall. The customer is right many times, especially when the club team makes a mistake, such as incorrect billing or missed appointments, which the club has to correct immediately.

But the member/customer is also wrong in many cases, and he often complains simply because he wants to work the system and take advantage of the club. Pricing is the area where club owners get worked the hardest and the pressure is to do whatever it takes to get someone into the system. But if an exception for one person is not offered to everyone, then your reputation and integrity are damaged and that will cost you a lot more money in the future than holding the line with members who want memberships designed just for them and won't join unless they get that special deal.

Successful pricing and membership collection should be fair to both sides. The members should have a number of membership options offered fairly to everyone and the club should have a system in place that allows it to collect the most money from the most members that is legally and ethically possible. If both sides win, then the business will endure and the club owner will make the most money he can in that market.

STAFFING

IT Stock

Chapter Nine

Staffing will be the hardest issue you deal with in your new fitness career and your success will be defined in the future by your ability to find, develop, and motivate your staff to drive revenue in your business and to provide legendary customer service.

When you first open your new business, you will have to build systems that can be carried out by a variety of people as your staff comes and goes through the first year. Some people will stick with you and be loyal over time, while others will simply pass through the business and end up leaving you at what seems like all the worst times.

It is almost a rite of passage in the business, and practically guaranteed, that the first person you lose will be your morning person, who just fails to show up one morning, and you find out brutally due to an irate member calling your cell at 4:30 a.m. while you are still asleep because you didn't get home from the club last night until after 11:00. It's the law in small business that most lessons are gifted to new owners the hard way and your introduction to staffing is definitely coming your way.

Building Systems From the Start

Systems can be defined as set procedures that are available in writing for each employee to learn and follow so that he can do any job required of him in your new business. When you hire someone new, all training is done through the set procedures for the area of the club where that person will work.

Your training will be easier, and you will make more money, if you develop a procedure manual for your business before you even open. Procedure manuals are simple notebooks that have each action an employee would do in his department clearly explained in less than two pages.

Sample pages for your manual might include:
- How to fill out a membership agreement correctly, with a sample of one that is well done and one that might show common errors circled in red
- How to open the club, defined in clear, simple-to-follow steps
- How to close the club at the end of the day
- How to troubleshoot the front-counter computers
- How to answer the phone, including sample scripts for everything from taking a membership inquiry to how to screen calls for the owner

Each one of these procedures should be in defined and written in the simplest and most straightforward of terms. For example, consider a situation in which you are not at the club and the front-counter computer isn't working. The employee would grab the manual, turn to the troubleshooting computer page, and read the following:
- Is the computer plugged in? Yes or no?
- Is the computer turned on? Yes or no?
- Are other things that are plugged in on the counter also not working?

- If other things are not working, go to the breaker box, which is located in the hall closet and marked "Breaker Box" in large letters on the front.
- Find the switch marked "Front Counter"
- Flip the switch back and forth to reset.

Do you have to be this anal-retentive with your employees? Come on, you say, how slow can these people really be? Most of them are not slow and, in fact, most of them are good people trying to do the right thing—if they just know what the right thing to do at the right time is. They are not you, they work for you, and to make sure good people can do a good job, you should clearly define how to do things the staff might not have experience with in their personal lives. And to verify if this is necessary, ask any long-term fitness business owner how much money he has spent on electricians who show up for a $150 fee simply to end up flipping a switch because the staff didn't know to try that solution. "Assume the best, but plan for the worst" works here too, as it does in any aspect of your business.

Developing procedure manuals early in the process makes your staff training much easier. You simply turn to the section for the department the person is working in and go through all of the key procedures he might encounter as the fundamental skills he needs to master for that position. In the training department, for example, a new trainer might spend the first few hours of the first day of training going through pages covering the following topics:

- Your (i.e., the club's) training philosophy
- What is expected of a trainer as part of his day-to-day job
- Dress codes for trainers
- How to meet, greet, and handle a client
- Selling a member on more sessions
- The steps of doing an assessment/first visit for a potential training client
- Meeting new members in the club

Each one of these topics could be covered in less than a page. The most important thing, however, is that everyone who starts in that department begins with the same basic knowledge, understands the fundamentals of that job, and knows where to look first if they have any questions. Your staff will perform much more efficiently if they share a base knowledge of the basic aspects of the job.

Establishing a Common Sales Language

It is very important to have all of your employees explaining everything in your business the same way each and every time. When you first open, things will be wild, but you want to be sure that every new member hears the same information about your offerings, services, and programming.

The fitness business has too many moving parts and it takes a build-up time for most employees to understand how everything works in the club. For example, how would a new employee working the front counter explain training to a new member? Or how would a salesperson who just does cardio explain training if she has never even worked with a trainer?

If we can't explain it, or don't do it, we can't sell it to anyone. Much of inside sales takes place through the simple method of a member quietly asking an employee about a program. It is not brochures or handouts that get someone excited; it is usually an employee telling the member how good the training is and who does it in the club.

Keeping this in mind, understand that staff left to their own devices will answer a question with whatever they think might be right, and their reply may be based not upon reality or what you hope they will say to properly explain the program, but on what their interpretation of the program or service is at the moment. Eliminate random answers by teaching the staff exactly what you want them to say when asked about any program or service. For example, whether someone asks a new counter person or a seasoned salesperson about training, both should be able to explain training according to a set script that simply describes what it is and who should do it. As a side note, all full-time key employees, such as members of the sales team, should be given a certain amount of time with a trainer as part of their job so they can reference their personal experience rather than stating, "No, I have never used a trainer, although I have been here three years." Remember the old adage: you can't sell the Ferrari if you haven't driven the Ferrari.

A simple tool to help employees master a common sales language from the start is the 4 x 5 card stack. This low-tech training tool consists of nothing more than a stack of index cards. On the front of each card is just one service, product, class, or customer-service issue. On the back are three benefits or responses necessary to explain the item on the front. For example:

[Front]

Cycle classes

[Back]

- **Low-impact cardio**
- **All the energy, excitement, and craziness of being in a small group**
- **Everyone can ride at his own level and still get the best cardio workout in the club**

Each employee would start with a stack of these cards the day they are hired. If you have a few minutes to train someone, just grab their cards and read the front of one and test that person on their knowledge of the back. This technique, usually referred to as spot training because it is done informally on the spot, allows you to coach as well if the new hire doesn't understand that product or service. Most of these spot training segments can be done in 10 minutes or less during the slower times of day.

Another benefit for the owner or manager is that spot training allows you to get a sense as to how the employee is thinking and handling the job. For example, if your new front counter hire has been there for several months and is still struggling with the cards, you now have a solid idea of how worthless this person might be and it also might indicate that it is time to send her home and try again.

When you first open the club, you might have a small stack of 30 or so cards, but as you progress through your first 90 days, keep adding to everyone's pile, striving to cover all products and services the club offers. It is important to develop a consistent sales talk in the club, as inconsistent messages are the easiest way to irritate your members when it comes to customer service. When members ask, they want to know right then and they do not tolerate employees that work in a business but don't really know anything about what is going on there.

Building a Team

At some point, if you want to become financially successful, and perhaps see your kids grow up before they leave home for college, you have to develop a team that can take responsibility for their own areas of the business, allowing you to spend more time working on the business rather than being trapped in it.

Most new owners, however, are slow to do this because they spend far too much time trying to do everything themselves. Hey, why spend an hour teaching a new person how to do something when I can do it myself in five minutes? The reality is that you will run out of "doing it myself" time before you run out of things that need to get done in the business. If you don't develop a staff, you will be forever trapped, doing nothing but a series of small, meaningless tasks all day.

If you have a small club, you will obviously end up carrying much more of the load yourself. As your club grows in size, your chances for success will be better if you can build a team of people who are responsible for generating revenue in the key areas of the club such as sales and training. You will make more money, and more quickly in this business, if you develop dedicated positions focused on creating revenue in their specific areas.

For example, one of the common mistakes a new owner usually makes is not having dedicated sales people for the membership and training departments. Both of these areas, depending on the size of the club, need separate sales teams instead of trying to use counter people to sell along with the other stuff they do everyday such as making smoothies, checking people into the club, and handling the phones.

A variety of management models are seen in the club business, but most fall into one of three classifications. The only one that will get you to the highest level of financial success, though, is the third one. Study these models carefully with the thought of avoiding the traps and try to build that production-based team as early as you can in your business.

The working *in* your business, not *on* your business model (single line business model)

TTTTTTOTTTTT

O = owner   T = team members and other staff

In this first model, the owner simply fills a routine job in his own club. This model is most common among trainers, who are better known as technicians because most are in the business because they enjoy working directly with clients. A trainer might start off with a small club where he trains almost every client, and, at some point, he then decides that his first club is just too small so he decides to build something larger, where he still trains most of the clients, but now in a larger space.

The model does have a direct application for mainstream fitness too. Many new owners have worked in other clubs, or at least should have at some point, and when they open their own model, they have a sense of their past job but don't really know much about moving from an employee to a manager or owner. These new owners are simply more comfortable doing what they know rather than adjusting to what they should be doing, which is learning to drive revenue in their new business with a team.

The least effective thing you can do in your own club is train members. You should manage your team with the goal of creating new revenue, you sell memberships, you develop staff, you greet people at the desk, and you take care of customer service, but you don't need to be training clients, which is time-consuming and has the least financial impact upon the business.

Most owners who are stuck in this model all say the same thing: "I am the best trainer and the members will all leave if I don't train them." Yes, you might lose a few when you transition away from being a trainer in your own business, but over time your business will grow if you spend those hours training the other trainers and the rest of your staff. The important consideration is that if you are a new owner, you should never get trapped into this situation anyway. You can't manage a team and grow your business if all you do is train a few clients hour after hour each day.

The Batman and Robin sidekick model

O (Batman)

S (Robin)

TTTTTTTTTTTTTTTT

O = owner   S = sidekick (your go-to person)   T = team members

In this second model, the owner still does most of the work, and then when he gets to the point where he can't get everything done, he hires a sidekick (hence, the Batman and Robin analogy) to do all the tasks that he doesn't want to do anymore. The limitation of this model is that you can never grow the business past your personal workload capacity.

Batman is you and Robin becomes the person who does nothing but handle all the day-to-day crap you can't or won't do yourself. Once you tap out at about 55 hours per week, you get yourself a Robin, who becomes your go-to person handling your overload. Another way to look at this model, which is the most common in the fitness industry, is that you simply try to clone yourself in the hopes that two of you can be enough to run the business.

Notice that in this model, every employee answers directly to the owner, which means that no one does anything unless you tell him what to do. There is no personal responsibility in this model because everything has to flow through the owner, who usually won't let anything happen without him being directly involved. The other big issue is what happens when Robin quits? You don't have systems in this model; you have simply tried to split yourself into two people who still make every decision and try to do most of the real business in the club.

The preferred and most financially successful model

O

M   M   M

TTTT   TTTT   TTTT

O = owner
M = managers (heads of moneymaking departments in the business)
T = team members

The preferred model is centered on hiring people who are in charge of the key revenue areas in the club and then spending the day working with them and helping them reach their numbers with their teams. In this model, the owner oversees the managers, who oversee the team members.

This is the most effective model because the owner, along with his managers, can stay focused on creating revenue. Their teams exist because each key moneymaking area in the club is separated and then covered with a dedicated team that is guided by a manager.

For example, in a mainstream business, you might have a dedicated sales manager and team, a lead trainer and team, a secondary sales team comprised of a trainer who can sell and who does nothing but create training revenue, and perhaps a front counter manager and team. Teams are created where the revenue occurs.

Keep in mind one of the most important rules in small business: There is no production without individual accountability. This rule is addressed several times in this book because it is important to understand that unless you have a dedicated person with sole responsibility for an area of production, such as sales or training, there will be no production.

Staffs that wear multiple hats trying to multitask always have the wrong hat on at the time you need to make money. For instance, you wonder why sales are bad and your team says they are too busy running the front desk or training people (the other hats they wear besides sales) and therefore, nothing gets done because no one is responsible. Another way to describe this rule is that when everyone has responsibility, no one takes responsibility.

In the training world, the first hire you almost always have to make is to get a dedicated salesperson who does nothing but take care of the acquisition of new members into the business. Most trainers who open their new business worry too much about getting another trainer, which you might need, but they don't worry enough about who is going to get new clients each month to feed the business.

This model still works in a training club, but you will simply have fewer departments to manage, and make sure acquisition is the first department you create. Another way to look at this is that if a trainer opens a 3,000-square-foot club, the only other employee in the business when he opens might be a salesperson in charge of new client acquisition. The old sales approach, where you shoot them and I skin them, seems to work in this case when you have a small business just starting out and you are wondering who to hire first.

The Key Positions in Your New Business

When you build your new management structure, start with the key areas of revenue and get someone in charge of those areas. Small clubs will have a smaller version of this system, but you must have someone take individual responsibility for the key areas of any business of any size.

A common mistake in most clubs is that too many people are on the operations side and not enough people are given the accountability and responsibility for production, or the creation of new revenue. In the fitness business, 95 percent of the job is production and 5 percent is operations. In other words, the main role for most staff in a gym business is to sell somebody something every day. You don't need many people to manage the details of the business if you don't have anyone out there making fresh money every day. Make it first and you can sit up in your underwear in the middle of the night counting it.

The following jobs are the key roles in most clubs. Note that the major areas where you will make money, such as sales, training, and nutrition, all have dedicated people who are responsible for the total production of that department. It does not matter how big your business is, or how small, you will have to have some variation of this model at some point to be successful.

Manager
(bottom-line responsibility, not just a sales guy with a cool title)

The manager, who works 45 to 50 hours per week, has two primary focuses. He handles the operational part of the business, such as budgeting, staffing,

Chris Clinton

and member service while also supervising and participating in the production side of the business, which is defined as creating fresh revenue on a daily basis. Most importantly, the manager is responsible for the club's total revenues.

The manager's role in operations is as follows:
- Hiring, developing, coaching, and firing staff
- Daily reporting and number analysis
- Advertising
- Budgeting (planning budgets and keeping the club within a set budget each month)
- Working the club during prime revenue hours (you do not make money going home at 6:00 p.m. on a Monday no matter what club you own or work at)
- Creating and maintaining a customer service program in the business with the goal of increasing member retention

Job Descriptions: Why and How to Use Them

Note: The following text is excerpted from an IHRSA publication

Generally, U.S. federal law does not require written job descriptions. However, these documents can be useful to employers, employees, and job applicants with respect to:

- Recruiting, interviewing, and selecting employees
- Training and orienting new employees
- Establishing performance requirements
- Evaluating the performance of employees
- Making decisions about compensation and/or job restructuring
- Checking for compliance with legal requirements related to equal opportunity, equal pay, overtime eligibility, etc.
- Providing proof of the essential functions of a job, for purposes of the Americans with Disabilities Act (ADA)
- Providing evidence that practices are fair, should an owner need to defend them in court

Components of effective job descriptions

Job descriptions document an employee's major functions or duties, responsibilities, and/or other critical features, such as skill, effort, and working conditions. Key components include:

- Title of the position
- Department
- Reports to (to whom the person directly reports)
- Overall responsibility
- Key areas of responsibility, with approximate percentage of time spent on each area (using action verbs when possible)
- Consults with (those people with whom the person works on a regular basis)
- Terms of employment (full-time, part-time, seasonal, etc.)
- Qualifications (educational, work experience, etc.)
- Disclaimers (to remind readers that the job description is not meant to be all-inclusive, that the job itself is subject to change, and that the document does not constitute an employment contract.) For example: "Nothing in this job description restricts management's right to assign or reassign duties and responsibilities to this job at any time. This job description does not constitute a written or implied contract of employment."

Note: This tip is intended to provide general information, and does not constitute legal advice.

Essential functions

Language in job descriptions should effectively establish the nature and importance of essential functions without being prejudicial to individuals with disabilities. Focus on essential functions in terms of what they actually require, not simply the ways in which they have customarily been performed. Give some notion of frequency, intensity, and/or duration (to help establish the level of the work demand). For example, the word "typically" can be used to acknowledge the possibility that alternate manners of performance of a function may be reasonable, as determined on a case-by-case basis.

For example, the essential functions may be written as follows:

- Frequently lifts, carries, or otherwise moves and positions objects weighing up to 50 pounds when stocking the supply room and setting up equipment
- Typically bends, stoops, and crouches on a regular basis to adjust settings on equipment

Clauses such as "performs other duties as assigned" are generally not suitable for covering essential functions. If a task is essential, it should be described.

Avoiding legal pitfalls

Job descriptions are generally regarded as legal documents. They have the potential to become the subject of contention, including grievances or litigation. It is critical that accuracy be maintained. Designate one party (for example, the supervisor or human resources director) as having primary responsibility for keeping job descriptions current, and have a plan for reviewing them on a regular basis.

Avoid any references in job descriptions to race, color, religion, age, sex, national origin or nationality, or physical or mental disability. Finally, to avoid claims of age discrimination, experience should not include an upper limit.

The manager's role in production is as follows:

- Selling memberships
  - ✓ The manager would do about 50 percent of all sales in clubs with fewer than 600 members.
  - ✓ The manager would do about 10 to 20 percent of all sales in larger clubs.
  - ✓ The manager would create and manage two sales teams in most mainstream clubs. The first team would be dedicated to the acquisition of new members and the second would be dedicated to creating long-term training revenue.
- Driving the revenues through action plans that are used to keep the managers and key players focused on production each day
- Budgeting and planning events
- Driving the revenues through sales and promotion of the club's profit centers such as weight management, smoothie bar, or massage

Sales manager

This person, who normally works 45 to 50 hours per week, has one function: Get the total number of membership sales needed each month. Even small training centers and small women's-only clubs have to have one person in charge of member acquisition. If your sales come together, the rest of the club will have a better chance of succeeding.

Not having a dedicated acquisition person is perhaps one of the biggest mistakes a new club owner makes, especially if they come from a training or service background. Most newbies just think prospective clients sort of turn themselves in each month in sufficient numbers. I don't advocate an old-style pressure system but you do have to have someone trained in presenting the business properly, asking for money (becoming a member), following up, and handling guests. Many potential members would like to become guests but they need guidance and education to make that happen, which is where your dedicated and professional acquisition person comes into play.

The sales manager should:

- Sell between 40 and 50 percent of the club's sales in a typical mainstream business and almost all the sales in a smaller business
- Provide daily training for the sales team and hold the daily sales and training meeting
- Train the entire staff, meaning counter people, janitors, and anyone else who works in the business, at least once a month on why and how we sell and the role all of the team members play in sales
- Manage the club's electronic marketing and all follow-up of the club's prospective members
- Have total responsibility for hitting the projected sales number for the month

The training department sales manager

Most clubs do not have this person in the system and this is a job seldom seen in mainstream fitness, but in many ways, this is the most important job in the club.

Most clubs that are based upon the traditional health club model of the 1990s use a sales manager and team that chase new sales each month. The weakness is that this team also ends up attempting to sell training, which, in reality, few sales people are really capable of selling training effectively. Selling training on a large scale involves the ability to explain a product that is fairly complicated while applying it to someone who has unique issues and needs.

Training, due to the emphasis put on just selling one-on-one by most club owners, is a hard sell in many ways. For most consumers, one-on-one training is either too expensive, too boring, or too elitist; and it can simply be a difficult sell because few who haven't had a lot of previous experience actually understand what a trainer can really do for them.

Club Business International, the IHRSA publication, cited a survey stating that 64 percent of the people who visit a fitness business would prefer to be toured by a trainer and not a salesperson. You can extrapolate a lot from this number, but the key takeaway is that selling training in your business would be more effective if you had a dedicated team to get someone signed up as a member and a secondary team that does nothing but sell training.

The goal, by splitting your team, is to build a training receivable base that is equal to or greater than your membership base, or in other words, putting the same emphasis into selling training as a receivable as you do into selling memberships.

The person who would lead this department should be a trainer/salesperson who is not afraid of the sales process or of asking for money. His primary job is to create revenue by getting new members into one of the layered training programs that was discussed in Chapter 8, although this tool is also great for selling one-on-one as well if needed.

The primary tool used to sell by this secondary sales team is the assessment. The assessment is a highly structured encounter between the potential client and the trainer/salesperson. The goal of the assessment is to properly place the person into the right training tool for them.

It is important to note that the assessment is a tool to start a conversation and get the person involved in training while demonstrating leadership. It is not a tool used to make someone feel bad about their current condition, such as doing a body fat assessment, during their initial visit. Save the pure assessment tools to use to establish a baseline once the client actually gets started in a program.

The assessment should look something like this (see Chapter 8 for more information and details):

- Each assessment should take about an hour to an hour and a half per person.
- The goal is to educate the client and inspire while demonstrating leadership. It is not to design a program for the person.
- Start with a 10-minute meet and greet to get to know the client. The purpose is to determine the client's goal, their time frame to accomplish that goal, and the days per week they can commit to accomplishing that goal.
- Use tools, such as a dynamic warm-up, that they should be using in other activities in the club.
- At the end of the assessment, the trainer/salesperson should apply what he has learned from the assessment to properly place the person into one of the layered training offerings.
- The goal for this team member is to close at least 33 percent of everyone he assesses into a higher-priced program. The ultimate goal is for the total receivable base in the training department to surpass the total receivable base in the membership department within one year.

Potential members will take general information about memberships and how the club works from a club salesperson but are less likely to take training information from a salesperson who is not a trainer or can't apply the many nuances of training to an individual. Separating the membership sales team from the training sales team allows you to develop dual income streams that help protect your business in competitive markets while maximizing your potential revenue.

Hemera/Thinkstock

Lead counter person

The lead counter person works 32 to 45 hours per week and is in many ways the most important person in the club, since he is your lead person at the front-counter area during the business's prime time. The importance of this person derives from the fact that this team member, in many ways, becomes the image of your club over time. Potential members coming through the door will often judge the club by the strength of the person behind that counter, and we also forget how important this person becomes to our regular members who expect to be welcomed and known at "their" club. This person also supervises the rest of the front-desk personnel, as well as drives the club's profit centers, including drinks, shakes, and supplement sales, which might be housed in the front-counter area.

The lead counter person should:

- Train and supervise all counter people as well as handle front-counter scheduling
- Be in the club during prime time Monday through Thursday night, because the members seek consistency and like to see a familiar face each day (It is an important side note to remember that constant change over in the service areas, or staffing your front counter with young, inexperienced, and ineffective people (often hired because they are young and dumb and will work cheap) sends a message to your clients that you are not running a good business that is likely to stay around long. In other words, if you can't keep front counter staff, why do you think you can keep members?)
- Meet, greet, and handle all potential members during prime time, setting a strong first impression for the club
- Assist in the promotion and revenue production of the club's profit centers during his shift

Special note for training clubs: Once a training club gets its client list up to about 100, it is time to start hiring at least a part-time person to work Monday through Thursday nights greeting clients, handling problems, and assisting with new client acquisition. Once your business becomes a "real" business, you also have to start answering the phone live and avoid voice mail or answering machines.

Weekend supervisor

This entry-level management job, which requires about 45 hours of work per week, allows the club to have a management-team member on duty during the prime production hours on Saturday morning. This person's schedule could be structured in several different ways over a three- or four-day workweek, depending on her other duties in the business, but her most important function is to generate revenue during the prime Saturday morning production hours.

The weekend supervisor should:

- Open and close the club on Saturdays
- Close the club on Sundays

- Be off every fifth weekend so she may have somewhat of a life
- Be in charge of the weekend production, including selling memberships and promoting profit centers. She can also be trained to sell training if she has a training background.
- Work the rest of her hours in the club early in the week as a regular staff person. This job still requires two to three days off per week as any regular employee would get.

Lead nutrition/weight management professional

This person, who works between 32 and 45 hours per week, is the liaison between your club and your nutrition/weight-loss management company. This person is also a trainer who specializes in weight management and who is passionate about helping members get their best results. This profit center is so important that one person from the training department should be dedicated to driving the revenues from this area.

The nutrition professional should:
- Work with your weight-loss management company to drive the revenues from this area and master all software and support materials needed to create revenue at the club level
- Educate the members and promote supplements in the club, resulting in the creation of ongoing revenue
- Educate and train the training staff on supplements and assist in their supplement sales

This job is becoming more important in the club business. In the past, most club owners have simply left this as something a trainer might recommend on a clipboard as part of a training session without the ability to generate any additional revenue.

In today's market, especially with the national awareness of obesity and the constant stream of weight loss articles in all the major media, many more members than ever are aware that they need weight management coaching. This should be offered on a per-hour basis as well as combined into the layered training programs. It is also important to offer every new member free online weight management support, which should be available through your chosen weight management company, as part of their membership. This gives the member added value and will help sell more weight management programs over time.

Lead conditioning professional/lead trainer (formerly called the head trainer)

This person, who works 32 to 50 hours per week, is responsible, along with the trainer/salesperson, for driving revenues in the personal training and semi-private group-training areas in the club. The lead trainer is responsible for all revenue in the conditioning department. The trainer/salesperson might be the lead trainer in smaller departments. What you must avoid is having a lead trainer that does nothing but train his own clients all day. You cannot be responsible for growing a department financially if all you do is train clients, which, as is the case for owners, is the least productive thing a lead trainer can do with his time. The job is to create revenue and that only happens by introducing a large number of potential clients to the benefits of working with a coach either in a group setting or one on one.

The lead trainer should:
- Acquire and develop trainers in the club
- Write protocol and then supervise the training department
- Train staff and then develop supplement sales in the training department

The group exercise director

This person, who works 20 to 45 hours per week, is responsible for driving the numbers in the group-exercise department. This person's ultimate goal is to get 30 to 40 percent of the club's daily traffic into some form of group exercise. This person does not have to be an instructor but can be anyone who loves group exercise, such as a salesperson or trainer. The main skill you are looking for in a director is that they have some business sense and understand the financial limitations and restrictions of running a department. They don't have to teach, but they should love group and be willing to take a lot of classes per month to control the quality of the product.

The group exercise director should:
- Attend a national group exercise director management-training workshop. Most of the major group exercise suppliers in the industry offer management training as part of their product. Most of this training is good because it centers on the basics, such as setting schedules, evaluating the classes, and incentivizing the instructors to grow the department.
- Do scheduling and class analysis for profitability for the entire program.
- Train and develop nontraditional instructors. Many new owners are held hostage by a core of already trained instructors that roam from club to club in their markets. More progressive owners break this chain by hiring a solid director that can develop nontraditional instructors, such as using the club's trainers or other staff members, based upon a core of pre-choreographed offerings that are usually part of using a national supplier.
- Complete roll-out and promotion of each of the club's offerings in the group-exercise department. Ultimately, the director has to be responsible for growing the program each month and for keeping it safe and current within the scope of your national supplier.

Note: National suppliers are companies that send you pre-packaged programs each month, or quarterly, that keep the owner in control of the program instead of being at the mercy of a director that has complete control of everything in the department and who could hurt the club by leaving suddenly. Group exercise should never be about the individual instructor, but about the quality of the overall program. National pre-packaged programs keep you in control since the club owner owns the materials and concepts.

When to Hire Your New Team

Do not hire your team and put them on the payroll until you have a definite opening date for your business. Owners that hire too soon, and too far in advance, will often lose money or staff if the club is delayed for whatever reason, and your opening, no matter what size club it is, will most likely be delayed at least slightly. Hire key people 30 days out and the rest of the staff the last two weeks prior to opening. Sometimes, you can make deals with your key people and leave them in place at their current jobs until you need them, but you definitely want them free and on your payroll at least two weeks prior to opening to allow time for training.

A rule that covers this very common phenomenon is called the Plummer 20/20 rule. This rules states that your new club will be 20 percent over budget and open at least 20 percent later than you planned. It's like building your own house. You see a tile that wasn't in your budget and you can't live without it, but hey, it's only a $1,000 more. After a few months, you are really over budget because those $1,000 hits add up over time, both in time and in the additional length it takes to get all changes added.

Clubs also seldom open on time for a variety of reasons, most of which are out of your control. Strikes, landlord issues, building permits, builders that can't handle the job, late additions or subtractions to the plans, and just bad luck all add up to not opening when you thought you would.

Few clubs open on time and even fewer open within budget, so be prepared and understand what you are getting into with this new project. Adhere to the following guidelines when hiring your team:

- Get your managers in place approximately 30 days out but leave them in their current jobs until two weeks out if you can.
- Always hire a salesperson first. Get someone on the team that can generate new memberships from the presale forward. This is a person whose sole job is acquisition of new members. Do not hire this person thinking he can do several other tasks in the club until business picks up. Business will not pick up unless someone is working full time to get new members and clients each day.
- Hire just a few people to handle presales. See Chapter 11 for more information.
- Concentrate on production and farm out the rest of the day-to-day functions. Your presale time and the first 90 days of your new business are extremely important. Anything that gets in the way of generating revenue, such as trying to do payroll or collecting your own memberships, needs to be handed out to the professional companies that specialize in those tasks. Your job is to expand the business, and that's where you need to focus. The perfect example would be using a third-party financial service company to service your membership agreements. Get one before you open and do not wait until you think you are big enough to use one. You won't get big enough unless you protect your membership and training revenue streams from the day you open.

- Get your entire team hired and on the payroll simultaneously two weeks out and start intense training. Follow the same steps a new member, and potential member, would go through in your business. For example, what will you give the potential member to take home if they become a new member? What will he take if he doesn't become a member? How will you answer the phone and greet people at the counter? Who has learned the software and can all the counter people use it effectively? Train for all the expected combinations. If you can get into your club before you open, try to train in the actual areas where everyone will be working.

- Set your new employees up to be paid twice a month, meaning the 15th and the last day of the month—never every other week. If you do fall in the every other week trap, you will end up with two months a year with triple payrolls due to the extra weeks in those months, which plays poorly on your budgeting and cash flow.

- Get employee manuals in place before you open. Keep the first versions simple. Do not open without one. There is more information at the end of the book about getting your first versions started.

- Become a member of IHRSA and get their information on hiring and firing. Every employee, including childcare providers and janitors, should sign a nonsolicitation agreement.

- Try to meet with your team at least once a day during your first month of operation to problem-solve. Issues will arise concerning such things as customer service, which need to be addressed and handled early, and you will also find a hundred small things that need to be adjusted as you get through your opening phase.

- Plan for at least two months, and possibly three months in more competitive areas, of reserve capital. This means that if you anticipate your monthly expense at being about $80,000, then you should have at least about $160,000 in reserve to cover operating losses until the club starts covering its own expenses, which should happen between the seven- to nine-month mark for most mainstream facilities. Training clubs also need two months put aside but they can break even at a slightly earlier date due to the higher return per member and the lower operating cost.

Your Role in Your Own Business

Learn to sell. If this is your first fitness business, learn to ethically sell memberships, and other services and products, in your business. During your first 90 days, personally sell as many memberships as you can. This practice will make it easier in the future to hire and train the sales staff, because you will have experience. Once you master membership sales, you can teach others how to do it and supervise the department at a higher level.

Your overall job is to drive revenue and keep your managers on track to hit their numbers. The important thing to remember is that you have to have a plan every day to make money. How much are you targeting today and how will you and your team make this money? Never start a day, or a month, without knowing the number you are trying to achieve, how that money is going to be made and who has responsibility for making it happen. Making money is a not a random act where you just sit on your butt and see what comes through the door. Making money is a proactive act that involves you creating a plan to generate revenue and new memberships each month and then attacking that plan daily, allowing for the need to adjust as you go forward.

The owners in the industry seem to fall into two distinct categories. On the passive side, and occupying about 90 percent of all owners, are those who live following the maintenance style of management.

These people just try to beat last year's numbers by a few dollars, hang on to equipment an extra year beyond its real life, put off painting for another six months because good enough is good enough. They manage by being reactive and only taking action when forced to in the market or by the members. For example, most owners managing with this style won't market until they are hurt a little and need members to survive or because their competitors run some aggressive advertising, forcing them to do something.

The other 10 percent is comprised of owners who are proactive and believe in attacking the market, their competition, and their own business. Their clubs are current, fresh, and always competitive, and they are the ones forcing their competitors to make mistakes due to their aggressive marketing, programming, and adaptation of what is current and on members' minds.

The key thought is that you can either drive the market or react to the market. You are safer, and will make more money, by being a proactive owner that continually works every day to create revenue in the business and to bring in new members as part of a profit plan rather than because you are desperate and need to market to stay alive.

The day you open your new business, you need to start having a daily meeting to drive revenue with your team. Keeping your staff focused on what has to happen each day is probably the single most important thing you do as an owner/operator. Don't let your team worry about the month; keep them focused on making revenue during the next 24 hours. Your managers can think "big picture" but keep the team focused on easier-to-obtain, shorter goals that build confidence and create daily cash flow in the business. Follow these guidelines for your daily meeting:

- Hold the meeting daily Monday through Friday (and on Saturday once you get big enough where you have a weekend manager in place).
  - ✓ Hold the meeting between 12:00 and 4:00 p.m. Make it the same time every day and never miss a day.
- Make the meeting mandatory for all full-time department heads.
  - ✓ A separate meeting should be held for the salespeople once you get two or more in place.
- Keep it to less than half an hour.
  - ✓ Keep it positive and focused. We chew out in private, we praise in public. Keep these meetings positive and keep people focused. Chewing them out every day in a group kills morale and defeats the purpose of building a team.

✓ Discuss how much money or how many sales are you going to make between now and tomorrow's meeting.

✓ No one leaves without a clear understanding of the number their department needs to hit and how they are going to make that number happen.

✓ Break the 30 minutes into a series of five-minute segments. For example:

⇨ Segment 1 is focused on reviewing the goals as they are today.

⇨ Segments 2 through 3 would be used to set goals in each department for the next 24 hours.

⇨ Segment 4 could be a review of something the team could do better, such as correcting a common mistake at the front counter.

⇨ Segment 5 could be the introduction of a new product and a team review of what the product is and how it will be sold in the club.

⇨ Segment 6 would be another review of the goals for the next 24 hours.

• Set goals for the next 24 hours.

✓ Set goals for the week and goals that are broken down for the month.

✓ Adjust goals for the heavier-volume days and reduce goals for the lesser days.

• Get to the point where no one works without a production goal.

✓ The owner/general manager should generate his own goals.

✓ The general manager generates goals for the department heads.

✓ The department heads generate goals for their teams.

✓ The manager, in smaller clubs, should generate plans for everyone if needed.

• Use performance contracts.

✓ You will get more from your employees if you transfer ownership of the work that is going to be done to the person responsible for the work. A simple performance contract, that merely states: I, the employee, agree to do this work this week, is often enough to get the employee thinking about the goal becoming his own to pursue. You can also add a small incentive for hitting the goal that week in addition to normal commissions and bonuses.

• Reward excessive success.

✓ Pay does not have to be fair. If someone is a strong achiever, he needs to get more for his work and get better side bonuses and rewards. Reward the players and fairly compensate the average. In a productive business, the manager is often not the highest paid employee as is the habit. The best money should go to the biggest producers, and if your sales manager and key training people generate big numbers, they should make big money, often exceeding what a manager would make.

• Punish failure.

✓ If an employee is not hitting goals, he needs to go away. One of the biggest mistakes an owner makes is carrying an employee too long after he stops producing. If you can't get an employee producing in 90 days, send them on their way and try a fresh person.

- Coach (teach) daily.
  - ✓ Understand the difference between training and teaching. Training people is what you do to get someone in place with the basics of their job. Coaching is the daily application of slight pressure that keeps the person moving ahead. Coaching is also the subtle daily correction of behaviors that leads to a higher level of performance.
  - ✓ Coaching must take place every day, every hour that you are in the business. Training, or the introduction or review of a skill, can be applied weekly or as needed.
- Have a plan to make money every day.
  - ✓ Money in the fitness business is made daily, and therefore should be planned daily. Money that is not planned becomes random and will always be less than planned money.

You have to understand where your money comes from in the business. Remember, you can control your revenue to a certain extent by keeping your team leaders focused on what they have to accomplish each day.

The Role of Partners

Partnerships usually work fine until the doors are open, and then all hell breaks loose in the partnership world. When the reality of the business sets in, most partnerships fail because there was never any substance or clarity in the relationship.

Each partner in your business should clearly, and in writing, state what he will do in the new business and what he is responsible for each day. Anger surfaces when two people think they are managing staff, for example, or when one partner realizes that he is carrying the load for the entire club and the other person is just training clients all day. Know who will do what, based upon the skill sets each partner should possess, before the business opens. It is too late to adjust once you are moving and in business.

You also need to clearly and legally define your partnership before you pool money and resources. Your attorney should help you develop a partnership/management agreement before you get too for into the new business. Ask your attorney to cover these issues:

- *What happens when someone wants out?* You need a predetermined buyout formula in place prior to starting the business. The standard formula is:

  [(EBITDA + owner's compensation) x 3.5] − debt = business value

  This might look more complicated than it is if you are new in business. Simply put, this means that the value of your business is based on the pre-tax income, depreciation (derived by your accountant), amortization, and the addition of owner's compensation. The total of those four numbers is then applied against a multiplier of 3.5; in other words, this is a way of saying that your business is worth about three-and-a-half years worth of net income before you subtract the debt.

This is a very simplistic explanation, and you want to talk to your attorney and accountant when you add this to your agreement. One key point to add is that you want to build in the ability to pay the buyout of the partner over five years. Many businesses are hurt because one partner will get himself into financial trouble and then want to be bought out of the business right away. It is usually unrealistic to come up with quick cash to buy someone out, so build in a five-year payout to keep the business and surviving partner from failing.

- *How do you agree to disagree?* Agree in advanced to third-party mediation prior to everyone getting attorneys and racking up huge bills that may not be necessary.

- *What if a partner dies or gets divorced?* You think the business is worth about $300,000 and the divorced spouse says it is worth about $3,000,000. The previous formula settles that issue by establishing a pre-set number to solve the dispute. The company would pay according to the formula and then the partner can buy back his share as needed.

- *What happens if you need to put more money in and one partner doesn't have his share?* Agree to dilute stock if needed if one partner has to add money but the other can't come up with his share.

- *What happens if you want to open another club?* Does every partner automatically have the right to be in the new business? Most clubs will always be set with separate corporations for each one. Your attorney and accountant will tell you when to move beyond that assumption. Do not automatically assume that every partner will have the same share in every new venture. Each club is new and there might be different percentages or different partners altogether in future projects.

- *One partner should have the final decision-making ability to run the business. Who is that in your partnership?* It is mandatory that one person has the final right to make a decision. If it fits, establish a number, such as $5,000, where the operating partner can make a decision if it is that number or less, but if the decision costs more than that number, the partners have to vote.

- *How do the partners get paid and take money out of the business?* Decide this in advance. You will always have one needy partner that is always broke, and you don't want to constantly weaken the business feeding someone's lifestyle. Start with paying base salaries for whoever is working in the club and then do owner's payouts quarterly. Run this by your business's support team as well.

- *Who manages the staff (only one person can do so at a time)?* You can't work for more than one boss and if you want to torture your staff, try to manage them using two or three different people, all giving the team conflicting directions and criticisms. Designate one person who runs the staff and do not try to team manage your business with too many partners giving too many directions. This is especially true when a husband and wife own and work in the same business and try to boss around the team separately. One spouse always feels a little left out in this concept of only having one direct report, but it is easier than having a staff trying to make two different bosses happy every day. Breaking down management by department and then letting each partner or spouse manage an area of strength or interest might help this situation.

There are other issues that will be addressed by your attorney when it comes to drafting your partnership agreements, but you do need to discuss these business-killer points with your business partners or spouse before you get very far into the deal. It is especially important that you come up with a way to buy out unhappy partners before the business gets going. Unhappy partners often want lots of money when they try to leave because they believe that the business was their "concept," and although it's not making money at the moment, they often expect to be paid on what the business might do in the future. You can't, nor should you, pay for future revenue that might never be made, so keep your documentation clear and define escape clauses up front so that no surprises occur if and when you have to break up your partnership.

Final Thoughts About Your Staffing Efforts

To be successful in competitive markets, you have to move toward an older, more mature, and more productive staff that matches the demographics of your club. Most club owners try to staff their businesses with people who are too young, inexperienced, and mostly ineffective, thinking that they are saving money by hiring cheaply in the market. When given a chance, always take effective at a slightly higher price than young and dumb at a bargain.

In most markets, paying about two dollars more than the local minimum wage will buy you talent, as opposed to just warm bodies filling job slots acquired at a lower rate. Local minimum wage is defined as what you would have to pay to get someone to take a front counter job in your city. In northern states, it might be as much as $12 to $15 per hour. In the southern states, it could be much less and sometimes actually closer to the Federal minimum wage guidelines.

Add two dollars to that amount, however, and you can usually upgrade your quality of hire. Two dollars an hour is about $340 a month, or the cost of one membership in most mainstream clubs. Buying the best talent you can afford, as opposed to stocking your business with the youngest and least experienced person you can hire because that person will work cheaply, will lead to increased revenue production, which is what you what to hire for and expect from your team in your new business. Remember that production is everything in a small business and you are hiring people to produce revenue while working rather than just hiring people to simply fill slots and shifts.

Also consider having fewer part-timers and more long-term employees who you have invested in through education and staff development. A hardworking former housewife returning to the work force who has had work experience in the past can often do more work in 40 hours than part-time people can do in 60 hours just from knowing how to approach a job. It is a simple rule, but a team of trained full-time people committed to your business can produce a lot more revenue over time than a slew of part-timers who are merely passing through your business on the way to other things.

Payroll, payroll taxes, bonuses, and commissions should be between 37 and 42 percent of the entire monthly operating expense, although that number will go higher if you are using the layered training model discussed in this section and in Chapter 8. Do not base your payroll on total gross sales for the club (total revenue). Basing staffing on gross sales was the model the industry used for decades but it has proven to be ineffective in a competitive market due to the fact that as revenue increases, you just keep adding more staff as a working percentage of the total. Over time, you erode the club's profit margin as well as developing a business that becomes bloated and hard to correct in slower periods.

The fitness business is a fixed-cost business, meaning that at some point, once you hit a certain level where the business's expenses become fairly stable (at about the 13th month of operation), everything generated above that level should become profit. In other words, at some point in time, the expenses of the business become fairly stable, resulting in the cost of running the business being covered by a fairly fixed membership base. Adding members beyond that base doesn't add a lot to the expense, but it will add a lot to the bottom line since the fixed expenses are covered by a consistent number of members.

Having payrolls that are too big, which is usually the result of not watching your budget or not adjusting your staff needs for the slower times of year, eats up the profitability of most new clubs, especially in the first year when the owners think that just throwing in more staff solves most issues with service. Run lean through your first six months and only add staff as needed.

The best staff is working and won't usually answer want ads, especially in competitive job markets. Look for people with business sense and not necessarily people who have prior fitness business experience, and then do your best to entice them away from their current jobs (steal them is the proper term here). You can teach fitness skills to almost anyone who is interested, but business sense is harder to teach. Managers at Gap® stores, people working in GNC® stores, and other folks who are working in customer service-centered jobs make great employees because they have had good training but are usually looking for jobs with better pay and more enjoyable atmospheres, such as fitness businesses. Also, look online for your new hires. Websites such as craigslist have proven to be very effective at attracting new employees nationwide.

The Key Concept in This Chapter

Staffing will be your biggest challenge in your business. Finding the right staff and motivating each person to produce is an important thing to learn early in your career. Attend all the seminars you can that feature a variety of speakers who address the unique concerns of staffing in this industry.

SALES AND MARKETING ARE PART OF ALL SMALL BUSINESSES

Note: Some of the material in this chapter is excerpted from *Anyone Can Sell*, by Thomas Plummer (Healthy Learning, 2007).

Chapter Ten

If owning a fitness business was only as simple as it sounds and looks. You run a little marketing, sign up the hundreds of folks driven crazy by your latest ad, and then spend the rest of the day counting money and working out. If this scenario were true, a lot more clubs would be making a lot more money around the country, and a lot more owners would be in better shape, too, because everyone would want to be in a business that appears to be such a dream job from the outside.

Marketing and sales are fundamental skills that every new owner will need to master to be successful over time, especially since you cannot separate these two fundamental business skills in a small business. Marketing can be simply defined as getting qualified butts—potential members is the commonly used term—in seats in front of your sales team or trainers. While this task sounds simple enough for an owner to accomplish, the job of actually getting qualified leads in the door of your new business takes two distinct skills—marketing and sales—that you must master to be successful.

But first, looking at the business from a higher level, you have to become a total businessperson to compete in the fitness business as a financially successful owner. The problem is that most new owners are usually one-dimensional when they start their new business. This means that they are heavily skilled in one area necessary for the business, such as training, but negligent in the other areas necessary to survive over time.

The total owner understands the business side, defined as basic banking skills, the ability to read statements, hiring and firing knowledge, as well as the ability to control marketing and create new business. He is also educated in training and should be a certified trainer, although he may never train people in the club; he should also have at least a basic certification in weight management.

For example, there are some owners that get into the business because they think it is a great investment. This owner understands the business component, but is usually not much of a trainer (although he might be an enthusiastic workout person) and is not educated even at a basic level as to weight management. It is important to note that being a training client does not, at any level, make you a qualified trainer who is able to help someone else.

The problems arise for this owner when he has to hire and manage a lead trainer, for example. This owner looks for a trainer who can manage, but since he has so little personal experience in training, he doesn't really understand what he is hiring and what he needs from this new hire. Instead of hiring a good person and then giving direction as to what he wants to accomplish, he is now totally dependent on the head trainer to create and manage the most important department in the club.

This new owner often is held hostage in his own business because he has such a low level of understanding of what we do for a living in this industry, which is to create an atmosphere where people can safely get healthier over time. If he doesn't understand what happens in the training department, then he can't effectively manage for profit and results. If you only know one part of the business, you will always be limited in your ability to manage and grow your business. Before you get into a new business, do everything you can to become a well-rounded businessperson, competent in the three areas (business, training, and weight management) necessary to successfully run a fitness business.

As mentioned previously, in addition to competence in these areas, you will also need to master the fundamental skills of marketing and sales. To master the first function (marketing), you have to have a marketing plan in place at all times designed to attract sufficient new prospective members to the gym each month. To master the second function (sales), you have to have a trained salesperson in place to take advantage, once the prospective member is in the facility, of the marketing dollars you spent to drive that person through the door. Included in this second point is the need to have a salesperson/trainer in place that can effectively place at least a third of your new members into some type of higher-priced training in the club.

Marketing and sales are totally dependent on each other in your club's business plan. Unlike other areas of the club, such as personal training and group exercise, where you can excel in one and be terrible in the other and still run a successful business, you cannot be strong in either marketing or sales and weak in the other and survive over time. You have to master both marketing and sales to be successful and these two areas, along with staffing, may be the most difficult areas of the fitness business.

You can, and most likely will, make a number of classic mistakes as a new, or even seasoned, owner. One of the most harmful business situations a new owner creates for himself over time is that he never realizes that everything he presents to the public—marketing, his personal image, the image of his staff and service, and even the first impression from the front of his building—becomes part of his overall brand in the market. You slowly become the image you create for yourself, and once this image is set in the community's mind, it is hard to change that image.

For example, an owner on the wrong track will run ads with a very short-term vision. The owner needs new members so he talks to the local newspaper person, for example; then he dashes out an ad using a price discount and a stock photo the newspaper guy found online. This type of ad is put together at the very last minute, has the standard components of a semi-naked model, a bulleted list of all the stuff in the club, and a price special. On the day the ad appears, you become that image and that image becomes the identity of your business.

Over time, your club becomes known for these poorly developed and presented ads that aren't consistent and don't build a positive brand over time, thereby often lowering the perceived value of your business. Marketing should be viewed as a long-term endeavor that increasingly gets better results over time and eventually leads to a strong and consistent identity in the marketplace. Every detail counts when it comes to your image, and just one poorly conceived ad can lower the value and perceived quality of your business.

You only really have two options for your new business when it comes to attracting new members. You can run price ads, which are based upon offering a sale or discount of some type, or exposure ads, which means that you use marketing to introduce your business to new people without them having to take on any risk or part with any money before getting a chance to try it.

Marketing for the fitness business has to lead to direct results. A direct result would be defined as advertising that creates immediate interest and response. Large companies, such as the major soft drink manufacturers, have the budget and can spend the money on what are called "image ads" that are designed to give a product name a positive association in the consumer's mind, but they don't always lead to immediate sales. In the fitness business, we usually do not have the time or the money to develop the long-term commitment it takes to use effective image advertising.

Marketing Basics

In the ancient days of the fitness industry, which means prior to 1990, marketing was somewhat simple. You ran an ad with a price special of some type and people showed up. You could also use draw boxes (enter here to win 50 gallons of gas, etc.) and people not only picked up the phone but also actually came in and joined. Even better were referrals from members, who gladly gave out lists of their friends who needed to join the gym and who really did respond to the club's calls.

These things worked because there was much less competition in a club's competitive ring and because the consumer was not yet jaded by the marketing overexposure he is subjected to 24 hours per day in today's culture. Marketing was new, fresh, and effective, but very little, if anything, works from the glory days of fitness.

All of these things that worked then are no longer effective today, because the market and the consumer has changed. This difference can be simply explained by the following formula:

$$\frac{\textbf{High demand}}{\textbf{Limited choices}} = \textbf{Almost any marketing will work}$$

Simply put, this equation means that if you own the only bar in a college town of 40,000 kids, you'll make a ton of money. In other words, if you have high demand (thousands of thirsty college students) coupled with limited choices (you own the only bar), you will make a fortune, no matter what specials you run or advertising you do, if indeed you have to do any at all.

This equation also represents the early days of the fitness industry. More people wanted to join gyms than there were options and choices in the marketplace. Therefore, if you owned one of the few fitness choices in the market, almost any fitness ad worked and you looked like a genius no matter what type of marketing you ran.

The problem is that no one ever realized that it wasn't the ads or other creative marketing that drove the business; it was the market conditions at the time that made the businesses successful despite what they did in advertising. Ads in those days were price-driven, which means that you ran some type of special that deviated from your normal pricing structure. For example, your club might have a regular membership fee of $69, but in your ad in the paper you feature a two-for-one summer special where two people can join for the price of just one membership.

This ad might work for a month or two and then the club owner would switch to another special, such as join now (during the summer) and get the fall for free. The member would join in the summer and defer the first payment until after the first of the year. This process would go on month after month as the owner grinded out deal after deal after deal. "Hey, what special are you guys running this week?" was a common customer question in those days.

Everything you did in those days worked, so it had to be the price-driven marketing, right? If you guessed yes, then you gave the wrong answer. Price-driven marketing, as illustrated in the earlier formula, will work as long as the demand stays higher than the choices available.

Another way to look at it is as follows: If you own something that is limited or rare, you can charge a lot more for it than you could if it was more common. If you have a high demand for fitness, which the industry did in the 1980s, and limited fitness choices compared to what the consumer currently has elsewhere in the market, then almost any ad or special you might run would work to create new business.

Things changed in the late 1990s and into the early 2000s. Demand stayed flat compared to the percentage of total population, but the number of clubs began increasing. The market was still somewhat strong, but it was becoming harder to do the old-style marketing and still drive big numbers. Other factors, such as increasingly sophisticated consumers, also started to change the way marketing worked. The new formula for those years looked as follows:

$$\frac{\textbf{Flat demand and growth}}{\textbf{Increasing consumer options}} = \textbf{Decline in the effectiveness of traditional marketing}$$

Pressure selling has always been a negative part of the industry to the consumer, but the use of this tool became even more aggressive when the marketing became less effective and the clubs became more desperate to get enough new members. If you have fewer people responding to your ads, then the pressure has to shift to the salespeople to create more sales from fewer leads.

The chains in the late 1980s and 1990s were notorious for the pressure their salespeople had to apply at the point of sale, as well as the stress felt by those sales teams to make their 100 cold calls a day and keep their personal appointment sheets filled. When the marketing began to fail, the pressure was on for the salespeople to fill the shortages. The current market follows yet another formula:

$$\frac{\text{Slightly increasing demand}}{\text{Virtually unlimited fitness choices}} = \text{Failure of traditional price ads to drive revenue}$$

This equation shows where the market is after the end of the first decade in the new century and where it will be for a number of years to come. When you have a slightly increasing demand for fitness by the consumer, yet not enough demand to keep up with the increase in club openings and the development of other fitness choices, such as the advent of the yoga studio, the Pilates studio, and the thousands of small training options, price-driven marketing becomes even less effective than in the previous models used during the earlier days of fitness when none of those options really existed in any real numbers.

Price-driven ads are by design meant to generate volume. You can't sell your product at the regular price so you discount it and hope to sell more to make up the difference in price, which was usually a false number anyway. In other words, if your price is $40 for an item and it doesn't sell, then can you discount it with hopes of selling a higher number of units to make up for lesser money earned through the lower price?

Two key elements are in play leading to the failure of price-driven advertising in this model. Only a finite number of people are joining a club at any given time. At this point in time, only about 16 percent of the population in this country belongs to a health club or fitness facility of any type, and even though this number might be slightly increasing, it is not rising as quickly as new clubs are opening and the other options are developing.

As an owner, you are locked into competing for a finite number of members that might join. If you are using price alone to attract new members, such as the $9- to $19-a-month membership clubs, which again is a system designed to generate a high volume of new memberships, your business plan will most likely fail because an insufficient number of new people are interested in joining a fitness facility in the first place. In other words, you are running ads to attract people who aren't there in big enough numbers to feed all the fitness businesses in the area.

The second reason you would be on the track to failure is that price ads work off a false assumption. This assumption states that price ads are created to attract people to the business that *already have* fitness experience and are now shopping for the best price. These ads are not designed to attract new people who have never been in a fitness facility in the past since all the components of the ads are targeted to people who "already get it." For example, a typical price ad might look as follows:

Join now and get the rest of the summer free!
- **Large free-weight area**
- **100 group classes a week**
- **Free childcare**
- **Certified personal trainers**
- **Weight loss available**
- **Tanning included with every membership**

Couple this typical ad copy with a picture of a semi-naked woman and you have the stereotypical fitness ad you would see in a shopper, newspaper, or Yellow Pages ad. Besides being somewhat illogical in the sense that a fitness center is advertising that it has fitness stuff in it, this ad is also ineffective because it targets the wrong market, or those who already probably belong to clubs because they are already fitness people. Think of a hotel advertising that it has beds or a car dealership advertising that it has cars for sale. "Hey, come to our fitness center, we have fitness stuff."

Think about this sample ad carefully. All of these bullet points are aimed at whom? Who is this ad designed for in the market? Would a deconditioned female respond to this ad? Or is the more likely respondent a person who already has fitness experience and is looking for these things in a gym?

Also think about the statistic that only about 16 percent of the population belongs to a fitness facility at this point in time. If all clubs run these types of ads, which again most do, then all fitness owners do is target that same small population of already fitness-educated people that have already sought out and joined the club near their home. This advertising is doing nothing to attract people who don't have any experience and who don't respond to these ads. In other words, these ads target existing fitness people but do nothing to develop future markets by going after a share of the 84 percent that don't currently belong to a club.

Exposure Marketing

If you don't advertise price, then all you have left is exposure marketing. Remember that only two ways exist to attract people to a fitness business. You either offer a price special of some type aimed at discounting your product or you let the person come and try your facility, see if he likes it, and then sign him up. Exposure marketing is similar to car companies that let you take the car home for several hours, or even overnight, with the hope that once you experience the car, you will be hard put to return it. Perhaps the most dramatic example of exposure marketing is the puppy store that lets you take the puppy home for the night before you decide to buy. It is doubtful too many kids have ever returned the new puppy the next day.

Some ads that aren't seeking direct results run pretty pictures and let people know the business exists without including any type of special offering. Coke® and its traditional bear ads during the holidays are a great example. These ads are cute, but they don't include any special offer. You watch, smile, and maybe connect with the company somehow, and Coke hopes that you remember their name when you are walking down the soft drink aisle in the future.

You aren't Coke and you don't have the money to run ads that merely look cute. In this business, you have to run ads that drive people to the door in big enough numbers to feed your business, so every ad has to have some device to elicit a response.

Exposure marketing means that you let someone come try your business for free and see if the person likes it enough to join. This type of marketing is called trial marketing, and it is a very common form of advertising for products that might be a little more high-end in nature or for products that aren't easily explained in a short period of time. We often forget that fitness has too many moving parts for the average consumer to grasp during a 20-minute sales encounter with an overly caffeinated sales dude. If the guest does not have previous fitness experience, it is hard to build a relationship, answer the necessary questions, and create interest within the potential member in less than 20 minutes.

Full trial memberships, meaning those trials that last 14 days or longer as opposed to just a single workout, have been used in the fitness business since about 1990 and are an effective way to attract people who normally wouldn't respond to any type of traditional fitness advertising. A sample trial ad might look as follows:

Never been in a fitness club before?

Afraid to take that first step?

Would you like to try the area's only upscale fitness center for 14 days with no risk or obligation?

We are so proud of our club that we would like you to come try us absolutely free for 14 days with no risk to you or any obligation. We're proud of our club and feel it is the best in town, but talk is cheap. We would like you to come meet our staff and meet the other members and try a full membership for a full 14 days.

At the end of this trial, if we haven't earned your business, then we don't deserve to have you as a member.

All trial memberships include a personal coach, a session with a nutrition professional, and a full membership to the club for 14 days.

This type of copy is aimed at the people in your market who aren't fitness people and who again don't respond to typical price-driven ads. The thing to remember is that people with fitness experience will find you anyway, since fitness is part of their lives. Those fitness folks are looking for a gym as soon as they move to a new area or when they become bored with their existing facility. These folks are in the clubs, know the clubs, and are self-contained when it comes to seeking a new place to work out, and they don't respond to your advertising.

Exposure ads also kill risk, which through the years has proven to be the biggest barrier to inquiry for those who don't have any fitness experience. Risk pops up in the form of, "What if I try this and don't like it? Will I still have to pay for it? Why can't I try it first and see if I like it?" The fear of risk prevents many new fitness people from even trying a club due to fear of getting talked into a membership during their first visit by an aggressive salesperson.

All of these concerns and questions are legitimate and don't get answered through traditional price-driven ads. Traditional ads, coupled with traditional sales techniques that slam hard on the first day a new person inquires about the club, set up an almost impenetrable wall for someone without fitness experience who might be nervous about inquiring at a fitness center for the first time.

The Trial Philosophy

The trial philosophy is really nothing more than stating that you have a good club and you'd like people to come try it because you know that once they do they'll want to become a member. The trial is also a way for a person who has little experience in fitness, or perhaps have had a negative experience, try fitness with little or no risk. Fitness again has a lot of moving parts and does not always translate as a positive experience the first time you try it.

People that do fitness for a living, or who are around fitness every day of their lives, lose their sensitivity to what it is like to be a beginner with all of the fears and self-doubts about whether you can do even basic exercise. Keeping this in mind, we have created, as an industry, the hardest way to actually sell someone on the prospect of doing fitness and getting involved in a club.

Take, for example, a 40-year-old guy who has been working hard in his career for 10 years; he has two young children, and has gained about 15 pounds over the last decade. He used to be in shape when he was young, but due to his job and his parental obligations, he hasn't done anything but play a little weekend golf over the last 10 years of his life.

Now, let's take this guy into a gym as a potential member. The salesperson gives him the 15-minute power tour where you walk the guy to the back of the club and then to an office. After he receives the pitch, he is turned over to a trainer for his first workout in 10 years. The trainer is young, dressed in a tight shirt to show off his physique, and he takes the guy through a standard circuit workout that has no relevance to the guy's life or goals. The trainer pushes the guy a little because he likes to leave everyone slightly beaten up to prove his expertise.

The potential member is dragged back to the office immediately and finds himself sitting across the desk getting pressured from the sales guy to buy today. The guy is whipped, questioning whether he can even do this at all because it was so hard, doubting he can do the full-hour workout three or four days a week the trainer says he needs, and feeling totally insecure around a young staff of hardbodies that are all in good shape.

Is this the best time to ask the guy for the sale? He is depressed, hurting, intimidated, and at his absolute lowest point in 10 years of being out of shape. Did the sales guy and trainer prove—as they think they did—that he really needs this, or did they actually prove that it is too hard and not for him, which is what he is really feeling?

The trial membership was designed for this guy. He needs several workouts at a slower pace, which you can do if you don't need to kill the guy in one shot, in order to gain a little confidence and to establish the feeling that he can do this and that this is the club for him. This can be done over a trial period. This cannot be done in one workout, which is why the industry has such a hard time getting anyone except experienced fitness people to commit to a club during the first visit.

The trial philosophy can be explained in relationship to our potential member in this example as:

Would you like to try our club absolutely free for a full 14 days, with no risk, no obligation, and no money up front? We'd like you to come try our club, meet our members, and meet our staff. At the end of 14 days, if we haven't earned your business, then we don't deserve to have you as a member.

This type of marketing not only generates a larger number of leads because it extends beyond the 16 percent who already belong to clubs, but also makes the salesperson's job a lot easier too. Trials are targeted at people who don't have a lot of fitness experience, which is a much larger number than those who do.

Trials done correctly feed the club sufficient leads as opposed to price-driven marketing that will always have limits in the marketplace, which allows the salespeople to concentrate on closing the ones already in the system rather than wasting time trying to develop appointments that never show. There are simply more people interested in trying a club if the risk and pressure are low compared to the number of people that will respond to price over time. The exception is the $9 price point that can continue to draw potential members if the density in the market and the turnover potential remain high.

Types of trials

A club owner could use two types of trials. A regular risk-free trial simply lets anyone in the market who is qualified try the club for the set trial period. The tool of choice for most markets is either a 14-day or 21-day risk-free trial period.

Qualification is usually determined through the following restrictions:
- Must be 18 or older (minimum age may depend upon the type of club)
- Must live in the club's market area (as shown with a driver's license or equivalent ID)
- Must show ability to buy at some point by flashing a credit card
- May be used once a year

These points represent the fine print. You will still have a small percentage, usually about 3 to 4 percent of all the people who take the trial, who don't really have any intention of actually becoming a member. This situation is acceptable for two reasons. First, the person might actually buy something while in the club, such as a bottle of water or personal training, so the risk is acceptable for these people.

The cost of actually servicing these members is low compared to the upside of what they might spend in the club during the trial visits. It is also important to remember that just because a person doesn't join during this trial period doesn't mean he might not consider joining in the future based upon his experience with your club.

Secondly, this number represents a very small percentage to worry about if indeed the volume of potential members walking through the door does increase. In other words, if the volume goes up for potential members, it doesn't really matter if a few of them are just passing through looking for a free workout or two. The key is to avoid losing focus on what you're trying to accomplish with a trial. The goal is to drive more guests, from a different target market than typical club advertising reaches, than you would get with regular advertising.

Length of trials in use

A number of variations can be used with trial memberships. The examples listed in this section are the most commonly used in today's market.

The 14-day trial. This trial length is the standard for most clubs that have never tried a trial offer before and want to start a little more cautiously. It's long enough to attract more people than the seven-day trial, which has lost its drawing power over the years, but the right length for most clubs to service without losing control as a first effort.

The 21-day trial. This is proving to be the most popular tool for most mainstream clubs. The 21-day trial attracts more prospects than a 14-day trial and is an easy length of time for most clubs' staff to handle, especially with tracking the member while in the club and following up.

This trial length is a tool a club owner might use in conjunction with the 30-day offer. The 30-day trial would be offered directly to small businesses or as a special pass arranged by a member of the sales team. For example, a sales manager might visit a small business and offer the owner and her eight employees a chance to come try the gym as a group. Rather than handing out almost worthless business-card size passes, and to show more value than the 14-day or 21-day trial available in the paper, the salesperson would hand the owner eight 30-day trials in the form of 4 x 5 cards with an employee's name handwritten on each.

Paid trials. Paid trials are a form of target-specific marketing, which means that you are using a specially designed tool to go after very small segments of the market. Another way to think about it is to imagine a single bullet rather than a shotgun approach. Traditional marketing done through newspaper ads, for example, works off the principle of sending a mass message to the entire market with hopes that someone reading the paper will see your message. Target-specific marketing, on the other hand, assumes that you can identify

one specific person, or group of people, who is an ideal candidate for your club and then you offer that person or group a specifically designed marketing piece targeting their needs and concerns.

Sample paid trials, such as 30 days for $19, also represent a finite course of action that still limits risk for the consumer. One of the problems with traditional fitness membership offerings is that they don't match what the consumer is actually looking for when she walks through the door. For example, a deconditioned female walks through the door with the specific concern of losing 10 pounds before being in her sister's wedding in a few months. She has a specific need, a specific goal, and a set timeline in mind when she comes through the door.

The sale breaks down when 30 minutes later a salesperson hammers her on a long-term commitment, or even a simple month-to-month membership, both of which fail to meet the goal she had in her mind when she came through the door.

She wants to buy a specific solution for a specific problem, which is what you should be selling her. Solve her problem first and she is more likely to stay beyond the initial program. The paid trial membership, which again is nothing more than a short-term finite course offered for a flat fee, gives her what she wants initially, making the process of getting her into the system easier. This use of a trial also helps the club in that it exposes its services and programs to someone who might not sign up through a traditional one-visit pressure close. Once she gets into the system, gains trust in the club and its staff, and sees some initial results, she is much more likely to become a long-term member that will stay longer and pay longer because she was slowly brought into the system at her own pace.

Paid trials can be used throughout the year and work especially well when alternated between the 21-day trial and a 30-day paid tool. Both trial tools work, but in most markets they pull two separate groups of people; therefore, it is recommended that you use the 21-day trial for 90 days and switch to the paid trial for 90 days. Some consumers don't trust 'free' and respond to the paid trial while others just like free. Use both tools throughout the year and you will eventually find the one that works best in your market.

Training clubs can stick with a variation of the paid trial as their primary tool. Most training facilities can offer a paid trial based upon 30 days for $49 to $129 depending on the market. This seems like a big range but clubs in markets where the training rate is about $40 to $50 per session will benefit from a paid trial of 30-days for $49, while clubs in more metro areas where the training rates get closer to a $100 per hour or more need to use a paid trial based upon a much higher monthly cost.

No matter where you live, you need new clients in your club. The paid trial will provide a trainer with more people to talk to over a 30-day time period compared to any other marketing you can do. Most trainers, for example, offer a discount on an initial package as their marketing, but these seldom pull because you are assuming the client understands the value of the offer, which always seems high if the potential client doesn't have any experience with you or has never worked with a trainer before.

The Law of Diminishing Returns

Price-driven ads do work for a short period of time in most markets, but ultimately fail in almost every market. This failure (i.e., inability to continue to pull sufficient leads to the business) happens because of the law of diminishing returns.

This theory, derived from an agriculture concept born in Europe, states that when you first plant a crop in a new field your harvest from that same crop in that same field will go down in each succeeding year. For example, you might plant corn and generate 20 bushels per acre the first year. If you plant corn again in the same field next year, your harvest will drop to maybe 18 bushels per acre and continue to drop each year after that until your harvest reaches a sustainable low point.

In other words, by repeating the same action over and over again you get lower and lower responses. Over time, you will ultimately hit a low point where the action generates the lowest possible number for that field or market. In the corn example, you might get to the point where you are down to a few bushels per acre, at which point it bottoms out. There is still corn, but not in the numbers you need to survive.

Price-driven ads emulate this same theory in the fitness business. Run the same type of ad over and over again and slowly that market is burned up and the ad fails. For example, when an owner first runs price-driven ads, he will get results, but if he continues to run them, the market becomes burned over time and the ad response continues to drop until it hits the lowest sustainable number.

In most markets, this drop occurs during the first six months the ads are run. It is interesting to note that this same falloff occurs with the low-price players if there is not huge density in the area or a constant turnover of new people filtering through providing a new market within the market.

For example, if an owner offers a year's membership at $249 in the paper, he will initially be successful by attracting everyone in the market looking for a membership who is willing to pay $249. After the owner burns up that segment, however, then what are his options? If everyone in his market who wants to, or can, pay $249 has responded, then each time he runs that ad it will be less successful as fewer people are left to respond.

This owner's next step would be to lower his price, perhaps to $229. He would thereby open up his market to a new segment that didn't respond to his previous ads at $249 per year and he might generate a little success with this ad for a short period of time.

But what happens when new sales falter again? When an owner is dependent on price-driven ads he will ultimately burn up his market, which is nothing more than the law of diminishing returns kicking in, and eventually he will be forced to lower his price to the lowest common denominator, which might be $149 or even less in this example.

Every market will have a limit, no matter what the price. It does not matter what price you use, you will at some point burn up everyone that is price-driven in the market. The only factors that change this formula are density within about five miles of your business and turnover of new people within your market who haven't yet seen your ads.

Can you use a low price based upon a monthly membership that resists the theory of diminishing returns? What happens, for example, if you run prices so low that everyone in the market who has ever thought about a fitness membership has no excuse left? The ads will still fail over time, but it will take longer for it to happen.

For example, an owner runs prices in the $9-per-month range. This price will obviously attract the widest number of potential members who are interested in price and the theory is that this price is so low that he should be able to attract new members practically forever. This type of pricing is the purest form of a volume-driven business plan because almost all his revenue is coming from building up a large membership check based upon thousands of people paying him $9 per month.

The reality is that every market still has a limit no matter what the price; it just takes a little more time to hit that bottom if the price is lower. If you use the low price of $9, then you might be targeting a huge initial number in your market that might take two years to fully realize. This number is called penetration rate and is the total percentage of the population you can attract to your business.

Penetration rate has two limiting factors: drive time from your business and turnover in your market. Research shows that the average person will only drive about 12 minutes from their home to get to a fitness facility. Typical facilities, for example, usually have about 85 to 90 percent of their membership living within a 12-minute drive time from their club. Specialty clubs, such as women's-only or sports performance centers, draw from a slightly larger area, with a drive-time potential of up to 20 minutes.

In other words, every club has a geographical range that limits its drawing power to an equivalent of about three to five miles from the club. Potential members simply won't drive any further than that to go to a club for a workout. Therefore, you are always at the mercy of the number of people who live in your defined marketplace and who are interested in fitness at any price.

The turnover in an area also is a factor. Some markets, such as parts of Orlando or Atlanta, have extremely high turnover in their younger segments. These areas have a larger than normal amount of apartments and other multifamily homes, which turn over often due to the large number of young workers coming into and out of the area. This number is usually constant, however, and once accounted for becomes a normal part of the business plan.

For example, the owner using the $9-per-month per-member price might be targeting 20 percent of his available market. If his five-mile market ring contains 60,000 people, then his business plan is based upon attracting about 12,000 members paying $9 per month. He would hit this number near the end of the second year if his business plan came together, meaning his monthly check before collection expenses and losses would be approximately $108,000. It is possible for the owner to get to this point and several low-cost chains have clubs that do these numbers. The hardest part of this business plan is sustaining these numbers over time.

Once this owner hits a certain penetration rate, then that point is as far as he can go with this type of business plan. If 20 percent is his number, then he has reached the market limit. Everyone who wants a membership at $9 has already joined and, over time, the owner will reap lower and lower responses from the same type of advertising unless people move out and others move in; but he still won't go over the 20 percent ceiling in this example.

Also remember that his market has geographical limits that prevent him from pulling more members from further away from the club. If his market has unusual turnover numbers, he might be able to sustain higher volume over time, but eventually that number will also top out because of the loss rate.

Price Ads vs. Trial Memberships

What everyone who uses price ads forgets is that price ads are designed to attract people who have previous experience with fitness and do nothing to develop new business. If you know about fitness and are looking for a place to workout, then price ads will work. Price ads won't work, however, for people who don't have this experience and aren't sure whether fitness is really for them or not.

Trial ads, on the other hand, are based upon an entirely different theory. Trial memberships, and the variety of copy that supports these ads, are designed to develop interest in people who have not yet taken the next step toward fitness. The most important thing to remember is that price ads fail over time and trial memberships don't, because the former are designed to capture people already interested in fitness and the latter are designed to develop new markets over time.

In summary, trial memberships done correctly help drive new sales because over time these ads will continue to increase the number of potential members who visit a gym. Trial ads also don't weaken over time because repeated use doesn't burn the market as price-driven ads do. The major weakness of price-driven ads is that eventually the responsibility to fill the club with potential members will fall upon the sales team, because the ads will fail to drive enough new bodies over time.

Sales teams in clubs using trial memberships should concentrate on getting these trial members into the club and then spend a great deal of their time and energy servicing these potential members. Keep in mind that trial members will usually revisit the club more than once, and clubs using trials will always have a combination of new business and recurring leads running through the business each day. The recurring aspect of a trial system eliminates the dependency on having to fill the club's appointment book each day with fresh leads that then have to be pressured into closing during their first visit or lost forever because you only had one shot at getting the sale.

The Marketing Budget

You should budget about 10 percent of your base operating expense each month for outside marketing to attract new leads to your business. The national average, according to research, is that the average club that is struggling only spends about 4 percent of its budget each month on marketing, while more financially successful clubs will spend about 10 percent.

It is also highly suggested that you start a relationship with a marketing company that specializes in the fitness industry. Your goal with your marketing company is to develop and control the image of your brand. Most owners who rely on the local marketing outlets, such as the local paper, end up letting the paper itself develop or create their ads. This ad represents the projection of your business into the community and you should become brand obsessive by making sure every single thing that goes to the public, both in and out of the club, is the highest quality possible and represents the best possible image to the public.

What should you spend this budget on each month?

You will be better off doing fewer things, but mastering these things in your market. Many owners take the shotgun approach and spend a little money on a lot of things over a year's time. Unfortunately, the combination of these things, because they all look a little different and are done by different ad people, doesn't lead to brand recognition and more sales in the market.

Consider track marketing when you first get started. Track marketing means that you start with an ad concept and then stay with that theme and colors over time. For example, maybe the best-known track marketing ads of all time are the ones starring the Pillsbury® Doughboy™. That company has run the Doughboy ads for about 40 years and it's hard for the average consumer to hear the word "Pillsbury" and not add "Doughboy" to the end.

The track concept means that Pillsbury changes their ads often, but has the same components in each ad. You always see the happy family, a warm kitchen, and the Doughboy somewhere in the ad. Each ad is different, but in reality each ad is always the same. This approach builds brand recognition over time. People are more likely to buy something from a company that has been around for a while and that they are familiar with as part of their life. Recognition and familiarity build trust and you are more likely to buy from a business that has been a constant part of the local market year after year rather than buying from a company that has a limited recognition factor in your head.

Marketing is also divided into two general categories. First of all, you have retro marketing, which is used for the slightly older crowd. Older is a sliding scale but the easy way to define it is where does a person get most of his information from in his life? If he reads the newspaper every morning, watches television, uses his cell phone mainly for calls, and maybe uses the computer as a basic work tool rather than a tool to enhance his life, he is a potential client who will respond to retro marketing.

If, on the other hand, the person gets most of his information from an electronic source, then he will most likely respond to electronic marketing. For instance, a person is a strong electronic candidate if you ask him a question and he whips out his smart phone and looks up the answer in a few seconds.

The age factor is a sliding scale because each year the number is getting a little higher. For example, as of this writing age 35 to 40 might be the crossover zone between retro and electronic. Those over this age limit might be stereotypically the people who live in a retro world and those under these ages might be people who are totally involved in the electronic world. In your marketing, it doesn't matter, just cover both sides aggressively throughout the year and you will be fine.

Retro marketing and the associated tools

Direct mail cards. These cards are sent directly to the consumer each month from the marketing company you choose. You can control where the cards are sent through the use of a carrier route radius report, which is usually free from the company you are working with for your marketing.

Carrier route radius reports list every mailing address in a radius from the club based upon mileage. You can also narrow your mailings down by household income. See Chapter 4 for more information on carrier route radius reports.

Several tricks can make your direct mail cards more successful. First of all, only use the oversized cards most companies feature. These cards cost a few cents more, but these bigger cards are long enough to stick out from the rest of the mail that typically crams your mailbox, and getting seen is the biggest part of getting results.

You should also drop your cards in the mail every Monday. Some companies want you to drop the entire month's mailing all at once, which is easier for them, but the risk of not getting seen is higher when using that technique. For example, suppose you drop 20,000 cards during the first week, which is your entire month's budget, but you catch a heavy direct mail day where Sears®, Radio Shack®, and Home Depot® are all dropping their pieces as well. You will be lost in the bulk and your ads for the month will be less effective simply because you were buried with everyone else's marketing.

Drop weekly and you are bound to get through more often, in addition to developing a steady stream of guests throughout the month rather than trying for a surge at the first of the month. Direct mail does not work in every market, but you should at least give your campaign three months once a year as a minimum to determine if it indeed works for you. Shop for prices. The cost will vary depending on how many cards you send each month and how long you commit to mailing each month.

The best times to drop your three-month card run are September, October, and November. You may also consider February, March, and April. If you have the budget, do both time frames. If you are short on cash, only do the fall and use other tools listed in this section for the spring. You do have to do cards at least once a year if you are a mainstream club to verify their effectiveness and to mix up your delivery system in the marketplace.

Training clubs should use a more sophisticated tool, such as a newsletter insert, as opposed to postcards. Your story is more complicated and doesn't lend itself to the smaller amount of information you can fit on a card.

Flyer inserts. Flyer inserts are the cheapest marketing you can do and are also good for presales. This tool is 8½ x 11 inches, one-sided, full-color, and is stuffed in the newspaper. The cost varies by newspaper, but you can control where your pieces go by zone or zip code, depending on which tool the paper chooses to use.

The best days to insert are Mondays, Tuesdays, and Thursdays, if possible. Avoid Wednesdays if you can because that is traditionally food day in most papers, meaning that they are stuffed with flyers from all the local grocery stores. Prices depend on the newspaper and the quality of the piece. If the paper lets you use the back, fill it up but don't pay double for it. You will usually have a choice as to who prints the card. It may be cheaper for your marketing company to print the cards and ship them to the paper, or the paper might give you a great rate on the printing and then you would simply use the marketing company to develop the piece.

There is another level of tool available in this class. Newsletter inserts are a more sophisticated form of a flyer insert. The difference is that the newsletter insert is four pages and resembles an actual newsletter. This allows the club owner to develop a more detailed story about the club, its members, and what it offers due to the increased space available. This is the tool of choice for most owners but it does cost more than a simple flyer insert.

The newsletter insert would include a positioning letter from the owner stressing the differences and uniqueness of his club, two to three testimonials from his members, a special highlight of one of the club's programs such as training, and a full page on how easy it is to get started using the trial membership. We sometimes assume that everyone knows what we mean by the trial, but assume that most people reading this insert don't have a clue. Clearly and simply state why you offer a trial and how the consumer would contact the club to get one for himself.

The newsletter inserts are used the same way as the flyers by simply inserting them into the newspaper on the days described in the previous section. These can also be mailed but that adds more expense, although trainer clubs and top-end mainstream facilities could do well by mailing these to select target demographics in their marketplace.

Internal marketing. This tool is often an overlooked part of the marketing plan. Each month, you should send a quality letter to all of your members, driving referrals through promotions, such as inviting them to bring a guest this month and choose from the following three things: three months added to your membership, a $150 personal-training package, or a $100 shopping spree in the club. Start this program the first month you are open and do it every month after that point. These letters, which your marketing company should help you generate, usually cost approximately $0.70 to $0.90 each.

Cable and radio ads. The cost of these ads depends upon the market. Radio is usually too expensive for a single club owner to afford, but it might be worth trying in smaller markets where the station choice is more limited and the ads are less expensive. Radio also might be part of your presale approach, since you are trying to flood the market during the first months you are open. The advent of satellite radio has decreased the effectiveness of radio as a marketing tool, but there is an exception to every rule, especially if you live in a rural market where radio is a bigger part of the community.

Cable ads are very much dependent on the local television stations and whether you have more than one club. If you would like to try these ads, the best time of the year is late September through early November. Don't spend extra money for direct placement in your favorite television show.

To get the most bang for your buck, ask for rotational advertising, where your ads might pop up any time during the day or night. You'll get more ads this way and a higher chance of being seen by a wider range of people. You will save money as well. Work with your cable advertising rep to get you on about five different stations, depending on the club's target demographics. For example, if you are a women's-only club, try to get your six-week ad campaign spread over five stations that cater to women as their primary target audience.

Newspaper ads. Large newspaper ads are a good tool for presales, especially if you have the budget to go big. Newspaper ads do not work in every market and are definitely a try-and-see venue. Most newspapers have a very large percentage of ads as compared to stories and pictures due to their increased cost of printing and it is very hard to get noticed in large, metro newspapers.

Smaller markets, however, still have some life and you can usually buy bigger ads for a reduced cost. If you commit to an annual contract in the smaller-market papers, you can often get a full-page ad once a month for less than $2,000 per insert. If the market is right, the ad combined with inserts is a strong tool to dominate your marketplace.

It is also worth exploring the newspaper's electronic version. Many papers are offering a web version of their product that a consumer can pull up on his iPad® or iPhone® and these versions often have a much lower ad cost.

Electronic marketing

The problem with discussing electronic marketing is that much that will be written about it might be out of date before the page is printed. Things change quickly in the world of electronic access, so this section will be restricted to general guidelines. Any products or tools discussed in this section might become obsolete in the near future, but the category that tool fills might just have a newer and more effective player that is worth looking at as you develop your marketing plan.

Web pages. Web pages are still a core tool, but how you create one has changed dramatically over the last several years. First of all, the cost has come down substantially in just a five-year window. What used to cost $30,000 to develop is now less than $5,000 in most markets. The second big change is that every good site has become completely video-driven. For example, even the introduction to the site, which should pop huge as the first thing the consumer sees, should be a 30-second to a minute-long clip that has a person talking about the club and how to use the site.

All your testimonials should also be videos as well, restricted to no more than a minute or two at the most. Consumers get bored after a couple of minutes, so keep the clips short and tight. Keep in mind that energy sells, so instead of simply panning a camera around the club, use action sequences that show the club in motion.

You might have luck going to a local tech school and getting your video needs handled there at a reasonable cost. The kids need projects and usually charge a reasonable rate. If you find a kid that can get it done, hire him for about 10 to 15 hours a week to take care of all of your tech needs.

You should get a site that changes copy every day, has a capture tool (e.g., to get this free trial, submit your email address now) that helps you get leads, and gives you the ability to post your own schedules and events. Your third-party financial service company probably has a scheduler that you can use that can be integrated into your website.

Make sure you own your own domain name and that you have clear documentation of where your site is being housed/served. If the company that does your page goes out of business, you want the ability to get your name and site moved to another server. This is a common rookie mistake. Make sure you register your own names and control the use of these names yourself. You also need all the codes and access information to the backside of your website in case your web master disappears or gets fired. If you can't get onto your site and make changes yourself, or if you have not registered the domain name and know where your site lives, you have a problem that will be hard to solve in the future.

Social networks. These sites, such as Facebook®, are becoming efficient tools to promote your business on a daily basis. Efficiently using these sites requires you to post something daily, preferably a video clip (up to about 30 seconds long) of the day of action in the club. The goal of using a social site to promote your business is to make it a daily part of someone's life where they feel they need to check in at least once a day to see what is going on at the club. This only works if you keep it current and post once a day (or more if you have something special going on at the club).

Most owners will find that this takes up too much time, therefore, hire someone to do this for you. It was recommended previously that you consider hiring someone from the local tech school to manage your daily tech needs, which could include posting to social networks. You could also use a person on your staff to do this if he has the time to keep the postings updated daily.

One marketing idea that works fairly well is to post a free 30-day trial for anyone that friends you on your social site. This pushes your members to get their friends to your site as well as helps you create an even bigger base for future marketing.

Video sites. You also need to create your own site within a site on video-driven websites such as YouTube®. For example, you could create a tip of the week for your web page and then create an ongoing accumulation of the tips on YouTube. Again, keep the site current and post often. Once you get people looking for your new clips, you need to deliver or you will lose them.

Coupon companies. Companies like Groupon® and LivingSocial represent an emerging category that is of interest to a club owner. This new marketing endeavor is based upon the use of electronic coupons. For example, the coupon company asks you to promote something at a special price, such as 20 workouts and a $20 smoothie bar voucher for only $20.

The coupon company does a blast to its proprietary email list. For example, they might sell 50 of these in an hour-long promotion. The company takes half the money as their share and you end up with the other half, in this case $500, and a chance to get 50 leads into your business that paid you to be there. The actual show rate of the 50 is all over the place and you might see 50 or 1, but it is worth doing something every month if you have the option in your market.

Learning to Sell Is the First Step to Success

You sell. It's what you do every day in the fitness business. It's been an inherent part of the business since it began and it will always be a vital part of what you do for a living. In fact, 95 percent of what you do in this business, and virtually any other small business, is sell somebody something every day. Sales are how you make money and how you keep cash flow, the lifeblood of small business, flowing through your ever-needy businesses every day, every week, and every month you are operating.

Once you make this money from sales you can then spend the other 5 percent of your time sitting up in your bed at 3:00 in the morning counting your money and trying to figure out just what happened in your business that day. Owners usually make most of their money in the fitness business on the workout floor or behind that front counter, helping their members and guests get what they want from their membership and solving the problems they bring as part of their expectations of being a member.

Most new owners drift away from this core philosophy at some point early in their careers. They start on the floor with the members, but it's just a matter of time before they move to the office. They sit and look at statements, make deposits, return phone calls, solve member service issues, make up their own ads, call the significant other, sneak a lunch, fix a toilet, run a few errands, and, at the end of the day, they're sitting on the couch feeling really tired from putting in a full day at the gym. These people are really busy, but they are not effective.

The problem is that they forgot to make any money that day because they were too busy being busy. They started as production-based people, but they eventually become "managers," and managers seldom make the money because they have lost their feel for daily production. This does not mean that you have to be selling memberships in your own business forever. It does mean that you often lose this production mentality by moving off the floor and into the office setting.

Any time you find a business that isn't performing, one of the first questions that has to be asked of the owner is, "How many memberships did you sell in your own business last month?" If the business is flat, the answer is usually zero. This owner, who probably started as a driven salesperson putting memberships down every night and growing the receivable base and cash flow, probably comes in at 10:00 in the morning, takes care of paperwork, checks the deposits, and is gone by 6:00 at the latest. It feels like a long day but it is not an effective day.

When times get tough, most owners just get more entrenched in their offices. "If I just sit here long enough and refigure these numbers, sooner or later they'll get better." The recommendation is get off your butt and go back to work, because one of the fundamental principles in this business is that no one ever made any money in the fitness business sitting at a computer in an office. Remember that busy is just that—busy—but effective is something entirely different. Most owners are busy but few are productive because they have lost the sense of production that you have to maintain in your business.

Even the owners who are running successful businesses and are far removed from sales need to sell a few memberships in their businesses each month just to keep the feel. You can ask your staff a lot of questions about what's going on with the potential members, but when you do a sale yourself you get instant feedback from the person's words and expressions, which gives you the powerful information you need to keep that business successful.

In the fitness business, you make your money on the floor, one membership at a time. You also make it selling training sessions, soft drinks, supplements, tanning, and any other profit centers the club offers. The old staff training line, "Can I get you a drink for the ride home?" is often more powerful than a whole lot of hours spent sitting at that desk wondering how much money the club will save switching from three-ply toilet paper to the cheap stuff. Small business owners must remember the following principle:

You can never save yourself into profitability.

Most fitness businesses can be cut back and waste exists in every small business. In fact, it is hard to find any fitness business that cannot trim 10 percent or so from its base operating cost.

The secret to running a successful fitness business, however, is not saving pennies. It's making dollars. You are in a production-based business, which means that every day the club is open someone has to sell someone else something. Again, 95 percent of what you do in the fitness business is produce. It takes work to keep this production happening in most small businesses, especially if you get into multiple units or get big enough where you actually do work as a manager in your own business.

One of the main obstacles to keeping this production-based environment going is that managers and owners often take too much on that gets in the way of making money. The basic rule of thumb is that if it gets in the way of production, farm it out. Think of keeping your business a lean, mean selling machine. If something gets in the way of that mentality, you probably shouldn't be doing it. Another way of looking at this is to ask yourself, "Is what I am doing at the moment $10-an-hour work or $500-an-hour work?" If you find yourself doing too much work at the lower end of the scale, then you need to learn how to delegate. Most owners work way too much in their business and way too little on it.

For example, many young owners, and even a few experienced ones, insist on collecting their own memberships. Why would you not farm this task out to a specialist and then manage the results instead of doing the work yourself? In many cases, owners simply can't help doing this work, since this industry attracts so many control freaks whose idea of running a business is, "Get the hell out of my way and I'll do this myself." The sad thing is that when this owner says, "I'll do this" it usually means he is doing everything in the business except the important things, such as selling memberships, training, and other high-dollar items that would give the club a cash flow boost that day.

The goal is to keep the business simple. Farm out everything that gets in the way of production and keep the business totally focused on putting numbers up on the board every day. In the fitness industry, you make your money one day at a time, and your focus should be to keep the business on a set production track each day.

Another mistake that owners make in their quest for building a superior production-based business is that they forget *when* they make the money. Most clubs have a prime time, and that key production slot is seldom between noon and 5:00 in the afternoon. In other words, most owners go home just when the business is starting to get good.

Numbers-wise, owners make about 70 percent of their money in a coed club between roughly 4:00 and 9:00 in the evening Monday through Thursday and on Saturday morning from about 8:00 to 1:00. If you have a women's-only club, you usually have a second prime time in the morning during the week, from about 8:00 to 11:00. Training clubs also have that surge in the morning, followed by a lull midday, and then go full speed from about 4:00 to late. You have to be there when the money is being made if you only own one club.

If you are going to score each day, then you have to have your best players, without exception, in the club during these prime hours. If you leave at 5:00 and let your worthless brother-in-law who is on his fifth job this year run your business for the rest of the evening, you will eventually fail, simply because no strong players are present to drive the business and to create revenue.

It's hard to make money when you're not in the business during those best production hours. Even if you've matured as a business and as an owner, you still have to have a powerful driver in the business during these times. If you are an owner with a single business, then it is absolutely mandatory that you are in your business for those key hours during which you will have the greatest chance of making money in this business.

When you explore ways to improve your business, always return to the key questions: "Am I doing everything possible to create a business that is totally production-based?" Another way to look at this question is to ask yourself: "Is what I am doing, or going to do, the best use of my time and my manager's time at this minute?" If what you're doing is not driving production and sales, then you should be doing something else. As you increase your knowledge about sales, always return to the most basic, but most powerful premise in the fitness business:

95 percent of what you do in this business is sell somebody something every day

Have this statement made into a huge sign that hangs over your desk. Also make this rule one of the first things all new employees learn, along with your new definition of sales, on their first day on the job.

If you want to be successful in this business, learn to sell and get some practical sales experience before you open your club. Do not assume that you can just hire a bunch of people to sell memberships for you or, worse, hire someone who learned to sell in another system when you can't tell if what he knows is good or bad for your business. A good sales effort takes training and leadership every single day, as well as an immense amount of follow-up.

If you can't sell memberships in your own club, it is unlikely that you can teach someone else to do it and manage the results. This statement is especially true of those trainers who want to open their own training facilities. Opening your own business doesn't mean that you simply get to train more people in a bigger room.

When you open this new business, you should be moving from the training floor to the sales and management floor as soon as possible, and the only training you should be doing is training other trainers to be successful and training the rest of your staff in what takes to be a financially solid production-based business.

How good do you have to be?

You need to be able to close at least 55 to 60 percent of all your qualified guests with an annual membership, or higher-priced layered option, over a 30-day period of time. This number assumes that you are using some type of trial membership and that some of your members will need more than one workout before they can buy. In other words, you should end up with 55 to 60 new members on annual memberships out of every 100 qualified guests who walk through the door.

Out of these 55 to 60 people, at least 30 percent should buy during their first visit. These sales come in form of buddy sales, referrals, or just folks who come into the club ready to buy. Remember, these sales are annual memberships, not a bunch of short-term or daily members. Your goal is to create a large receivable base, and adding annual members each month is how it is done. This rule also strongly applies to training facilities as well since we are trying to move away from sessions and packages into 3- to 12-month obligations.

The national average is that the typical club only closes approximately 38 percent of all its qualified traffic over a 30-day period. This low number is due to lack of training, poor systems, and the absence of a set follow-up that goes beyond just calling and harassing people on the phone. If you are using a different system, such as more open-ended memberships, adjust accordingly, but you still have to establish a standard that will help you get the most members possible from your leads.

You will be more effective in your sales efforts if you learn to enhance rather than discount. Enhancing the sale means that you recognize that the person is graciously giving you his business and that you reward that choice

Stockbyte

by giving him a gym bag, T-shirt, a personal-training package, and a few other gifts as a way of saying thanks. Enhancement is treating the new member with respect by acknowledging that he is investing his hard-earned time and money into your business as a new member.

The old sales closing method, which is less effective and very insulting to most potential members, is to "drop close" the person by dropping $100 or some other equally unbelievable number from the membership fee if he joins today. If the person comes back the next day, he supposedly has to pay the full price. Dropping the price the first day is meant to force the potential member to buy now rather than risk losing the $100 deal.

This worked about 50 years ago when the potential members weren't nearly as sophisticated as they are today. Everyone knows that no one ever paid the full price, and if the guest comes back the next day he can probably pay just about anything he wants to get started. Try enhancing first and offer packages to help people get started. People like to look smart, and if the customer receives a nice gift package for joining, he feels good about what he just bought.

Get control of the leads during the presale.

If you are on top of your business, then you know your leads for the day, the week, the month, the same month last year, the average per month, and maybe even the most common first name among all of your potential customers. Leads are where it all begins, and you need to get control of them from the first time the door is open for sales.

Figure 10-1 provides a sample inquiry sheet, which can be used for both walk-in traffic and phone inquiries. This is just a sample and most clubs will shortly find their own version that matches the club and the owner. The key is to always gently ask about the person's goal, his time frame to reach that goal, and the commitment he can make in time each week to accomplish that goal.

Do not have the guest fill this form out while he is waiting for a salesperson. The salesperson needs to be able to ask the questions as part of a normal conversation with the guest. Over time, these questions will be a routine part of every conversation between the club's sales rep and the potential member, and the sheets will become secondary tools that can be filled out after the client leaves the club, but there still has to be one sheet for every lead in the club each day.

At the end of the day, the leads go to the sales manager, who is in charge of the club's follow-up procedures. Every phone call about membership and every guest that walks in, whether qualified or not, has to have a matching inquiry sheet on the sales manager's desk at the end of the working day.

Your third-party financial-service company should be able to provide you with sales tracking software. All leads need to be added to your ongoing file for use throughout the year, such as when sending invitations to a party or special event.

Guest Profile

Today's date _____ Date recorded by manager _____

Did the person: ❑ Visit the club   or   ❑ Phone

Guest's or inquiry's name:

Have you heard about our trial membership? _____

Before we get started, may I offer you a gift from the club? _____

How did you hear about us? _____

Do you know any of our members? If so, who? _____

Have you ever been in the club before? _____

Do you work or live near the gym? _____

What type of workout are you doing now? _____

How would you classify yourself as an exerciser?

❑ I currently work out.

What are you doing? _____

How long? _____

How many days a week? _____

How is it working? _____

What are you looking for that your current program doesn't provide? _____

_____

❑ I used to work out.

What did you do at that time? _____

Were you consistent? _____

How did it work? _____

Why did you stop? _____

How are you feeling since you stopped? _____

How long have you been thinking about getting back to a regular program?

_____

What's kept you from getting back in the past? _____

Is that still a problem? _____

❑ I don't work out.

What has gotten you interested in working out? _____

How do you feel about your health and condition? _____

What was the best you ever felt? _____

What was different at that time? _____

How long have you been thinking about getting into a fitness program?

_____

What's kept you from getting started in the past? _____

Is that still a problem? _____

Figure 10-1. Sample inquiry sheet

We've found over the years people that who want to join a gym and begin a regular exercise program usually fall into one of three categories. Which one of these is your primary goal?

❏ Improve your appearance

❏ Improve your health

❏ Improve things in your life, such as energy level, or reduce stress

Keeping this goal in mind, what is the single most important thing you want to get out of a gym membership? _____

_____

_____

What are some other things you would like to accomplish with us?

How would you like to change your body? _____

Is your weight something you are concerned about? _____

What's the timeframe you've set for your fitness program? _____

On a scale of 1 to 10, how important is it for you to reach your personal fitness objective? _____

Is that enough to get you started and keep you coming to the gym on a regular basis? _____

Now that I have a little information about you and what you're looking for in an exercise program, may I show you the club?

Profile notes so we can best help our guest: _____

_____

_____

Most of our guests or phone inquiries want to know more about what we do here. May we have your email address so that we can send you ongoing information about the club as well as our electronic newsletter?

Email address: _____

To thank you for taking the time to visit the club, we'd like to send you a gift. May we have your address? _____

_____

What is the best phone number with which to reach you? _____

_____

Office use only:

Club representative _____

New member _____

Trial member _____

Figure 10-1. Sample inquiry sheet (cont.)

The Key Concept in This Chapter

Marketing and sales are not separable. To be successful, you have to bring the qualified leads into the club and then give yourself the best chance possible to make each guest a new member while still maintaining proper business ethics.

New owners need to master both components in this business. They must be able to direct their marketing company regarding what they want to accomplish and be able to hire, train, and supervise an effective sales staff.

Marketing is dynamic in nature, meaning that it is constantly changing. Your goal is to work each month to bring in enough qualified leads to feed your business, which requires you to change marketing, try new tools, and constantly tinker with the tools and options you have at your disposal.

Also, it is important to remember that without sales, marketing dollars are wasted. If you only convert 40 percent or less of your leads into new business, you will fail because a typical club owner doesn't have enough money to keep buying leads he can't do anything with. Learn to market, but also learn to convert at least 60 percent of all leads into real members.

PRESALES

Jack Hollingsworth

Chapter Eleven

In the old days, presales were often months, or even years, long. In the modern market, the combination of angry attorney generals in many states, club owners who took money but never opened, and a jaded consumer who would rather just wait until the club really opens before he is willing to give it money force new owners to consider other strategies.

Old presales were based upon the idea of selling a lot of memberships before the club opened and then using that money to actually build the club. If presales fell short, however, the club wouldn't open, which caused tremendous problems to both the consumer who lost money and the state, which had to intervene at some point.

Large presales often had long-term negative consequences as well. If you sold 800 memberships in your presale, about 80 percent of those members will show up during the first two weeks you are open, leading to members who are upset because the club is too crowded and the staff doesn't know what is going on. Too many, too soon is also a problem when it comes to renewals 12 months later, when a lot of those early numbers drop away due to such a poor initial experience.

Soft presales are a better tool in today's market. Having a soft presale means that you only plan on preselling your club for 60 days or less and then putting most of your anticipated marketing money into the market during the first 90 days you are actually open. In this system, you will still get the same number of members paying dues, but you will keep more and have better word-of-mouth than you would if you were trying to make all the money before you open.

Using a Step Presale Process

A mainstream fitness center can use a two- or three-step presale strategy depending on your market and the time of year you open. This strategy is not the desirable course for a training center, however; an appropriate training center strategy will be discussed separately.

The best time to open your new mainstream fitness business is between August 15 and February 15, because opening in that time frame allows you to develop a strong receivable base (the large accumulation of member payments made monthly) going into the summer months of the first year you are in business.

Once you establish your opening membership rate, you can then start with one of the step options. For example, if you are opening on August 15, you might use a full, 60-day presale based on three steps. If your opening price was going to be $49, you would start presales in May/June at $34 and then raise it slowly, five dollars at a time ($34/$39/$44 = three steps), to get back to $49 when you open.

Two-step programs are used when your presale is shorter. It often makes sense to only presell for 30 days and get to the full price sooner, especially if you are opening a top-end club or if you don't have a lot of competition in your area. Less competition simply means you don't need to discount as much, or as early, to get memberships into your new business.

Truly upscale clubs that are basing their membership on a higher price base might only want to do a single step and presell for only 30 days. If you are basing your club on getting a higher price, then no reason exists to give memberships away early just to get your first generation of members.

Low-price clubs can usually presell for a longer period of time, if needed, since you are only trying to create awareness and go after the highest numbers possible. If you are using this model, have your attorney check the local laws to make sure you can legally presell for 90 days or longer and whether you must escrow the money generated from the presale in your state.

Presale Budgets

Budget the equivalent of about 20 percent of your fixed expenses for each month you are preselling memberships. For example, if you expect to have a fixed budget of $70,000, and plan to resale for two months, then budget $14,000 per month for each of those months. This seems like a lot of money, but you are trying to start a business dependent on a constant flow of new leads with no base. Budgeting this much money for a presale helps get the process jump started, especially if the money is focused within your three- to five-mile market area for several month's worth of consistent marketing.

Once you open the club for actual business, budget the equivalent of 15 percent of your fixed expenses for the first 90 days and then move to 10 percent from that point forward. You should always be spending about 10 percent of your fixed budget each month to buy new leads and to protect your market.

Staff/Location

Most presales are done in a space adjacent to your club or in trailers (nice ones you can rent). Once you start the presale, you must have your presale location manned during the stated hours. This process can usually be handled by one or two people. Make sure your phone is answered live and that you have messaging for after-hours calls.

Larger facilities that take over a year to build or longer sometimes rent 10,000 feet or so near the new location and actually operate a functioning club while they are waiting for the building to be completed. This works in more suburban locations or smaller markets and should be considered if you are building from the ground up and expect the project to take 18 months or longer.

Create the best visuals you can about your new club. Video clips from your new group programs, actual equipment, drawings and color samples from your architect, and layouts of the club all help sell memberships. You should have a website up and running before you open, and you should start on the social sites as well, posting information each day as to how the club is progressing.

Your Target Number

Your target number for presales is 10 percent of the members you expect to have at the end of your second year (the twenty-fifth month). If your pro formas anticipate 2,000 members at the end of the second year, then you would work toward a 200-member presale. You might do better in many markets, but this number represents the minimum you need to start your club the right way.

Keep in mind that presales are not guaranteed income. In some markets, you just can't get the numbers that were generated a decade ago due to the heavy competition in the area and the number of clubs that keep opening each year. Every time a new club opens that is overlapping your market, it takes a small bite out of your potential presale. Many members are also jaded and won't leave their current club until you are open and can prove you are the better choice.

The First-Year Overview

Perhaps the best thing about opening your new fitness business is that you should be able to cover your monthly operating expenses between months seven through nine of operation. This assumption is based upon opening the club sometime in the August 15 to February 15 window.

You will also need approximately three months of reserve capital to cover your operating losses until your business plan comes together. The recommendation used to be two months of reserve, but higher rents and payroll, coupled with more competitors per market, has driven the monthly cost of operation higher and lowered the amount of new sales you can gain initially through presales.

These factors have necessitated having a higher reserve of at least three months. For example, if your anticipated cost of operation is going to be $60,000, then you need to have at least $180,000 in reserve as opposed to the $120,000 you would have needed a few years ago. Figure 11-1 illustrates a fitness business in a rental space and represents what should happen during your first year of operation from the day you formally open.

The expense line appears somewhat constant, showing just a 5 to 10 percent increase during your first year. Most clubs are running almost at full expense when opened, because items such as the rent, bank notes, equipment leases, and utilities are already in place. The slight rise comes from adding classes or perhaps trainers as those departments grow toward their peaks.

Do not open with a full schedule of group classes. You are better off having fewer classes that are packed than having too many classes with just a few people in each. Add classes as needed, but always err toward classes being too full as opposed to too empty. Post all schedules for only three months in advance (four your first year of operation), giving you the chance to add as needed while still keeping the members informed.

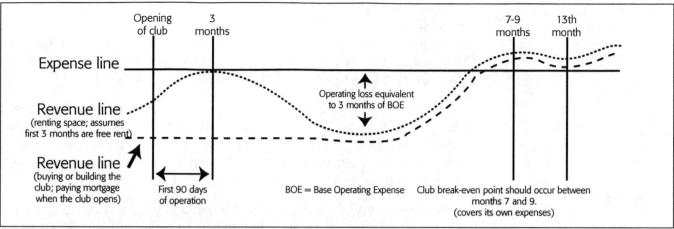

Figure 11-1. Updated maturation chart

You should have revenue from day one, since you will be enrolling new members and already have the ones from your presale working out. Each guest who becomes a new member will generate revenue in the form of a membership fee and each member workout should also generate a usage fee from the club's profit centers.

The usage fee is the relationship between members who visit the club to work out (daily traffic/member check-ins) and what those same members spend in the club during each of those visits. For example, a good smoothie bar/coffee bar can generate $1.00 to $1.20 per member visit. This profit comes from just shakes and coffee and doesn't include cooler drinks or munchies, which have their own tracking numbers.

The good thing about profit centers is that this number should hold true even when you first open because it is based upon member visits per day and not on a total amount of members the club might have in the system. For example, if a newly opened club has 100 member check-ins for the day, it should be able to generate between $100 and 120 for the day in shakes and coffee (100 visits x $1.00 to $1.20 per visit).

Figure 11-1 shows that the expenses and revenues are close together for the first three months, and then the revenue line seems to dip. Most club owners will get the first three months free of rent when they are in rental space, meaning that the overall expenses are lower during the first three months and the revenue that is coming in will almost cover the total operating expenses.

Once the rent kicks in, however, the revenue is still below a level where it will completely cover operating expense. In Figure 11-1, the expenses don't rise, but a bigger gap appears between what is coming in and what is going out due to the rent factor.

You will also notice that this club needs three months of operating reserve (as illustrated by the dip/operating loss) before the club breaks even (incoming revenue covers total operating expense). This chart illustrates that the club covering its expenses somewhere in the seven- to nine-month period.

Revenue continues to grow and you should notice a second rise going into the thirteenth month, which is the point where the club's first wave of renewals hits the system. During that month, the club will add another wave of members into the system, as well as keep a certain number of members from the same month during the previous year that are still paying.

For example, the club might have signed up 100 new members during January. The following January, the club might have only 50 of those members still paying due to losses and normal retention. The club owner does, however, add another 100 members during this January, for a net of 50 extra members paying monthly dues.

An easier way to think about it is that the club added 100 members, but had only 50 left after adjustments. If it adds 100 new members, 50 cover the revenue from the lost members and the club is a total of net 50 ahead. In other words, the club now has 150 members paying monthly dues instead of the 100 it had from last year's memberships during the same month.

Opening during the typically slow months in the club business, such as May and June, will usually extend the break-even point out to about 10 months. The initial higher sales that come during the busier months are going to be lower during the slower months, which leads to a longer buildup of revenue from member payments.

Training Club Presales

Most training clubs would be better served by not doing a traditional presale. It is difficult to convey the energy and professional training a client can expect in your new business prior to being open. Most of what a trainer does needs to be experienced rather than just discussed in an advertisement.

Many trainers have had success with creating a boot camp or other group activity near their anticipated location during the year prior to their opening. Other trainers have also had success working as an independent contractor in a club near their anticipated location and then taking their stable of clients with them to their new club; although, the ethics of this move could be debated.

The safe plan for most training facilities would be to budget between $5,000 to $10,000 per month for marketing for the first three months they are open, using a paid-trial membership as their primary marketing tool. The goal would be to flood the center during your first few months so you can get better word of mouth from your guests and new members who get caught up in the action and new faces.

Handpick your first testimonial as a representative of what you hope your target market will be. This person, in reality, should be someone you have trained, who lives in your marketplace, and is somewhat visible in the community, such as a banker or schoolteacher. Rotate your testimonials every 90 days so you avoid letting your marketing become stale and dated.

The Key Concept in This Chapter

Modern presales are usually just 60 days or less. The old goal was to sell as many new memberships as you could and then collect the big membership dollars once you open.

Your goal should be to go into month five of your business with a healthy, satisfied membership rather than going into your first month with members who received large discounts many months before the club opened as incentives to join early. Be patient and go for the bigger membership dollars closer to opening.

The goal is to stabilize the business with a solid receivable base, no matter if you are mainstream or a training club, as quickly as you can. Be patient with your presale and concentrate on putting more money into your new member acquisition once you are open as opposed to attempting to sell empty space too far out for a lower dollar.

About the Author

Thomas Plummer has been working in the fitness business for over 30 years. He is the founder of the Thomas Plummer Company, as well as the National Fitness Business Alliance (NFBA), a group of industry vendors and suppliers who have banded together to provide education and tradeshows to the independent club owner. Currently, the NFBA offers over 20 seminars a year across the country.

Plummer is in front of more than 5,000 people a year, through numerous speaking engagements as a keynote speaker and event host, and he also gives lectures and workshops worldwide. He has authored six books on the business of fitness, which have remained the bestselling books in the industry for over 12 years, and several of the books are currently used as textbooks in numerous college programs.

Due to the over 70,000 people who attended his seminars during the past decade and beyond, coupled with the continuing popularity of his books, many industry experts feel that Plummer is the most influential person working in the fitness industry today. He has dedicated his life to helping the young fitness professionals in this industry become financially successful doing what they love. During his 30-year trek, he has shown thousands of people how to make money ethically while still creating their own lives in fitness.

In the early 1980s, he was the vice president of marketing for American Service Finance, the largest third-party financial-service provider in the industry. Soon afterward, he became the executive director of the National Health Club Association, which was founded by the owner of American Service Finance to capture the independent market.

He created Thomas Plummer and Associates in 1991, and started a small, limited tour with industry sponsorship. In 2003, he reformed the company and moved it to Cape Cod, Massachusetts. The NFBA, which was founded in 2004, is currently the largest provider of education for the independent owner in the world.

Plummer attended Western Illinois University and then attended graduate school at the University of Arkansas. He started working in the martial arts (Taekwondo) in 1976. He worked as a ski instructor in Colorado for 10 years, raced bicycles in the 1970s, reached a third-degree black belt in the 1980s, and loves music, books, and the water. He currently lives on Cape Cod with his family, travels extensively, and is presently working on his next book project.